To the client, for their trust and enthusiasm.

To the makers, colleagues, mentors, and partners,
without whom this vision would not be possible.

Thank you.

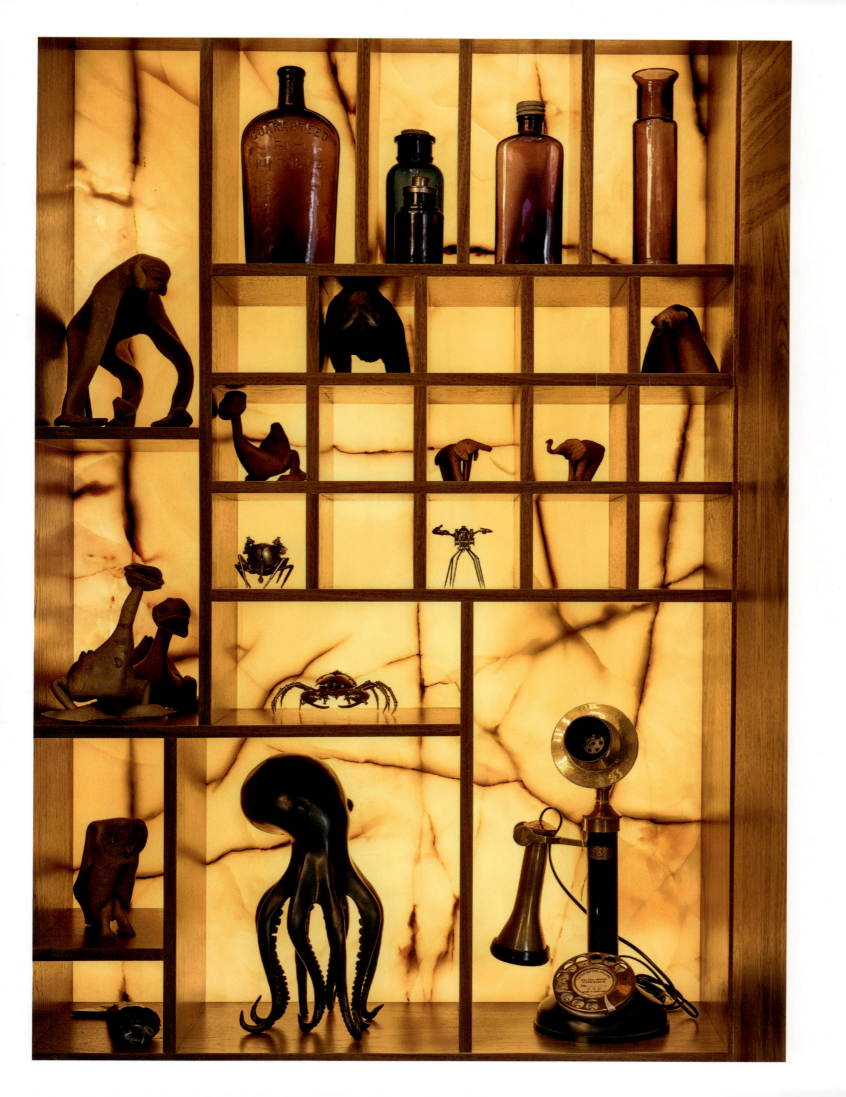

Collaborations:
A Houston Penthouse

By 212box and Saxon Henry

images
Publishing

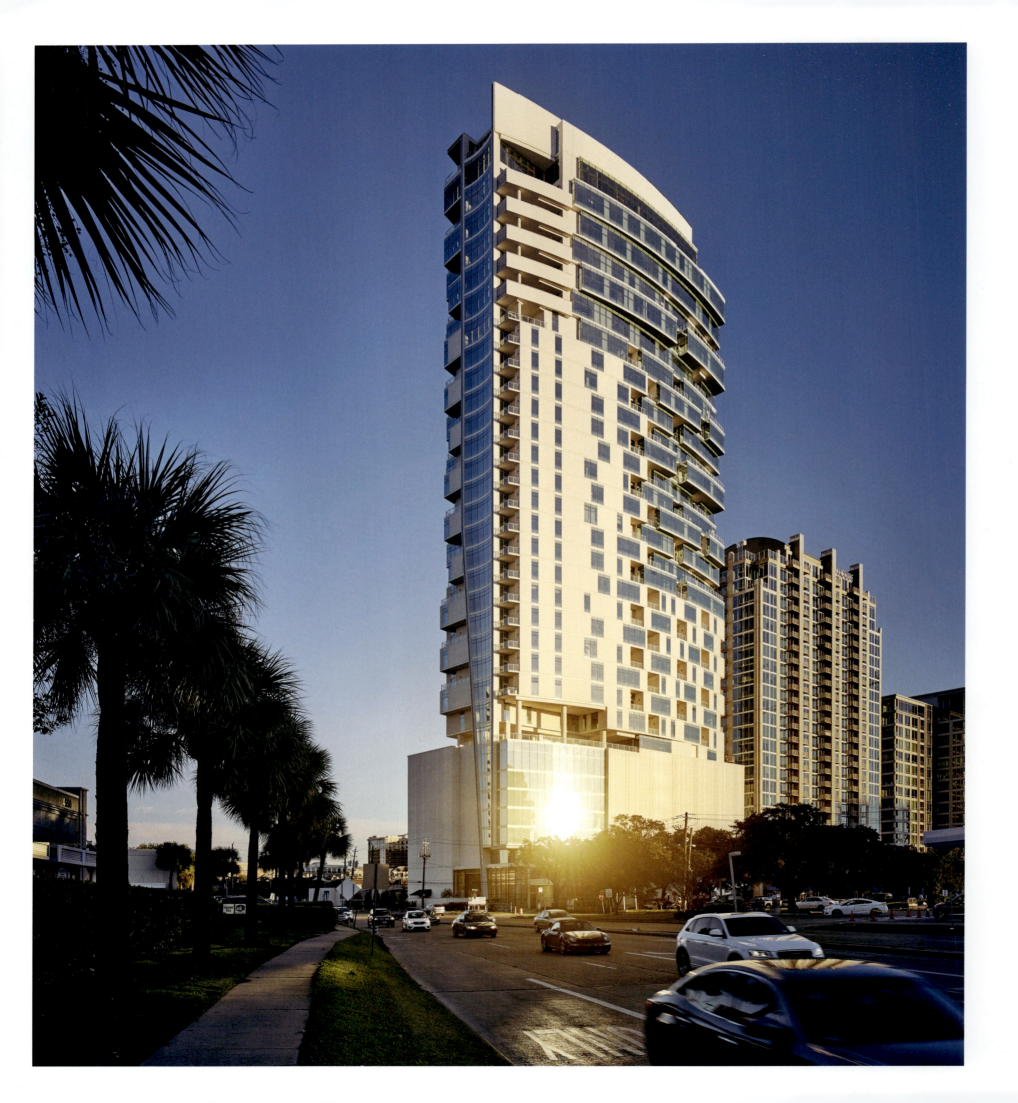

Contents

This is an inspired book born of an exceptional layer of collaborations, initially with our clients, the homeowners of this penthouse; then with the array of artisans and artisanal brands whose efforts coalesced within the residence overlooking the Houston cityscape. Our clients are patrons of the arts, though not simply patrons; they are inquisitive and talented supporters who requested more information about the objects curated and created by our office in tandem with so many collaborators. "Show us the makers," they said. This book is our answer: a lifting of the veil that reveals our trusted confidants who exemplify pure talent, skill, and passion.

Our aim at publishing *Collaborations: A Houston Penthouse* is to bring makers and curators into focus in order to give readers a look behind the scenes of the partnerships we formed. These ranged from deeply involved collaborations that brought new elements to life to forages through a variety of retail domains as we sourced furnishings and materials. The remarkable perceptiveness that flowed as the process unfolded resulted in an enchanting milieu, one that reflects a 212box way of thinking. This perspective of creating is dependent upon relationships within our own team and with others we choose as our co-creators. Whether internally or externally directed, the 212box narrative is a continuing series of questions that we call "What if" moments: "What if we exert ourselves more or employ deeper thinking and make it this way?" we ask. "What if the harder way has a better payoff?" we wonder. "What if this old technique can be beneficial when used on a new material or vice versa?" we ask.

With these prompts we continually push ourselves to provide the finest-quality products and services to our clients because we know it is this rigor of putting more thought and perseverance into the process as it is ongoing that will bring us the most nuanced result. The penthouse with its utmost level of detail, and enriched base of conceptual and bespoke work is an example of the storytelling we employ through the making of objects and experiences. We hope this resonates through and through.

The "we" in this book is the collective voice of 212box, its principals for this project Eric Clough and Eun Sun Chun, who have asked Saxon Henry to shape and compose the narrative of this book. She has written for myriad publications during her career as a journalist, including the *New York Times* and a number of interior design and travel magazines. She is a seasoned author with a passion for storytelling that we find is resonant with ours. Along with presenting the building containing the penthouse and the residence itself, she introduces readers to each maker as a character in the story. The property is presented and the apartment is unveiled as if the residence is being toured, room by room. The complexity of each space deepens when the stories of those whose creations furnish the tableaux are told.

The works themselves create subtle layers that may feel at once dynamic and mysterious. The forcefulness rests in the fact that, for use, intentionality is a truth that runs deeper than any trend, and relationships form the nucleus of our broader sense of creativity. The mystery exists because the visceral encounter is infused with the human energy of the many contributors whose works are installed or exhibited within each room. All in all, this bespoke residence illustrates our commitment to the connection between the value of materials and the value of an experience, and our dedication to the mastery of the finely executed space.

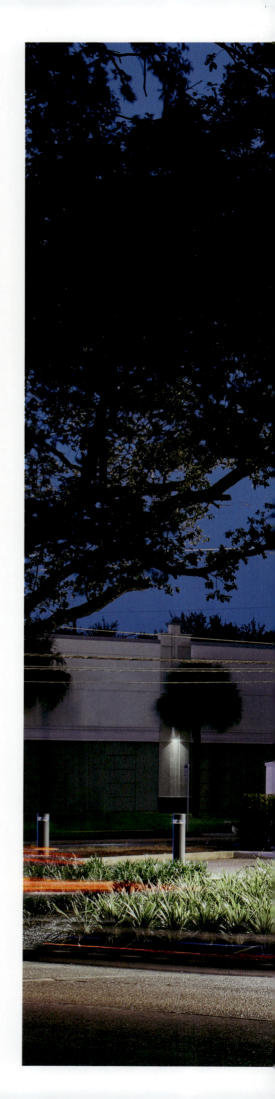

Finely detailed elements speak for themselves. When Randall Davis, the developer of Arabella in partnership with Roberto Contreras, walked into the Christian Louboutin men's boutique that sits below an abandoned section of the West Village's landmark Highline in New York City, he was so attracted to the embroidered, embossed, and pleated leather surfaces he saw cladding the walls, he asked the manager for the name of the firm who had designed the space. His response was validation given we created the shop with its rich, exotic tones and textures for "the traveling man who has everything" in mind. To achieve this, we sourced artisanal elements from around the world, which we combined to evoke a sensuous, masculine ambiance with the rustic, regal edge of New York's Meatpacking District.

We would take the same approach of tapping into our global network of luxury makers and talented artisans when Davis asked us to design the public spaces on the first floor and a number of areas on the amenities floor of Arabella, which rises above the River Oaks section of Houston. As we worked with him during the design phase, we were impressed with his commitment to creating an identity and a brand for each project he realized—the previous high-rise we had just completed together was an art deco building inspired by the Pantages Theatre in Los Angeles. For the Arabella, we showed him one of our favorite projects in Singapore that had a similar vibe to the atmosphere we would create for the Houston building. It resonated with his ideas, particularly the dynamic black-and-white floor he had in mind for the

entry of Arabella—a coursing pattern that we tweaked to flow through the long corridor from the front doors to the concierge desk.

Though the public spaces have one coherent design aesthetic, there are four areas within it that evoke different moods. The entry is quite grand. Hanging from its twenty-two-foot ceilings are two statuesque chandeliers that we designed and had custom-made just outside Hong Kong—quite an undertaking since each fixture is around eight feet tall. Accent walls clad in book-matched Delmata marble provide a vibrant abstract visual relief to the steady geometric pattern of the floor while echoing them in tone. Bringing warmth to these gleaming surfaces are leather panels stitched with brass staples—a favorite detail of ours.

We intended the waiting lounge, tucked into a bright corner of the large volume, to feel like a gallery on a luxury liner that has just embarked for parts unknown. Here we introduced tranquil blues that glow when the sun shines through the windows so the area would feel serene for visitors while they wait to connect with residents. Room dividers with panels of mottled glass in calming shades of brown, blue, and cream accomplish this, as does an intricately patterned metal screen with transparent, semi-transparent, and opaque sections that undulates at the edge of the space. Due to its open design, the implied boundary allows visitors to see who approaches, while it also provides guests and residents a processional to the elevator bank.

In the elevator lobby, we mixed black and white with grays and browns, and chose leather panels and rich woods that include walnut and Tiikeri to clad the walls. A second screen in this area, identical to the one skirting the waiting lounge, complements the Italian brass furniture in the space. This section of the lobby is one of our all-time favorite spaces because it has such a gorgeous feel to it. Adjacent to it is the mail room, which is normally treated as a utilitarian space. We felt it should be just as highly considered as the rest of the building. It gleams like a gold jewel box hidden behind the largest leather-tiled wall in this section of the first floor.

Also off the lobby is a sitting area with a massive curved sofa and a six-foot-long linear fireplace with a single horizontal flame. After the broad expanses of the entry, this space has an intimate feel to it that draws residents for morning beverages from the adjacent coffee bar. It's a beautiful moment in the building that we envisioned being as enticing as it has proven to be. It evokes the timeless elegance of the gilded age with a modern twist thanks to the combined patterns in the carpets, the upholstery, and the numerous wall panels. Several of these are undulant installations that appear to be pleated. When combined, each element brings the room a complex mix of textures that makes it feel warm and inviting.

We placed a mural by artist Karen Darling, manufactured by Area Environments, above the fireplace. We chose the pattern by the Toronto-based artist because we wanted to

evoke a traditional fireplace. Titled *Smoke on the Water*, the pattern created the perfect imitation of billowing embers. Darling, whom president Diane Perry describes as a prolific and popular artist for their company and one of their longest-standing collaborators, says she is committed to creating with abandon because that's when the real magic happens.

"I have always been interested in interior design so to see my artwork used in beautifully designed spaces is a real thrill," Darling says. "The use of *Smoke on the Water* in this space couldn't be more perfect. It creates drama above the linear fireplace but also sets the mood for quiet contemplation. I am very happy to see my work used in such a beautiful way." Adjacent to this space are the card room and the conference room—the former beckoning residents for rounds of poker, bridge, or mahjong; and the latter providing privacy for important meetings.

We chose two patterns by Aaron De La Cruz, also produced by Area Environments, for these spaces, one titled "Option One (Light Gray)," which we placed in the card room; the other called "Disconnect," which we included in the conference room. "Disconnect" resembles a sophisticated rendering of dripping graffiti, which we feel gives the lobby area a youthful vibe. If you visit the chapter featuring the guest suite, we delve deeper into the story of Area Environments and another of their artists in an essay that describes our favorite aspects of the brand.

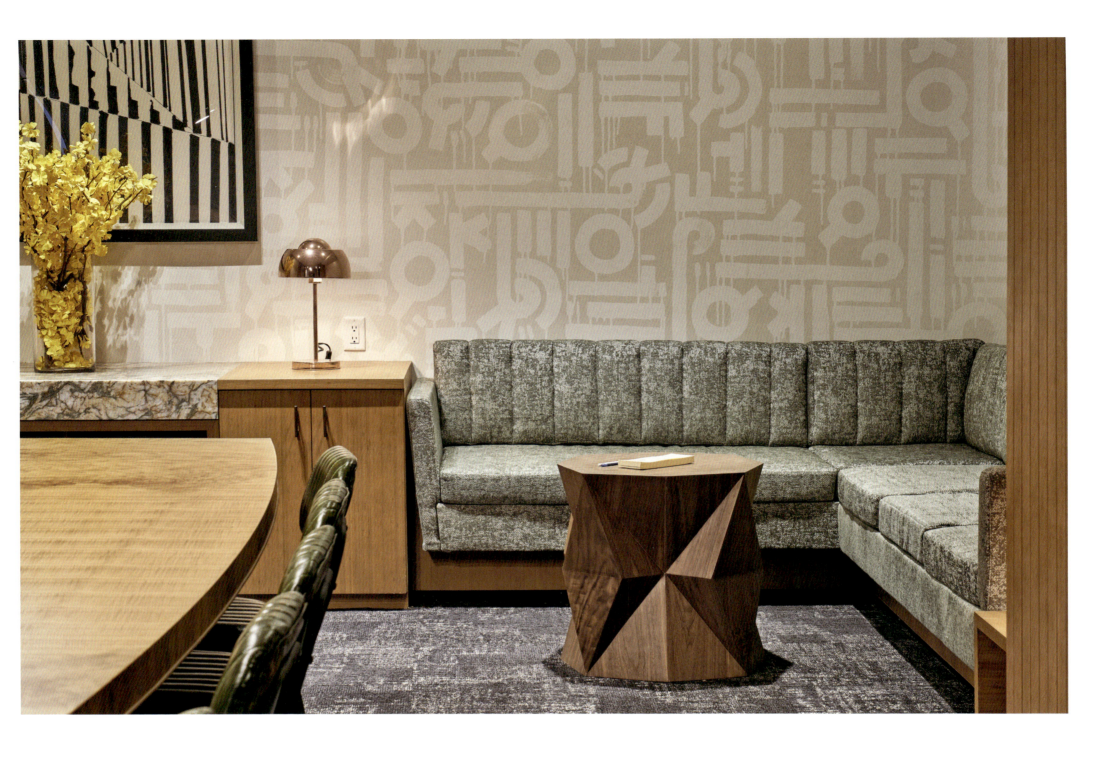

Reiki Starchild (Black) & (White) by Prodip Leung; artworks procured through Absolut Art.

We also designed the amenities floor of the Arabella, which is ensconced in the ninth floor of the building. Here, there are indoor and outdoor pools with a wraparound terrace. The centerpiece of the interior is a resident lounge with a bar and a screening room that serves as one large private entertaining space available to homeowners for sizable parties. Many of the furnishings are custom, such as the banquettes that line one wall, and the rainbow-colored marble and onyx tops on the bar and smaller tables, which introduce those gathered around them to a vibrant pattern experience. The pendant lights are transparent and shaped like diamonds. When illuminated, they effervesce just as brightly as the faceted stones that inspired their profiles.

Among the special material considerations is a saddle-stitched leather detail that wraps the top of a room divider. The indoor pool area is elegant and sleek with its black and gold tiles, which take on a sheen when light washes over them.

Each of these design notes was chosen to bring the feeling of sophistication to the spaces in which residents will gather, whether they are convening to mark the passing of important milestones or merely celebrating the big game in which their favorite sports team is competing.

Each space we've mentioned elicits its own experience, the scale growing more intimate once the breathtaking entry with its powerful black-and-white patterns coursing through the voluminous space has been traversed. The journey through these environments evokes a hint of things to come. Culminating with the final visceral responses we hope to inspire on the highest floor—in a penthouse filled with finely wrought materials and furnishings. It is into this collection of spaces we draw you as the excursion continues …

Kintsugi—Chanoyu wallcovering by Fromental; torn wallpaper
reassembled with hand–gilded lines over waxed paper.

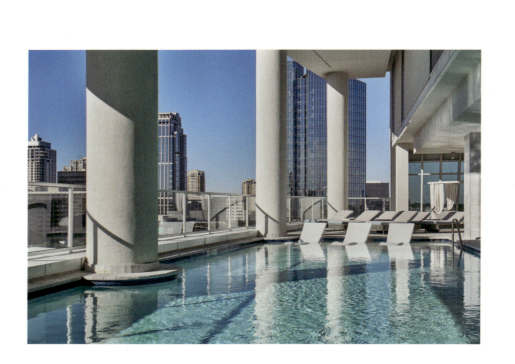
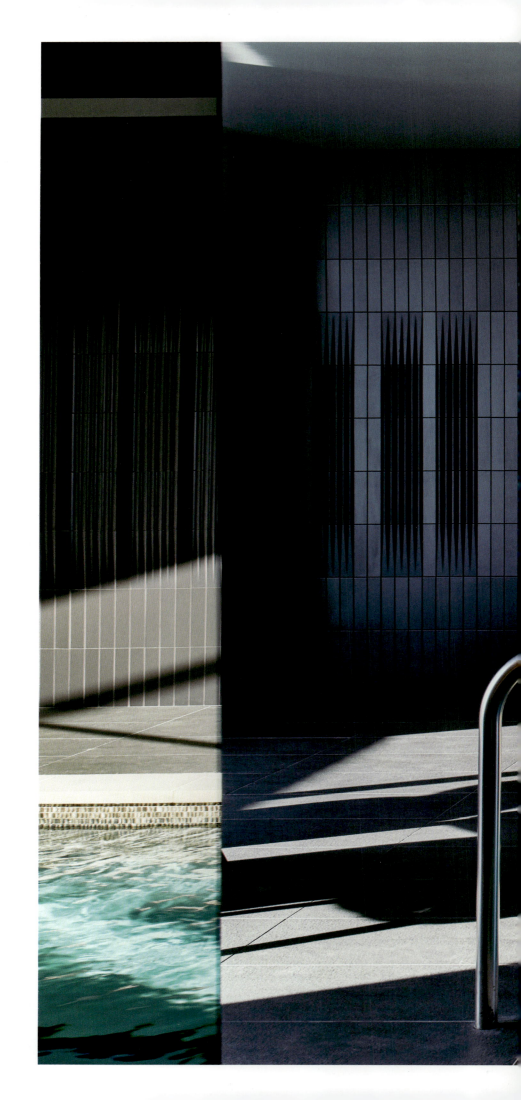

After seeing the public spaces in the lobby area and on the amenities floor of Arabella, the owners of this 6,000-square-foot penthouse chose us to design the *pied-à-terre* that would serve as a place to entertain friends and family, and to host visitors and business associates who have traveled to town. Due to this immediate confidence in our aesthetic, the project was an extremely satisfying one. But it was also a dynamic one because it was undertaken in a true collaborative spirit between our team and the homeowners. The fact that the couple was just as eager as we were to create a bespoke environment in which artists and artisans could shine was nothing short of a gift.

Returning to tried-and-true relationships we had solidified as we created so many projects, including the 161 Christian Louboutin stores we designed between 2004 and 2019, we began sourcing elements we had seen over the course of a decade and a half to bring a level of richness to the penthouse that we'd only dreamed we could achieve in a residential setting until this point. We also had the opportunity to forge new collaborations with artisans and luxury purveyors we discovered as we were traveling, at times with the homeowners, which brought new artisanal elements into our design aesthetic. Each returning artist with whom we'd collaborated before and each new talent we found have created elements that make this Houston penthouse one of the most sophisticated residences in our global portfolio.

Arabella was still under construction when we were commissioned for this project so we were able to rethink the developer's floor plan, which would have hampered our idea of open circulation for the main living spaces. Among our material choices were twenty-five different types of onyx and marble, mainly from Italy; a stunning variety of woods; and an opulent mix of leathers and hides. The array of craft techniques we employed span a dizzying lapse of time—from a young German artist creating avant-garde wood curtains that move like fabric to one of the oldest screen makers in Japan, whose team crafted a kitchen ceiling with the traditional *kumiko* woodworking methods they'd been practicing for many decades.

The custom furnishings we designed, the vintage elements we found, and the art we chose in diverse media coalesce in this residence to make it a rare place in the world that holds everything we love in one *mise-en-scène*. Rather than reveal the full thrust of the story that unfolds within this stage set now, we invite you to enjoy each act that follows as each space speaks for itself. From this point forward in the book, the backdrop we've created for the narrative will reveal itself room by room and artisan by artisan so that by the end you'll see why we felt so compelled to realize this veritable creative mecca.

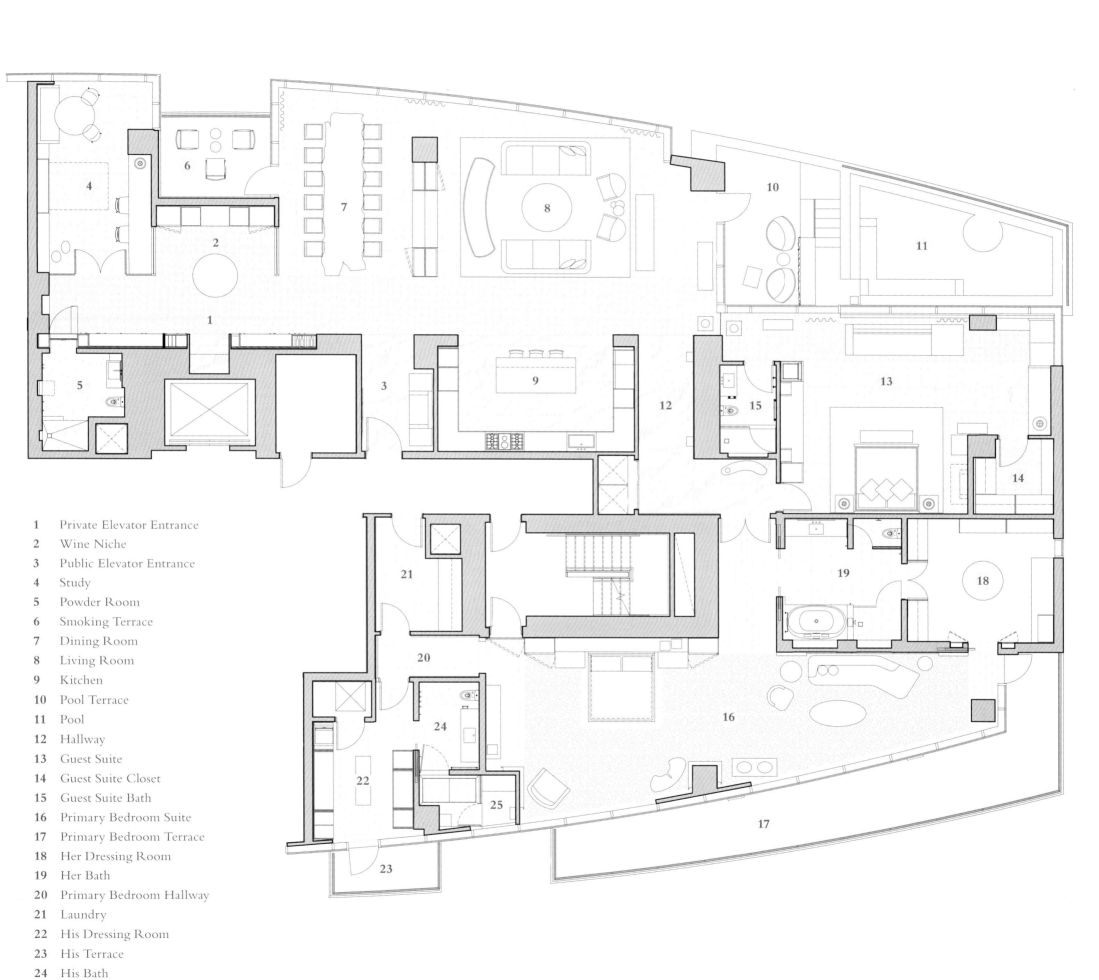

1   Private Elevator Entrance
2   Wine Niche
3   Public Elevator Entrance
4   Study
5   Powder Room
6   Smoking Terrace
7   Dining Room
8   Living Room
9   Kitchen
10 Pool Terrace
11 Pool
12 Hallway
13 Guest Suite
14 Guest Suite Closet
15 Guest Suite Bath
16 Primary Bedroom Suite
17 Primary Bedroom Terrace
18 Her Dressing Room
19 Her Bath
20 Primary Bedroom Hallway
21 Laundry
22 His Dressing Room
23 His Terrace
24 His Bath
25 His Sauna

Cordiality, affability, and geniality are synonyms for warmth. For the array of social gatherings this penthouse was born to accommodate, the meanings of these words are also resonant. There are two points of access to this residence—a private entrance in sultry shades of brown and dark gray, and a public entrance in resplendent white. The darker tones prevail in the private ingress. The patterns swirling along the surfaces of the torched-wood vertical elements and the staccato terrazzo flooring produce a magnetic sense of movement in the area. But only the long spine of timber flooring that creates a runway through the entire length of the main living spaces and extends into the guest bedroom is obvious when the doors to the elevator open.

One has to turn around to realize this entrance to the penthouse unfolds through mystifying millwork that disguises intriguing elements while also being a model of form and function. It's a Curiosity Cabinet with an array of doors, drawers, and insets that make up a twenty-five-foot-long installation, a necessity we employed to create harmony from irregularity. Between the columns on the wall where the cabinet is installed, volume widths and depths varied dramatically, at times offering as little as eighteen inches of space. This built-in allowed us to save every inch possible while also actualizing a highly refined feature that became a puzzled linear composition of boxes in a pinwheel pattern.

Once the exterior was strategized in size and scope, we went carcass-by-carcass to introduce function, designing a logical storage system where there is a place for every single item. If the homeowners need an adhesive bandage from a first-aid kit, we reasoned, why not make the drawer as beautiful as possible? It was the same for many other hideaways, such as the compartment holding the tool kit, which includes perfectly

fitted recesses so that every instrument stays in place. By putting so much thought into the cabinet before we fabricated it, we were able to cleverly conceal objects and create small surprises.

The latter includes the fact that the cabinet doors open in differing directions, which makes interacting with them an exercise in riddling through a puzzle. The surfaces are solid wood, and after the front faces of the walnut were torched so that the sugars in the grains burned off to accentuate the textures, they were clear-coated. To make the composition more complex aesthetically, we flipped the direction of the graining so that each panel was perpendicular to the one adjacent, following a logic system that jumped from one flat surface to the next to create a dynamic layer of patternmaking.

We turned to the talented Gregory Madzio, the founder of HIICompany Corp., to help us build these into a solid working whole. In fact, the millwork in every room in the penthouse except the kitchen was realized by his talented team. Madzio's passion for woodworking, which we share later in this chapter, has been all-consuming for most of his adult life. Into the framework that his team built, we fitted varying stones, brass and glass shelving, and extremely thick ribbed glass panels created by Nathan Allan Glass Studios. The textured pieces of the latter run behind one section of the bookshelves and are inset into the powder room door. We tapped this Canadian firm, whose profile is included in this chapter, because they are master craftspeople at producing kiln-formed glass. The sheets we included throughout the penthouse are a half-inch thick. The quality and purity of the material given this depth, and the fact that it is at times fluted, fritted, or smoked, is impressive.

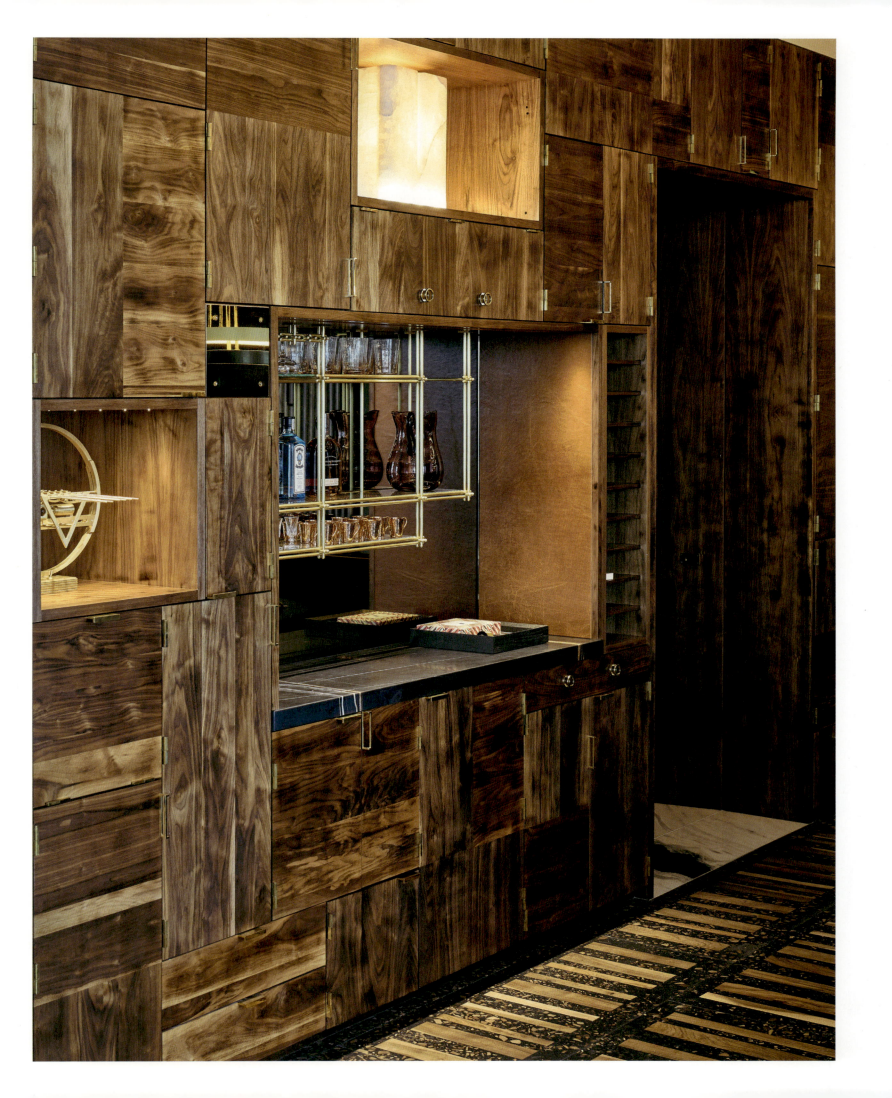

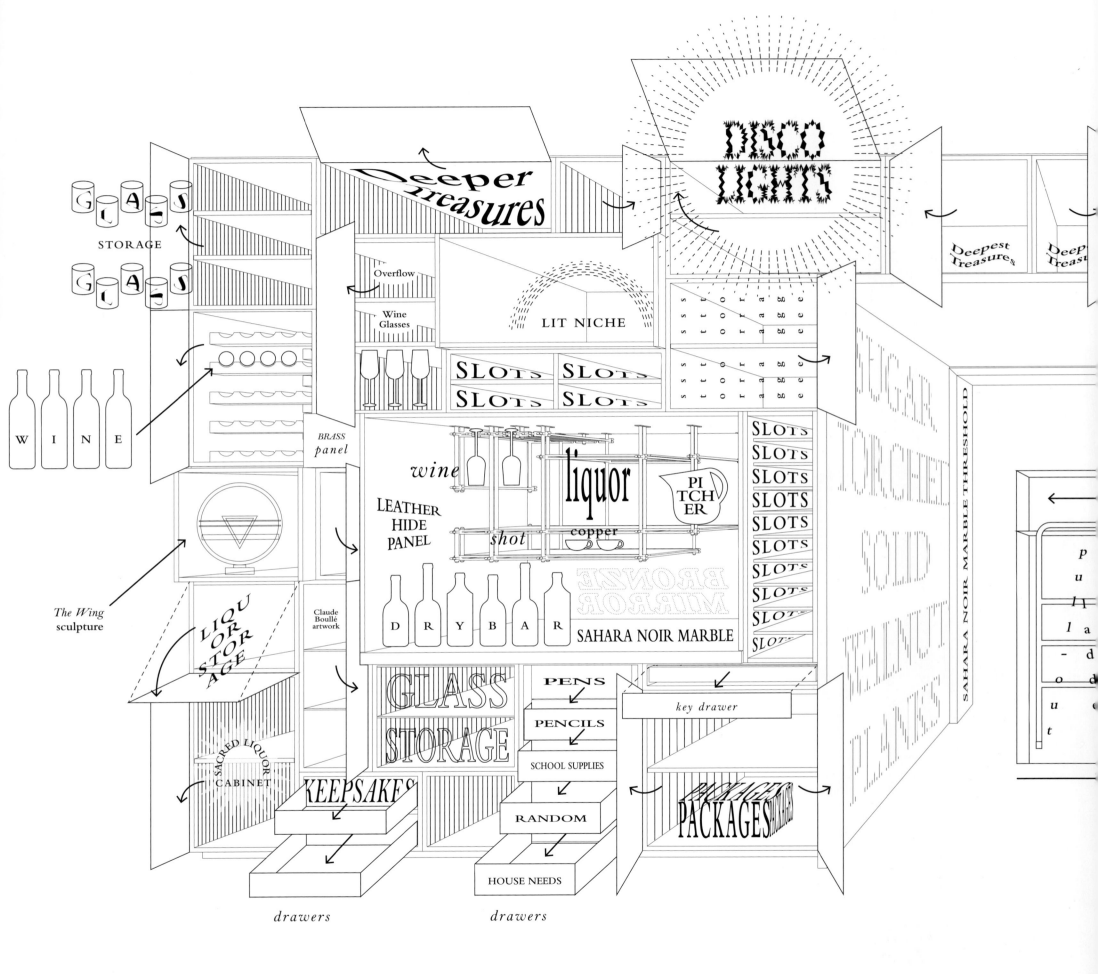

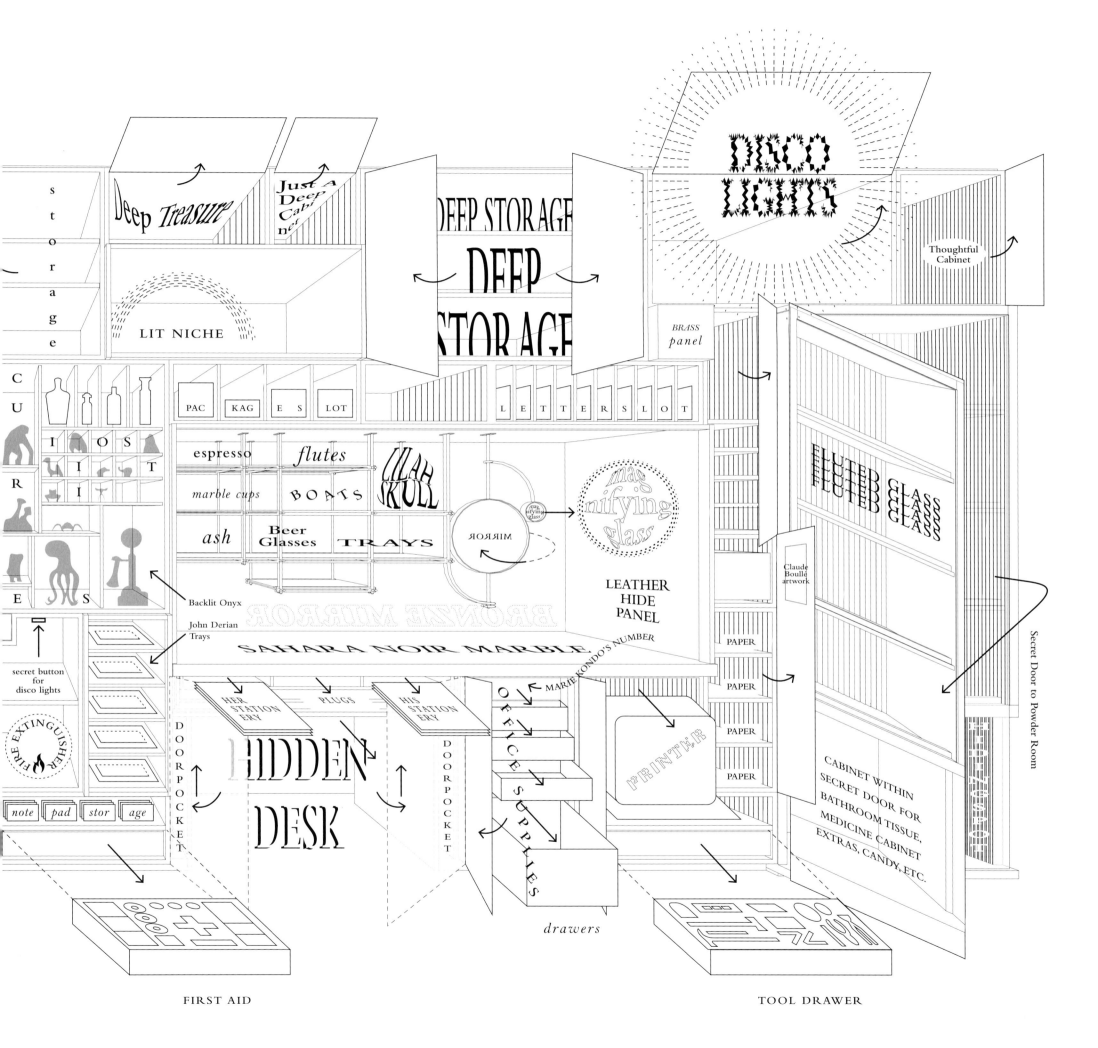

storage

Deep Treasure

Just A Deep Cabinet

DEEP STORAGE

DEEP STORAGE

DISCO LIGHTS

LIT NICHE

Thoughtful Cabinet

BRASS *panel*

CURIOSITIES

PAC KAG E S LOT

L E T T E R S L O T

espresso   *flutes*   LILAH SKULL

marble cups   BOATS

ash   Beer Glasses   TRAYS

MIRROR

mag nifying glass

mag nifying glass

LEATHER HIDE PANEL

FLUTED GLASS
FLUTED GLASS
FLUTED GLASS

Backlit Onyx

John Derian Trays

BRONZE MIRROR

Claude Boullé artwork

secret button for disco lights

SAHARA NOIR MARBLE

MARIE KONDO'S NUMBER

PAPER

PAPER

PAPER

PAPER

Secret Door to Powder Room

FIRE EXTINGUISHER

DOORPOCKET

HER STATION ERY

PLUGS

HIS STATION ERY

OFFICE SUPPLIES

DOORPOCKET

PRINTER

note pad stor age

HIDDEN DESK

drawers

CABINET WITHIN
SECRET DOOR FOR
BATHROOM TISSUE,
MEDICINE CABINET
EXTRAS, CANDY, ETC.

FIRST AID

TOOL DRAWER

We amped up our sense of playfulness in the inner formations of the cabinet with secret buttons behind the lower doors that open the tallest compartments. When one button is pressed, for instance, doors swing open and Siri declares "party mode," which triggers music to blast through Bose speakers, and laser lights to pop on and rotate. Suddenly, the penthouse has become a disco! Other features of this labyrinthian built-in include a ladder that pulls out to allow easy access to the upper cabinets meant for storage; and stationery trays next to a flip-down desk. A stool with a minimal handle-like backrest is tucked away in the study, the t-shaped back making it a breeze to retrieve.

The door to the powder room at one end of the Curiosity Cabinet isn't obvious because it is deeply inset; at the opposite end are shelves in front of a backlit onyx panel. The private elevator is tucked into the cabinetry between a dry bar and a hard-liquor bar, each of which is ornamented with shelving we designed to showcase contemporary art, glass decorative pieces, vintage and antique bottles, liquor, demitasse cups, wine goblets, and other cocktail-hour paraphernalia. The shaping of the shelving was based on a gift Eric's son gave him, a brass triple-cross puzzle like a small jack with six cylinders that come together to make a cross. It sits on his desk so he often studies it when he's talking on the phone or contemplating projects.

One day while he was staring at it, he realized it held the answer to an artful way he could design the multiple cylinders and support systems for the glass shelves in the Curiosity Cabinet. It was great in theory, as ideas like this often are, but

when we tried to build it, it was a conundrum. Fortunately, we were able to turn to Rhett Butler and Kiki Clark of E.R. Butler, one of the oldest hardware manufacturers in New York—the profile that shares Butler's point of view to follow is a fascinating story. Though the company has evolved into so much more, the deep knowledge their metalsmiths have in problem-solving makes them an important resource; and though knobs, pulls, and handles are still at the heart of this manufacturer's offerings, the showroom is filled with an array of furnishings that include sculptures, housewares, tabletop items, and lighting.

Coming to our rescue in this instance was a talented fabricator Butler had on staff who was able to strategize a process to connect the shelving that wasn't obvious to us. The challenge was in welding the metal pieces together because they needed to be soldered multiple times. By the second weld, the first weld was being undone by the heat. As he problem-solved the design, he discovered that the first connections could be welded and each one thereafter could be fastened by hidden screws. This was one of those moments in the realization of this project when we appreciated the skill of those involved. These shelves made of brass and glass have a minimal feel thanks to the thinness of the tubes. This is one of many examples of how E.R. Butler's products and team helped us achieve the pared-down aesthetics we sought to create, which unfold during so many lovely moments throughout the rooms in the penthouse. It is this company's handsome hardware that gleams on the doors and drawers of the Curiosity Cabinet.

Stone "pupil" found at Boullé Claude Galerie in Paris, and all glassware,
including marble goblets, collected from various antique markets.

Inside many of the sections of the installation, a treasure trove of playfulness awaits. Among the featured decorative accessories are leather animals made by the German company Deru during the 1960s; and pieces by Claude Boullé, the French artist and mineralogist who slices stone to fool the eye into thinking the sections he harvests are landscape paintings. We found his work in Paris and grew fascinated with his process. He goes on location and tells his men to begin digging where he senses fine specimens of stone may be. They then unearth them and split them on-site so he can judge whether any given stone holds a worthy composition. We fastened the small marble vignettes we bought to the backs of cabinet doors where they read so convincingly as intricate landscape paintings.

One piece of art that is visible in an exterior niche was sourced when we were traveling in Hong Kong. We came upon Upoint Studio, represented by a dynamic shop in Pacific Place where we were mesmerized by an eclectic mix of kinetic sculptures, particularly *The Wing*. We were just in time to purchase the last of the limited-edition run, as only one hundred were made and all but two were sold. The mechanical work of art has appendages that mimic the feel of thin rowing oars within a supporting sphere. The brass sculpture was designed by two architects who were inspired by the idea of combining motion and eternity.

Also sourced from Upoint Studio are assemblages of cast brass that depict animals and insects. These are backlit in a warm glow as light filters through the amber-hued onyx behind them. We became even more enthralled with the brand when we learned they provide opportunities for students to actualize their ideas, the creatives given carte blanche to realize anything they can dream up as long as they can prove it can be engineered. The atelier is known for its rigorous experimentation, such as using 3D printers to develop new technology that will replicate old casting techniques. This is a move that perfectly melds with our philosophy of using innovative know-how to transform solutions invented during the industrial age.

We also chose the decoupaged glass trays by John Derian because we appreciate how he has resurrected a traditional technique to create unique decorative elements. Handmade

in his New York City studio, the trays bring new life to reproduced imagery from his vast collection of antique and vintage prints. Trained artisans cut and collage the designs onto the handblown glass and each piece is made-to-order. Another colorful element displayed in an exterior niche is *Lilah*, a feathered skull by Laurence Le Constant, which we found at Galerie Géraldine Banier in Paris. The clients for whom we designed the penthouse were with us on the trip abroad when we came upon the sculpture. We had a jam-packed day of scheduled stops but as we were walking down rue Jacob, which is one of our favorite Left Bank streets for sourcing interior elements, the wife seemed to be riveted by the array of art in the window of this gallery. When she stopped to study it, we decided to take the time to look around, and we came away with the piece by Le Constant and another composition by a different artist featured in one of the hallways.

You will find a fuller profile on Le Constant after this presentation of the room. She is a fascinating artist who learned the art of *plumassière* in the haute couture studios of Chanel and Dior. She sculpts the skulls over which she wraps guinea fowl, duck, and pheasant feathers from resin, creating pieces of art that exude mystery and power in the process. The idea of displaying this very special piece of art, along with *The Wing*, in exposed niches was inspired by our sixteen-year relationship with Christian Louboutin. One of his signature concepts is singly showcasing each of his shoes in an entire wall of arched niches. When the arches are filled, the effect reads like a dovecote, each shoe reminiscent of the birds that would normally be perched within them. This wasn't merely an aesthetic move on his part; it was born from his love of each object he crafts: he wants every design to stand out, to be its own work of art.

In fact, he gives every shoe a name, one that reflects its personality. Just as the doves are to those who care for them, each of his creations is a soul exhibiting every nuance of emotion. Laurence's sculpture is similarly showcased on its own glass shelf because it is aesthetically dynamic. Each of her creations is slightly different than the next, which is why they remind us of Christian's shoes. Examine the skull for any length of time and it will transform to exhibit fabled features, as if it has its very own mythology. This enthralling section

Backlit onyx silhouettes, purple glass vessels circa 1885–1914 (top);
Deru leather animals—crafted from origami-like techniques of
crimping, cutting, and folding a single piece of leather (throughout);
antique candlestick phone (bottom right); *Octopus* bronze sculpture by
Upoint Studio (bottom middle); mechanical brass insects (throughout);
fish bottle-opener in mother-of-pearl (bottom left).

of the entrance to the penthouse is one of the most nuanced we've ever produced. The scope of the experimental as it evolved made us push ourselves to design what is in essence a storage system, but one that is so much more than this because it is loaded with meaning.

On the wall where the Curiosity Cabinet ends is an illuminating element: a massive split-faced geode shimmers from a niche clad in pale marble. Behind this is hung a white hair-on-hide mural created by Kyle Bunting named *Crossfire*. The white tone-on-tone leather piece softens the cold white marble while working in concert with it to create a bright contrast to all the warm elements in the entrance. Kyle's journey to working with this time-honored material is described in this chapter after we've completed the tour of the area. The alcove holding the mural and the geode is lit to draw the eye to the elements as soon as the threshold to the penthouse from the private elevator is crossed.

Leading the eye away from the mural is the plank bridge created by the Foresso flooring, which one passes over each time the central core of the penthouse is traversed from any number of rooms. The products the company creates were born of a dynamic collaboration we had with the United Kingdom–based manufacturer whose profile we feature later in this chapter. Design-wise, their participation

was ideal because we were able to produce a new product to break up the seventy-five-foot-long passageway that spanned the interior of the penthouse.This spine came to life when we specified their terrazzo floor to be embedded with plank tiles in varying sizes in a track pattern. These were accentuated with the smaller chips of wood that would normally be sprinkled into their surfacing materials. The varied shapes create a beautiful rhythm, as if sheet music was left on the floor so that each step could produce a cohesive cadence. To assure that the flooring would maintain a cohesion throughout the main living spaces, we chose the Foresso terrazzo with the small wood chips flecked into it for the rest of the living room and dining room, and for the study and guest suite.

One of our favorite aspects of the path the planks create is how the darker background contrasts with the brightness of the walnut. And, like many of the elements in the penthouse, there was a deeper meaning to the use of reclaimed wood elements in the interiors because the husband owns a lumber company he founded with a friend that is dedicated to sourcing reclaimed and salvaged wood. They scour the East Coast and Europe to find exemplary specimens, so including as much reclaimed wood in the residence as the aesthetics would support was our homage to this effort.

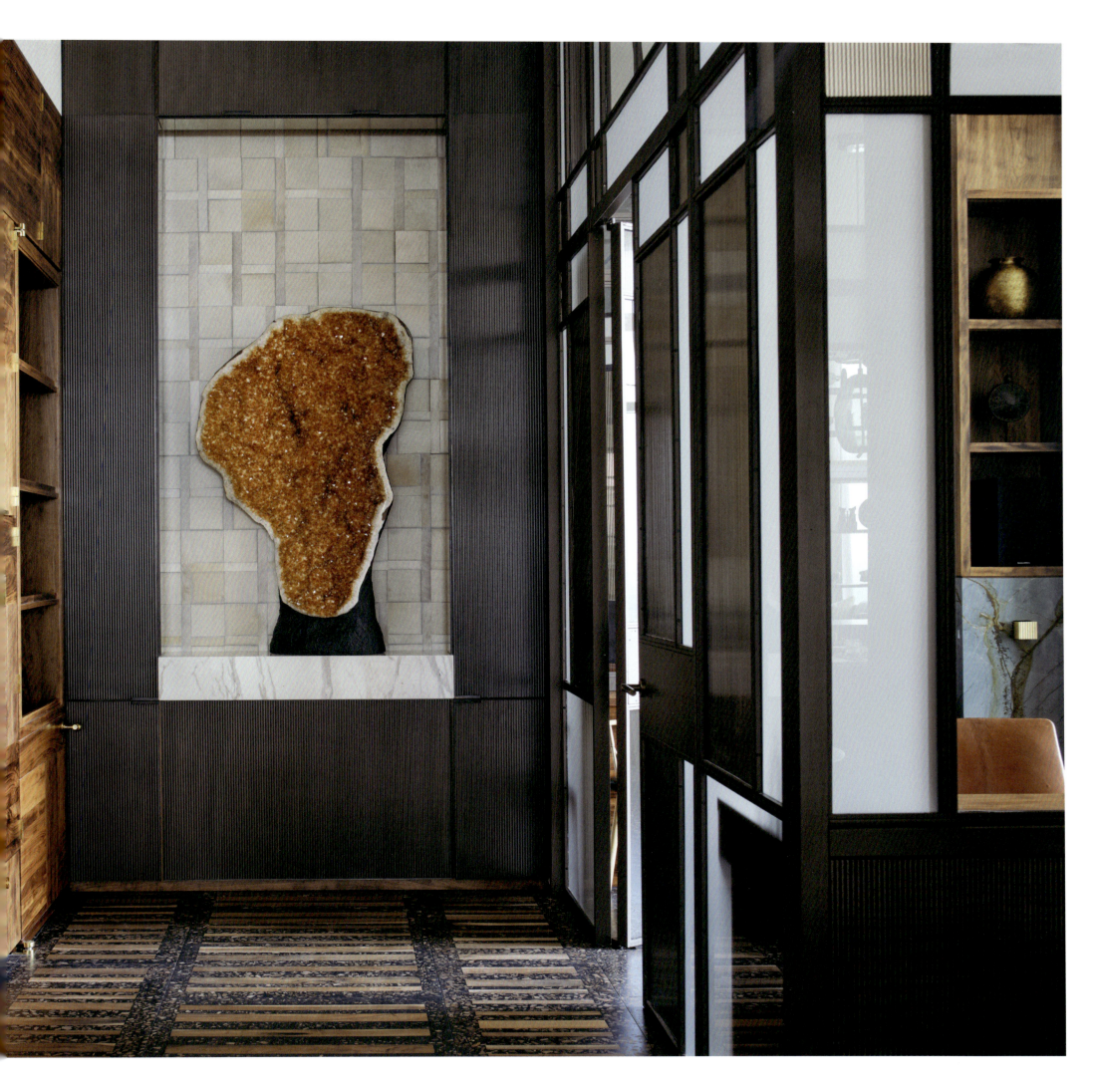

Gregory Madzio, HIICompany Corp.

Millwork Throughout Penthouse

It was Oliver Wendell Holmes who said he didn't give a fig for the simplicity this side of complexity but he would give his life for the simplicity the other side of complexity. Gregory Madzio of HIICompany Corp., who contributed so many solid yet intricate elements to the interiors of the penthouse, has dedicated his career to the same quest. He's done so by creating beauty from one primary material: wood. In every room in this residence but the kitchen, the refined millwork was crafted by Madzio's team of cabinetmakers. "Our work can be very complicated," he says. "I like challenging projects in terms of technical skills, as well as creative projects that require imagination. When these come in one package, everything we do is prototypical."

About the team who helps him achieve these involved projects, he says, "I'm very fortunate that my crew is made up of old-fashioned European cabinetmakers who have amazing intelligence in their hands." Though they are not great in number, each professional can do "pretty much anything a client can conceptualize with a piece of lumber." He believes this is because they have an ability to think three-dimensionally, which he says is a must for a good craftsperson working in wood. The sophisticated quality for which his brand is known and Madzio's drive to concentrate on making beautiful things propelled us to want to work with him, and we are proud to be among those clients who push his team to achieve inventive interior elements.

We knew him for several years before we found the right projects that would do his artistry justice. "A few years after I met Eun, I met Eric and we began collaborating on bringing his visions into being," Madzio says. "We had long afternoons looking at handmade sketches—wild sketches in some cases—and he would ask, 'Can you make this?' I would counter, 'Out of what?' He would up the ante by asking, 'And what happens if we do this?' I would answer, 'It would collapse!' He's very expressive so that kept the conversations going and we spent many afternoons moving through these types of exchanges."

It is the depth of Madzio's know-how that enabled us to bring the many complex ideas for the spaces in the penthouse to life. He is remarkable at suggesting materials that could be used and is adept at explaining to us how we can accomplish what we have in mind. "I enjoy working with clients like Eun and Eric because they like to collaborate, and they are curious about different possibilities," Madzio says. "Our role is to help them to execute their vision."

In this particular project, only a few of the elements had custom veneers; most of the millwork was made from solid wood, which can be extremely demanding. "It is challenging to make a nine-foot door that is three feet wide and one inch thick out of solid wood that will actually work and stay true," Madzio explains. "That's pure craftsmanship because of the stress and the pressure within the material. You have to have the ability to recognize what wood will do. If you treat it with respect, you can make it do what you want it to do. We have developed techniques that release all the pressure from the material, and this takes skill and patience and time, which is similar to other aspects of life if you think about it."

Madzio is most often called in on projects as early as the design phase because his knowledge of what can and can't be accomplished within certain budgets is key to the success of a collaboration. He not only works with interior designers and architects, he creates the backdrops in which fine art is shown for an A-list of New York City galleries. Looking back on a career that has amassed him an impressively sophisticated clientele, he can trace his passion for wood back to his childhood in Warsaw, Poland, where he began making model airplanes as a young boy.

"I was working with wood and parchment paper, and I kept trying to make them more complicated," he explains. "As a young man, I set my sights on furniture and took a year off from my studies in law to make pieces." When he graduated from this coursework, earning his law degree, he left Poland for a year in London. The pleasure in experiencing another culture spurred him on, this time to America, which had always held a fascination for him. He made his dream of coming to the United States a reality in 1986. "In London, I worked for a company that made old-fashioned millwork on-site, installing it then and there," he says. "I learned how to make staircases and such, and I continued to build interior elements in the United States so I could travel around the country. I went to Alaska, which was a dream, and spent a few months there. I liked this country very much so I decided to stay."

At twenty-five years old, Madzio made his way to New York City. "I wanted to see two things in the city—Central Park and the Museum of Modern Art," he remembers. "When I went to MoMA, they had on display some wonderful pieces of furniture. I still have the pictures of the specimens on view, which were beautiful, and were made of solid wood and veneers. I already knew that doing intricate veneer-work takes great skill, but seeing these furnishings in the Museum of Modern Art made me realize how furniture could be considered artful; and how showing it wasn't merely a celebration of the designers who envisioned the pieces. The great craftsmen who built them were respected as well."

A similar experience took place when he visited an extensive exhibition at the Metropolitan Museum of Art. "It was filled with furnishings made by French craftsmen, who were artists, though they didn't call themselves artists," he explains. "These people created original things that we still value. That's what drives me to do what I do; to make things that I would enjoy looking at myself." All those years ago, when Madzio was settling in New York City, one circumstance more than any other helped put him on the path that has led him to this moment in time.

It was a chance meeting with an elderly Italian cabinetmaker at a Brooklyn woodworking show. "I'm part Italian, and that's how we established a relationship," Madzio explains. "He was in the business all his life, and I mean all his life—as a kid, he straightened nails for his father! He was significantly older than I was and was a one-man shop. I soon figured out that this was because no one was good enough to work with him: he was so difficult, it was 'his way or the highway.' Because there were zero compromises, it was impossible for him to keep help."

Madzio was wise enough to know just how much he could learn from the curmudgeon, who was fond of telling the eager young man that he had no talent. Because he had never been employed in a woodworking shop at that point, Madzio does admit there was some truth to the elder's claims that he lacked skill, but the success he has achieved debunks the man's claims that talent was lacking. As Madzio soaked in these new opportunities to grow, his curiosity kicked into overdrive.

"I would sneak into the shop at night to learn the machines so that when he asked me, I could say, 'Of course I've worked on this one,'" he explains. "He would tell me I was doing it all wrong and so the lessons began." By the time his tutorial ended, he had learned a myriad of things from the master craftsman. Madzio still celebrates the year he had with the gentleman. Fast forward three-and-a-half decades, and most of the jobs Madzio takes on skew heavily toward custom millwork. "I want to concentrate on my core strength and I want to do pieces that I like, beautiful pieces," he notes. "My main goal is to go to work and do what I love to do. I have no problem getting up in the morning or dealing with normal work issues because I know I am going to be doing what I love."

This is so drilled into his DNA, it is the first piece of advice he would give to young artists or those who are new at trying to create artisanal brands. "You have to like what you do and do what you like: That's a must," he says. "Pay attention to things that inspire you in everyday life, such as seeing the beauty of nature. I'm a sailor and I love studying how the unique old boats are made: they are so wonderful and are super strong. Look into the past, and not just for inspiration, but for wisdom. Look at how beautiful and how well-made older pieces are. If you study a French bureau made with marquetry and fine veneers, it is amazing."

He advises anyone wanting to work with wood to attend exhibitions, and not just of contemporary woodwork but of a more historical nature like ones showing Renaissance pieces from Italy. "Looking for a longer-view perspective could also be a metaphor for anything else," he adds. "And do not compromise. If you think something doesn't look good: Do it again. Don't be lazy in your thinking. Put hard work into it; just redo it." He cites a wise man he once knew who was lamenting that young people didn't want to read or study to further their understanding of their craft. He had a right to his grievances because he was trying to teach the inexperienced apprentices woodworking skills.

Frustrated to no end, the man finally gave his students a book on Victorian millwork and said they had to learn how to make what they saw in its pages. This example taught Madzio how important it is for not only new hires to understand how to grow, but everyone on his team, including himself. "Look for challenges in everything you do," he explains. "I'm considering making furniture for yachts now. I'm going to travel to Fort Lauderdale in the near future to meet the interior designers and architects of a project. Do I need to do it? No! I can happily sleep in my own bed, but having the experience segues with my motto: keep your life interesting and you'll never want to retire!"

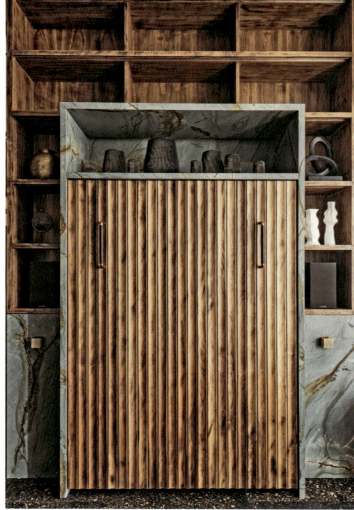

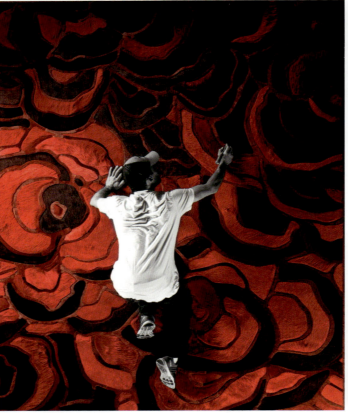

While creating the precursor to the layered piece of wall art that brightens a niche in the private elevator entrance, Kyle Bunting was caught in a crossfire. He wasn't at war with himself or anyone else; he was rocking out to an edgy song that inspired the name of the carpet he was creating at that time. "About a decade ago, David Sutherland launched a line of outdoor furniture with Phillipe Starck, and we were invited to produce some carpets to help merchandise the launch," he explains. "As I was designing one in our studio, it grew into a pattern of different geometric pieces with an irregular edge in an amoeba shape. Stevie Ray Vaughan's song "Crossfire" came on the radio and that clicked with me because it felt like the title of the song described the way the pattern looked."

He says the word also encapsulated the joint effort in which he was involved: "There was a crossfire of sorts to the collaboration, not in that we didn't get along, but it was something about working from Austin, Texas, with the Sutherlands in Dallas, and Starck in France that made the project feel very dynamic." This is the perfect word to describe how we feel about working with Bunting, as well. We've been tapping him for projects since 2006, enjoying the collaborations because he is such a charismatic and talented guy. The first time we worked with him, we chose his leather for a Christian Louboutin men's store we were designing in Paris because the sophisticated material with its elegant, gentlemanly feel was perfect for the boutique.

Bunting visited our offices, which had looked out on the twin towers before 9/11, in order to brainstorm with us. "I distinctly remember standing in the space overlooking the construction site of One World Trade," Bunting says. "It was very meaningful to be there, and getting to know the 212box team was exciting because of the innovation they bring to their projects. I was thrilled to be asked to create border inlays in the carpeting with Kyle Bunting hide for that Christian Louboutin boutique. They were thinking about us in such an innovative way, and it was gratifying to meld our experience with theirs because the result was something special."

Bunting says that this initial satisfaction has never wavered: "My first experience was so enlightening, and every opportunity since then has fulfilled that original excitement and idea. It has always been interesting to work with 212box, and never mundane." We feel the same about Bunting, whose draw to work in hide had its beginnings in his heritage. "I started the company twenty years ago, inspired by some work my dad had done when I was a kid," he explains. "Both sides of my family are from North Carolina: Dad was in textiles and ran operations; mom's family consisted of furniture makers, and she was a painter."

He says it's no surprise he would found a company dedicated to working with a supple material for the home décor industry: "With all the cotton mills and textile factories, if you grew up in North Carolina, you'd end up in some type of business that revolved around these." Though his interest in interior elements was born in these early associations, he didn't think of building a career in the design arena until 2000 when he was buying and renovating real estate.

"Before that I was in television and media so I was always steeped in creative businesses," he explains. "I didn't understand the home furnishings industry but I did have a unique appreciation for it given my background. I believe interior design is one of the highest forms of artistic expressions in the arts. I was attracted to the business due to an appreciation for the artisanship, the psychology, and the attention to detail. I also learned that being an artist and creating within a non-distracted vacuum in order to be creative is really hard!"

This comment, which reflects his own prior experience as an artist, references a time in his life when he was painting, a period when he learned firsthand how challenging maintaining a creative flow can be. "In solitude, a writer with a blank sheet of paper or a painter with a blank canvas can maintain a smooth flow unless there are interruptions, like having kids pulling at your leg or having other aspects of life swirling around you," he explains. That said, he knew he wouldn't be happy if he didn't opt for a stimulating life so he decided it was imperative for him to establish a creatively focused business.

"My dad used to say, 'If all you have is a hammer, everything looks like a nail,'" he says. This adage continues to spur him on in leading a broadly experiential and collaborative existence. His partners in this effort are the designers who keep the creativity flowing in. "It's fulfilling to see how inspired our clients are when they work with our products," he explains. "Our philosophy is not an 'it was invented here' mentality, and we feel gratitude that so many people take our hides and make magic with them." As one of the firms benefitting from the compelling business model he has created, which has allowed us to manipulate his materials in unique ways, we knew he would be a wonderful collaborator for the penthouse.

We chose him to create the hair-on-hide mural in white-on-white because it had a luxurious, tactile feel to it but it didn't compete with the massive geode sculpture in front of it. We also knew that placing it behind the big split-faced stone with its jeweled insides would soften the feel of the hard rock and serve as a light counterpoint to the heavy stone. We also appreciate that Bunting sources exemplary hides, as the materials from which his artful creations are made are overwhelmingly Italian in origin with the follicles remaining so that the leathers continue to breathe.

Bunting celebrates how the installation came together: "We are always inspired and amazed at what talented professionals do with our materials; and this project with the 212box team is a classic example of that because you found a way to use our product in a vertical niche as a backdrop to showcase a piece of art in a way that we wouldn't have imagined. Looking back, I knew we could create a material solution that didn't exist before, and we have." He says he enjoys this mindful aspect of what he does because each time his team makes a decorative hide carpet or wallcovering in collaboration with a designer, they are deeply involved in the partner's creative process.

It's apparent from the pleasure he derives in using his imagination that he has invented the right existence for his temperament. There is a symbol from his past that, looking back, might have foretold he would be doing what he's doing now. The serendipity exists in a wall-hanging of the map of Texas that was rendered in small pieces of cowhide by his father, Jim Bunting, many years ago. This piece represents the beginning of a legacy in the design industry that has made him a successful businessman.

We asked if he had any advice for someone wanting to create a business with as much heart and soul behind it as his has. "It sounds like a cliché, but I think people need to truly remember to trust their instincts," he answers. "How you feel about something creatively the first time you do it is usually the right path to pursue. Let's assume that it's a universal truth: my advice would be to follow that direction but with a wide-open mind so you can perceive what you want to do to create better outcomes. If you have enough humility to be mindful, you're better off listening to those who are in creative fields because you'll come up with something that will be more compelling to a broader audience and it will also be more fulfilling."

Bunting also believes that deferential design creates a more satisfying place to live. "What we as a creative company achieve can't be reflected in a catalog filled with black-and-white photographs of people staring off into the distance with dreamy looks in their eyes—it just doesn't work that way. Those of us running creative businesses may be fewer and farther between, but our reality is more genuine and honest. I would advise those who want to make a career in the home furnishings industry to embrace those around them in order to take advantage of what they have to offer; and to be more collaborative and holistic in their approach. This is especially true with young designers. The first reaction should be, 'What do we have here?' And then, 'Let's do something!' They'll have better ideas and innovation will follow."

Foresso

Timber Terrazzo Floors and Drawer Inserts

It thrums like a heartbeat pulsing along the core of the penthouse, a rhythmic ribbon sliding forward in a tempo that buoys one along until it disappears beneath a peek-a-boo window separating the guest bedroom from the living room. We've already described why the choice of Foresso flooring was perfect for the penthouse; we'd now like to introduce you to aspects of the brand that make us proud collaborators with the dynamic duo behind it.

The forward-thinking manufacturer of surfacing materials, which is based in Birmingham, England, was founded by Jake Solomon and Conor Taylor. We first met Solomon when he owned a company called Solomon & Wu, which made incredible architectural materials with lacquered finishes we specified for a number of the Christian Louboutin boutiques. We also sourced his metal elements covered with resin for several yachts we designed. We had worked with him for many years by the time he founded Foresso with Taylor.

Their combined knowledge was a dynamic catalyst that resulted in an alchemical transformation of wood and resin into a durable terrazzo, which would normally be made of more fragile stone and concrete. The drive the duo had to realize avant-garde materials makes them a dream team for experimentations we want to undertake. We also felt energized to work with them because they are seriously

dedicated to sustainability and ethical manufacturing. One of their declarations is that they extend their ethics to every aspect of their business, and we've seen this firsthand. Their secret-sauce of materials includes offcut timber, wood waste, mineral powders, 0 percent VOC bio-resin, and FSC birch plywood. Their products are plastic-free, and less than 5 percent of their waste goes into landfill; the rest is recycled.

A partnership with the City of London enables them to sustainably source the volume of wood chips they require because they buy bags of the mulch made from trees that have fallen in or are harvested from the city's parks. They are environmentally focused down to the packaging in which their sheets are shipped. These materials are not only recyclable, they are biodegradable as well. They will also accept discarded products they produced for reuse, as it can be ground up and poured into future batches.

We were so inspired by their commitment to ethics, we became ambassadors for the brand, and we feel fortunate we were able to champion them with this project because we had a client who was eager to support small businesses, and to be a patron to artists and artisans. The flooring for the penthouse was the first substantial order for Foresso, and we have enjoyed watching them grow and continue to thrive for several years since.

A person of deep curiosity, a brand with a dedication to refinement, a company that inspires accolades for its collaborative vivacity. These descriptions illuminate the reputation of a trio of entities: Rhett Butler, the man behind the curtain whose medium is metal; E.R. Butler, a name synonymous with precision and allure; and a retail gallery space that includes some of the world's most astute designs. The mark of perfection that he and his team achieve can be seen at every turn in this penthouse.

Though many of the pieces of hardware and arrangements of shelving the E.R. Butler team developed for the residence have minimal profiles, the breadth of knowledge required to reach a place at which metal implements become functioning works of art includes a thorough knowledge of the history of hardware. Not only has Butler amassed a stockpile of artifacts that make up one of the world's largest collections of fine architectural fittings, he has accumulated 40,000 catalogs produced by nearly every hardware manufacturer in the world.

Illustrating his respect for the fittings he produces, he says that hardware incorporates everything: "It's art, architecture, history, design, technology, manufacturing." He adds that it is in every building on the planet and there is simply no end to its importance. His think-tank is a voluminous factory along the Brooklyn waterfront with 130,000 square feet of space that holds a mix of machinery, storage, and workrooms. From here, he and his team not only craft superlative hardware, Butler explores avant-garde concepts.

He approached artist Christopher Kurtz (whose profile follows the presentation of the dining room) when he saw the needling wooden sculptures the artist created and asked if they could collaborate to produce them in metal. "To maintain the fidelity of my wood sculptures, Rhett digitized one and made a computer file," Kurtz says. "He then figured out a way to construct one, which was technically challenging and incredibly impractical." How impractical? There are only a handful of machines in the world that can achieve the delicacy and precision the sculpture would demand, and Butler located one. It was originally designed to make needles for endoscopic surgeons. Kurtz calls this project one of the most special collaborations he's had to date.

The level of creative thinking was similar for us, as Butler was able to take a number of Eric's ideas and create custom solutions, such as the complex shelving system in the Curiosity Cabinet, as you will have just read in the presentation of the private elevator entrance. We also found a number of decorative objets d'art in his boutique, such as the Ted Muehling candlesticks that enliven the dining room table with their slender profiles and Christopher Kurtz's sculpture.

Butler's path to manufacturing was not a given. He had doubts that he wanted to devote his life to the rigor he maintains, a hesitancy that continued well into his graduate studies in architecture at Rice University in Houston. When his father, who was in the hardware business for many years, retired, his clients were keen to have his son continue in his footsteps. Giving in to destiny, he left university and began E.R. Butler in a two-bedroom apartment on New York City's Lower East Side. He then set about acquiring other storied manufacturing firms, such as Enoch Robinson and W.C. Vaughan, moving to larger digs each time he outgrew the square footage.

In the early 2000s, he opened a showroom in a landmark building on Prince Street in Manhattan and based his headquarters there. The boutique is a shopping destination that includes an art gallery and serves as a mecca for design and architecture professionals thirsty for high-quality hardware. He's so popular with arbiters of taste because his designs are superb and the options in materials, shapes, and finishes are extensive—this is the case even before the subject of custom is broached. When window displays are changed, the neighborhood and visitors alike eagerly flock to see what's new in the E.R. Butler universe.

His designs are included in the homes of a long list of cultural icons like Lenny Kravitz and Bill Gates; former presidents have tapped him for products for their homes, as have leading fashion designers, Nobel Prize Laureates, tech and financial giants, and Oscar-winning actors and directors. These visionaries with endless resources turn to him because he is fearless in his experimentation. "We can do just about anything," he notes. This anything includes being a veritable 007 of hardware because he finds solutions for those who want to secure safe rooms on their properties. His virtuosity has developed through life experience; during his master's degree in architecture, which he did go on to earn; and through the company he keeps, which includes architect-, artist-, and fashion designer–friends who keep him immersed in design philosophy.

Stimulation is important in his life because his level of curiosity is vigorous. "As a child, my younger brother and I were not allowed to watch television but were given books to read," he explains. "These were not children's books, mind you, but sets of encyclopedias and other weighty volumes. Our father was a dealer in antiques, so we went to many antiques auctions and markets. Sifting through the millions of remnants and artifacts for more than a decade, we learned a great deal about so many things. I spent quite a few summers with either my mother's mother in a very small town in Germany, or my father's parents in an equally small town in South Carolina."

He describes a few of the experiences that he credits for the sensibilities he has developed: "During those summers with my grandmother in Germany, we would travel all over Europe; she had lived through the war and her house had been occupied twice, once by the Nazis and then by the American forces, so she was eager to be free, to see as much as she could, and to share it with us. We experienced everything: museums, castles, mountains, cities, farms, gardens; literally everything." Illustrating the intensity of his grandmother's experiences, he notes, "I once found a spoon in the basement crawl-space with a swastika insignia on it."

When Butler stayed with his father's parents, the experiences were quite different from those he had in Germany: "My grandfather taught me to drive a car, a tractor, and a truck by the time I was nine years old. It was in South Carolina where I received my first driver's license. My job was to pick up the farm workers from town, which was three miles away. My grandfather is the one who is responsible for teaching me a great deal about how to treat others with respect." Anecdotes from those summers bring to light the depth of his inquisitiveness and how long it has been embedded in his psyche. "Every day my grandparents would take a nap after lunch, and my brother and I would have the time to ourselves to do whatever we wanted," he explains. "We could take a nap or we could explore, as long as it was outside of the house."

As young boys are wont to do, it seemed an obvious choice to unleash their curiosity instead of giving in to unsuccessful attempts to take naps, which resulted in the painful frustration of hearing the seconds click by on the living room clock. After finding a book on making bombs, these outings would turn into explosive exploits: "I loved to blow things up! Creating hydrogen bombs was the most impressive—I guess I'd be in jail in today's world, but growing up on a farm has its privileges! It didn't help that my grandfather would specifically task me with burning huge mountains of trees after he cleared land for farming."

We asked Butler what drives his passion for precision and he didn't mince words: "I'm not really sure what drives the need for perfection. Could be that I got it from my German mother; could be that I can't understand the endless amount of garbage we generate because we are so focused on everything being cheap. Then again, maybe it's driven from a perspective of permanence. I need to feel as if what I spend my time making will outlive me." As to his favorite thing about the life he has orchestrated for himself, he says, "Being happy and content. It took a long time to get to where I am. I don't need anything and I'm happy with having little." He so wisely adds, "There is peace that comes from not needing or wanting."

Laurence Le Constant

Lilah Sculpture

Is it possible to harness the wind; to capture the essence of an entity that has no physical appearance without an object to oscillate? Notice how the plumed skull swirls with movement, how the striations buzz with energy as they flow along the surface. This is how currents of air wish they could present themselves in concrete form had they a choice. Let us introduce you to the enchantress who has taken mysterious breezes captive in her art that is festooned with feathers: her name is Laurence Le Constant, and she created *Lilah*, a sculpture we chose to ornament a prominent shelf in the Curiosity Cabinet.

Le Constant's initial inspiration that led her to layer plumage onto a cranial construct is as powerful as the sculpture itself: "The skull is a symbol of death—powerful, repulsive, and hypnotic—and the feather has played a bewitching role throughout history, as a symbol to communicate with the other world during tribal rites and as the standard value used when weighing the soul in ancient Egypt," she explains. "For me, colors represent sound frequencies; and feather types with differing degrees of pliability, from stiff to nimble, correspond to character traits."

Like the other sculptures in the "My Lovely Bones" series, *Lilah* had a very personal beginning: "When my grandmother passed away, her death was a significant turning point in my life. To both mourn and pay tribute to her, I began working on the feathered skulls. The name 'My Lovely Bones' came to me because each one is a portrait of a woman who mattered to me." Le Constant is an avid writer and especially enjoys putting her own poems down on paper, which will often

find their way into aspects of her art. "My works are poetry translated into volume, materials, and colors," she explains. "The inspiration comes from childhood memories or myths and legends, the latter two among my great passions. The notion of roots and the link to genealogy are the backbone of my creative process."

The relationship she has with her sculptures is a very dynamic one: "I consider my creations as beings with souls. I lovingly create them over many weeks, sometimes months, as I infuse them with life energy. Seeing them integrated into the living spaces of collectors deeply touches me because they are entering a new family and radiating in a space that gives them a new dimension." Le Constant was not always elbow deep in feathers in her atelier. "My background is as a painter and sculptor," she says. "I learned to work with feathers in a basic way during lunch hours while working in the haute couture workshops. I combine the techniques of sculpture and painting as I am manipulating the plumage, perfecting my methods of construction by watching how the birds nest."

She adds that the question of beauty is a fundamental one for her: "How far can I push that symbol or material to reveal its essence? Is it attractive or repulsive? Is it beautiful or ugly? What feeling does this work arouse in me?" The artist had a long relationship with elegance before she began cementing her legacy in art. After studying at the Sorbonne and the Chambre Syndicale de la Couture Parisienne, she signed on at Dior where she spent her days ornamenting opulent ensembles. Once she embraced being a maker of art, embroidery and sequin techniques morphed to feathers as

she explored her way into sculpture. "While I was working in the haute couture workshops, I befriended a retired lady," she says. "During our lunch hours, this beautiful woman taught me the basics of this technique that I perfected with practice and through studying how birds make their nests in nature. It is a unique and rich process that she helped me to understand."

Le Constant has known since she was a child that she would create, saying the impulse is so strong for her, she sees it as written in her destiny. What would she say to others who feel equally passionate about cementing their own legacies in art? "My advice to dreamers and creators is this: Stay true to yourself," she says. "You will meet people throughout your journey who will want to force you to create in a certain way so that you are in line with everyone else. Whatever the pressures, remain focused on what is your essence and stay the course, as it is your difference that will bring wealth to your work." We asked Le Constant to describe for us what excites her the most about how she spends her days: "The thing I prefer to do is look for new colors—in magazines, books, nature, everywhere and all the time. I try to imagine the sounds to which they correspond; to hear the celestial music that ancient people spoke."

Given the primeval intensity that *Lilah* arouses from her place in the penthouse, we marvel at the fact that Le Constant's dialogue with prehistoric souls is being transmuted into an intoxicating new lexicon.

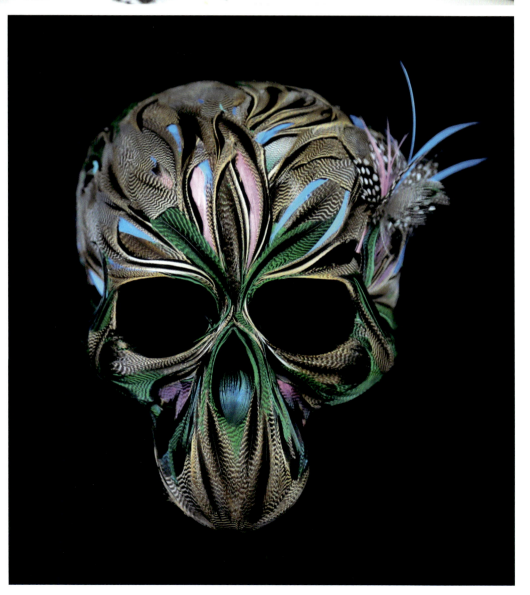

Who would be so bold as to draw lines in light—to take luminosity to task and striate it so that it explains itself in peaks and valleys? The rays of the sun are unaccustomed to being forced into form, but this is exactly what Nathan Allan Glass Studios achieved with the cathedral glass panels we included in the penthouse. The remarkably thick material brings an architectonic sophistication to the back of the powder room door tucked into the Curiosity Cabinet and to a corner of the guest suite where the ripples effervesce when bathed in natural light from adjacent windows. After dark, the surfaces change their personality completely, glowing golden when the egg-shaped night-lights are switched on.

Barry Allan, who founded the Canadian company and serves as its director, explains his inspiration for the vast array of materials he produces: "Just look at the planets, the ocean, the mountains: inspiration comes from everywhere! I might see a wallcovering produced in a completely different material and wonder how it would appear in glass-form. I take my ideas to my two lead artists, and we come up with our plans to create a design while also making sure the new product can be safely and functionally used."

His goal in creating the beautiful, linear cathedral glass was to see it in the highest-end projects to which he contributes. "It has the flavor of the old-style Greek columns, ridges like you would see in the pillars of buildings like the Parthenon," he says. "The surface pattern is deep, wavy, and very three-dimensional—attributes that are distinctive and are not seen anywhere else. I believe that our efforts to create uniqueness is one of the most winning aspects of our glass designs." We resoundingly agree, which is why we chose one for this residence.

Allan decided to go into business for himself out of great necessity. "I founded my company because my employer at that time (not a glass company) would not pay me a decent salary, even though I was setting sales records each year,"

he explains. "I remember going into the office of one of the owners who looked after their finances to request a very small raise. His answer to me was, 'You're actually selling too much product so our profit margins are going down.' I was young and stupid at the time, but not that stupid, so I quit and set off on my own."

He wasn't consciously aware at the beginning that he would become known for producing artisanal offerings. "At the start, I just wanted to survive," he says. "Then, with some limited success, I saw that the opportunity to grow was available; and with growth, it would bring us the revenue we needed to perform more extensive and expensive research and development. Our success allowed us to realize that we could become a brand, and we've certainly achieved that."

As he took these realizations and ran with them, he continued to push himself and his team into new territory that would result in some of the most authentically original products in his category. "So many others in our industry just copy what we do, or at least they try to copy and are mostly unsuccessful," he says. "They quickly discover how difficult it is to produce the innovative designs we manufacture, so we stay ahead of everyone by introducing multiple new designs on a yearly basis."

Because each piece of glass the company creates is individually crafted, the Nathan Allan studio has also become a go-to source for designers and architects wanting to achieve a vintage vibe or needing to replicate panes from bygone eras. "As with every industry, retro materials come into vogue at times and we are approached to match them," he explains. "We also receive quite a few requests to reproduce antique glass that has broken and is no longer safe to keep in a project. Because all our glass is handmade, we can customize it to appear very similar to the antique panes. There is one difference, though: it will look old but it will be safety glass, which is a great bonus."

Through the vivacity of his drive to always stretch and grow, Allan has built a rewarding existence for himself with an array of daily pleasures. "Every morning I get to go to work and collaborate with the same people I've known for over twenty-five years—bonds are created, even when we don't realize it," he says, calling this team talented and hardworking. Bringing him further satisfaction is the fact that he is steeped in natural beauty every day: "My factory/showroom/office is in a beautiful building located near horse country."

Though his love of travel was interrupted by the pandemic, he says his experiences of meeting talented interior designers and architects, and discovering new cities are treasured memories. But when pressed to describe his absolute favorite thing about what he does day in/day out, he reveals, "It is the freedom to design and create, bringing my thoughts and visions to fruition, and knowing our glass designs are being specified and installed in beautiful buildings. To go and visit a stunning office space or high-end hotel, casino, or restaurant, and see my glass installed everywhere—in settings where it looks incredible and is seriously functional—is most rewarding!"

What advice would he have for the person struggling as he was when he created his company while also knowing there must be something better? "Whatever you do, work as hard as you can; be grateful for the opportunity you have; don't complain; get up every day and go to work even when life has you down; never give up; and don't expect to make much money for the first five to ten years," he advises. "Also, be grateful for the free countries we live in here in Canada and the United States, and the opportunities our countries still provide if we want to be successful."

A mesmerizing piece of stone with such a volatile pattern, it must have once been the sky in which Zeus was waging war. The heft of time as staggering as the eons it took for it to age has a gravitational pull, one that has resulted in a contemporary mythic tale in this penthouse. The refined surfaces of straw marquetry surrounding it and the marble itself are counter-opposites to the modernity of the refrigerators that hum in the wine niche.

Unifying these paradoxical elements are antique bronze art deco plates we created from castings with E.R. Butler. The straw marquetry panels are by Alexander Lamont, whose tailored applications of materials are wonderful paintbrushes in our tool belt, which we enjoy introducing as we compose them in contemporary ways. You'll see why we admire him when you read about his constant quest for excellence, later in this chapter. The wine bar is tucked into a large niche that measures seven feet by six feet. Inset into this is the alcove of marble we sourced from Aria Stone Gallery (with showrooms in Houston and Dallas), and whose profile follows this presentation of the room. The handpicked slabs here were curated by founder Vinny Tavares.

We learned of the company when we were designing the lobby spaces in the building. Not only were we attracted to the aesthetic values of the stone he sourced, we appreciated the fact that he specializes in, in Tavares's own words, "pieces of art that nature has created so slowly over centuries." This particular point has great depth that resonates throughout the rooms in the penthouse, as the owner has spent his career in the natural gas and oil industries, and was educated in engineering and geology. He responded passionately to each stone we sourced, though he was particularly enamored with the slab in this area, which he handpicked for the niche.

We watched as he studied it, completely enthralled by its veining. It was like watching an art historian taking in a lauded painting from far in the past. He talked about how platelets had transformed into marble, the patterns inspiring him to tell stories about geological specimens he had studied. We felt that in tapping into his passion, we created a special owner's alcove—a blank slate for him to tell stories about geology as he welcomes guests in for cocktails or a glass of wine. These are the moments that become new mythic tales and keep the tradition of storytelling alive—one man whose fascination with natural resources fully on display in a penthouse overlooking a city inseparable from petroleum in its own legendary way.

Furthering the bountiful theme of hospitality set by the wine niche, is a circular table surrounded by stools, its shape perfectly echoed by a ringed chandelier that flows down from the ceiling. The pairing of the statuesque chandelier by Dimore Studio Lighting with the table is kinetic because the tiered stone base of the latter telescopes up from the floor as the chandelier trickles down. The two coalesce to act as a balancing element that aligns circular shapes in the space and introduces a pleasant dose of *chi* energy that flows evenly through the rest of the apartment. The table is placed to serve a purpose beyond its aesthetic power: it is a convenient place to deposit purses, keys, scarves, and briefcases, making it a helpmate for shaking off a day in the world as a glass of whisky or wine is poured—the first sip made all the more satisfying under the glow of the vibrant circular bands.

We have always been taken by this Italian company's beautiful lampadas because we appreciate the manufacturer's design prowess and thoughtfulness in how its products are assembled. The dynamic series of rings over the entrance table compose Lampada 028 in the Dimoremilano Collection. Aesthetically, we chose it because it personifies movement and activates the space. Added interest is created by the intermingling of oxidized brass and painted brass finishes on the rings. The table beneath the chandelier is a piece by Tyler Hays of BDDW, whom you will get to know in his profile that follows.

Hays topped the carved marble piece, which extends from its widest circular element on the floor toward smaller tiers at its apex, with a disc of reclaimed walnut peppered with fissures and joinery. The widest cracks in the wood are artfully secured with bow tie inlays, the placement of which illustrate the designer's nuanced eye. The opportunity to make a sophisticated design statement with salvaged wood as a focal point furthers our agenda of honoring the homeowner's love of the material and sets the tone for similar moves we make in a number of spaces to come. All in all, nature's artistry sings here.

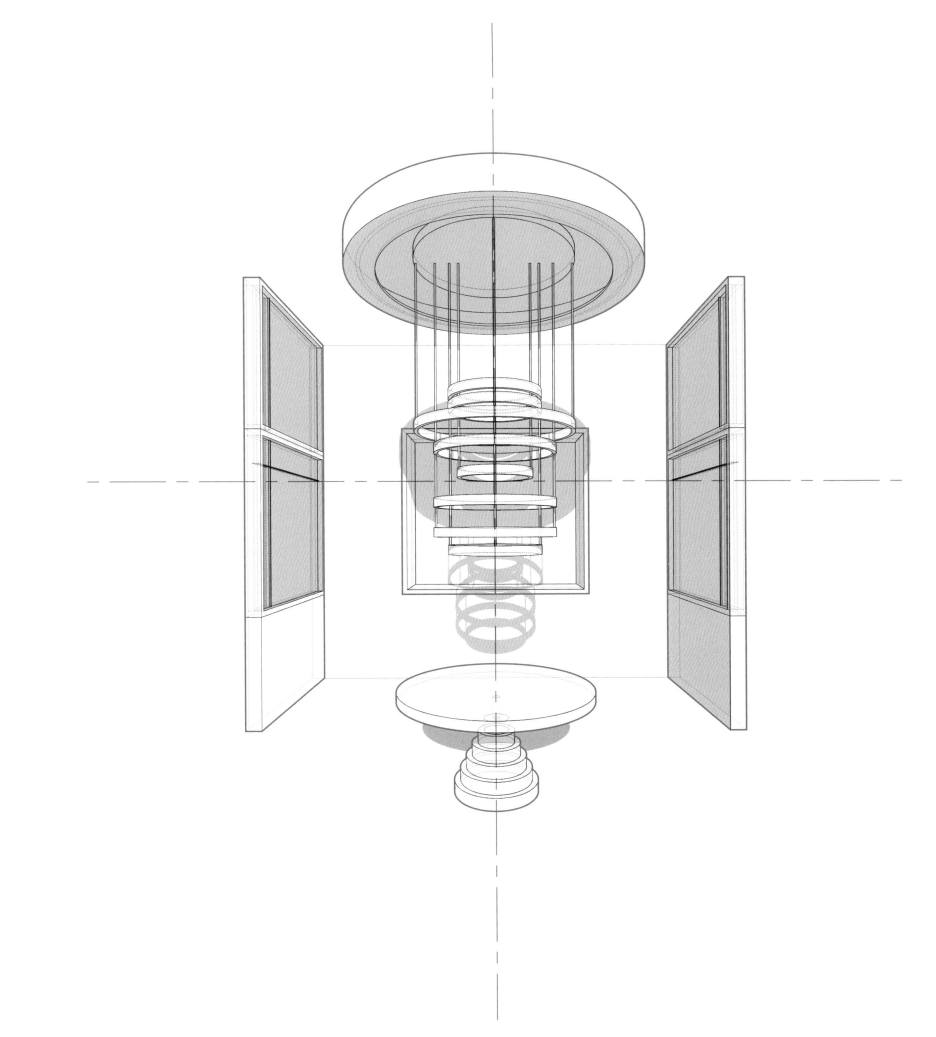

Alexander Lamont

Le Mur Straw Marquetry Panels

The concept of philosophy is defined as the point at which the fundamental nature of knowledge, reality, and existence comingle. When an artisanal brand has philosophically declared that it strives to live "between the stories of the past and the ideas of the future," it stands at another intersection: the one where art and design meet. Alexander Lamont's point of view is expressed in the above ideals. The British designer has always been interested in enigmatic textures, forms, and materials; or, as he describes the actualization of these, "surfaces that call out to be touched."

We came across Lamont's incredible offerings through Angela Brown Limited, a connoisseur of handcrafted elements who has been sourcing for us for over twenty years. Lamont's journey toward the realization of these refined furnishings took the passionate maker to Thailand where he has built workshops that are celebrated for the pieces that flow from them. Lamont believes that objects have power; that they connect us to our most intimate selves, as well as to the people, places, stories, and memories of our lives. He has an affinity for natural resources that grow old with grace. "I want the pieces and surfacing that I create to become lifelong companions, friends of the house, each with its own energy, beauty, and spirit," he says. "I seek to bring a fresh point of view to the world of decorative arts, fine furniture, and traditional materials with luxurious and contemporary forms."

This requires an uncompromising approach to innovation, craftsmanship, and quality. "These have been achieved in my workshops through the mastery of ancient skills and techniques," he adds, "and a willingness to break through those same traditions through our research and development work." He believes that in a world of increasing speed and mass production, we are in danger of seeing the disappearance of many things long considered essential to the designer and maker in times past: "These include hand drawing; the lived understanding of techniques and materials; and the years of patience and practice that build the skills needed to make something superlative."

He is building on the legacy of the craftspeople and makers in Europe and Asia who have been refining their techniques for centuries. "Our minimal, organic, and tailored designs show a contemporary reverence for the rituals of craftsmanship and the energy that human skills impart into every piece," he explains. These include the straw marquetry surfacing we sourced for the penthouse, which was handmade in his ateliers. "Straw is loved particularly by the French," he says. "I'm proud to say that mine is the only contemporary workshop to have mastered this exceptional material, from its natural raw state covered in mud and husk; through all the processes of cleaning and dyeing; up to the final stages of ironing and application."

He traces the provenance of straw marquetry to the villages and towns of rural France. "The earliest uses of straw for decorative purposes can be found in the seventeenth century in intricate sewing boxes and hand mirrors depicting marquetry floral patterning or landscapes that would have taken many days to complete. Favored above all others for this art form is rye straw because the stems are longer than wheat and oat, and the natural cellulose that covers it (and creates the wonderful reflectivity beloved in straw) is particularly resilient."

He explains that straw marquetry had an unexpected "boom" during the Napoleonic wars between France and Britain (and its allies) because French prisoners of war incarcerated by the king asked for straw so they could ward off the boredom they experienced as they languished in prisons like Dartmoor and Leicester. This also allowed them to create income by selling their creations. "As a result, exquisite works from their hands can be seen in various museums in England," he notes, pinpointing straw marquetry's next rise to fame three centuries later.

"Sometime during the early twentieth century, decorators in Paris rediscovered straw," he explains. "It is not known where the spark struck first, but Clément Rousseau and Jean-Michel Frank both began to use straw marquetry in their projects, the latter covering entire rooms with it in glowing bronze-dyed or natural tones. It is difficult to imagine the great rooms of this era accepting a 'peasant' material, but Frank was not bound by such strictures, and saw nobility in the straw itself. He believed that the gorgeous glowing effect of thousands of natural ribbons reflected light and color to elevate it."

Illustrating why Lamont's philosophy is so resonant with ours, he sees the delicate nuance of fine things made from elements in nature as nothing less than physical poetry. "It is only natural, excuse the pun, that straw should find its way from Burgundy by the container to my leafy Bangkok yards and rooms!" he quips. He says the journey that instilled in him the desire to source to this extent began when he grew conscious of his father's business when he was six years old.

"In 1975, my father started a business importing folk art and traditional handicrafts from India, Africa, and South America into a small village in southwest England," he explains. "The company grew, and over the years, I would work and travel with my dad to many places in search of what was authentic and beautiful; elements that reflected the spirit of the people and the resources of that place. I grew to have a great appreciation for these crafts, the vast majority of which have disappeared or are very rare now. My education in design came from these simple-yet-complex things—the vibrant imperfections of handmade objects that are made very well; pieces that spoke of culture, belief, and the local environment."

These experiences drove Lamont to pursue a path toward reviving these in contemporary works that "hold all the deep beauty found only in things made by highly skilled hands." The country in which he chose to do so was essential to his success. "When I started my business, I chose to base myself in Thailand because this is a refined and fascinating country, very rich in crafts and skills," he explains. "I had studied anthropology and Southeast Asian languages at university but wanted to begin to make things of real beauty—things I felt were relevant for a modern age, and particularly things that we're in great danger of losing as we've been propelled toward living with objects that have no human or natural connection. In a way, it has been more of a journey of respect, homage, and refinement to these traditions than about new design."

For the past twenty-two years, he has focused on what he regards as the epitome of the greatest craft traditions via the most beautiful surfaces known to us. "In Thailand we have many workshops for these, including shagreen, parchment, gilding, mica, woodwork, natural lacquer, eggshell, to name a few," he adds. "I also constantly travel throughout Asia to find artisans who have traditional craft skills that could benefit from reimagining." When he began working with straw, he asked himself, "How do I bring forth the greatest rendition of it; how do I prepare it, color it, abrade it, and bring an artistic dimensionality to this most 'alive' of materials?" He found the answer "within tiny fractions of techniques through which entirely new ways of presenting straw exist."

This quest has intermingled science, art, an understanding of culture, and travel. "Each moment," he explains, "has been filled with adventure and rich creative moments. My eyes are focusing on every step, knowing where I want to arrive." Having his work inform the beauty of glorious rooms on par with those he has held in high esteem spurs him on: "Within interiors, the designer is often searching for a balance of drama and quiet that is like finding a rare elixir; something that will *wow* the client but also be reassuringly beautiful over the years. Straw marquetry represents this balance in microcosm."

He has a clear vision for the experience he wants the shining panels in his "Le Mur" collection to offer: "As you approach or walk past, the light flashes and moves, following the myriad silvered lines that sit on every straw. It is beguiling and intriguing; it has an energy and vitality different from any vinyl or synthetic substitute. The only way to achieve this level of contemporary surface artistry is to slowly and painstakingly select every straw; apply it perfectly with glue and scalpel, and then give it sheen with an agate burnishing stone. Also critical is selecting colors that throb evenly to exhibit a tonal range without any jarring point."

We asked Lamont if he had always known he wanted to be a maker and to build an artisanal brand. "Like many people growing up in a family business, I didn't initially want to do what my dad was doing," he answers. "I loved the travel but I had 'bigger dreams' than just making crafts. But when I started working in an antiques gallery in Hong Kong after university, I began to realize that I had absorbed a huge amount of knowledge over the years, and that I loved and responded to the patinas, surfaces, and forms of crafts—both ancient and contemporary. I mean really loved them; was fascinated by how hands and tools and age had built such beautiful surfaces."

From this initial *aha* moment, he says, the idea to form a creative business gradually took shape. "There is no career that I would choose above what I have done," he explains. "It has allowed me to travel to every country that fascinates me and to collaborate with artisans who are making beautiful works. That, for me, combines the best holiday with the best way to spend my time! When I look at the type of mass synthetic products that fill most homes, I feel very lucky to spend my hours with these rare and gorgeous things—the same things that so many centuries of artists and designers have loved before me."

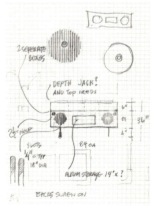

Straight lines and arcs, concaves and curves, the brilliant green of a leaf on a canvas or in a bowl, the haunting strains of a song that wafts into a room as a long skirt flows to the melody with a body's progress, the grating sound of metal when a lever is pulled after being bolted in place, a planer scraping the surface of a fine species of wood. Any one of these may hold the attentive absorption of Tyler Hays on any given day. In fact, trying to typecast him is a lesson in futility because his fascinations are boundless.

Hays sees BDDW as an amalgamation of performance, sculpture, furniture, and design fabrication; and himself as an engineer, inventor, architect, chef, musician, and furniture and fashion designer. His deeper enjoyment is derived from the time he spends on the engineering that results in more sophisticated furniture tooling and processes, and the explorations he undertakes as he problem-solves other projects, mostly heating systems and brewery systems. During the last several years, his art has been a very dynamic slice of his success, which means he's been able to spend more time concentrating on an art form he has long valued—painting.

We enjoy seeing a creative of his caliber continue to stretch and grow, and we are thrilled that the furniture we purchased for this penthouse captured his attention when it did so that we could buy it! Our respect for him is immense: time and again, the refined aesthetics of his creations draw us in; it is only after living with them that we realize how meticulously produced they are. The tailored perfection of the pieces we chose for this residence elevates everything we place near them.

We have a running joke among our team that it is dangerous to take clients into the BDDW store because by the time we have made the list of the elements they would like to see in their interiors, they will have a home filled with only BDDW's products! But take them in we do, as it's important for them to understand why his creations are superior. Each time we demonstrate the architectonic brilliance, peeling away the layers that go into his work as we open a drawer, unlatch a door, or encourage them to run their hands along a surface, we watch as the excitement builds. As design purists ourselves, we have collected furnishings for our own homes. They are personal artifacts that we know will become family heirlooms and remain treasured works of art.

Seeing the list of his preferred creative activities above makes it obvious that he is always experimenting in everything he does. He says that in each of these undertakings, including his furniture making, there is engineering at its core. It is this sophistication of invention that keeps us coming back to BDDW, and we often purchase pieces during his auctions, as they are trials that he has decided not to produce in quantity so they become valuable one-offs or limited editions. Hays once told us that we buy the very best things he makes, which is quite a compliment coming from him.

We took the couple who owns this penthouse through BDDW separately and watched as each of them took different directions in the articles they loved. As we worked within the schematic, we identified eight pieces that we spread throughout the residence from a mix of their choices.

These include the table in the center of the entrance near the wine niche, the large live-edge maple dining table, a credenza in the living room, the two bedside tables (prototypes!) in the guest suite, a bench in front of the windows overlooking the pool, the tall bookcase above the credenza that separates the dining room and living room, and the bleached wood hutch in the primary bedroom—each of which is a gem in the space it inhabits.

Knowing we would be including a number of his finely designed elements in the interiors, we pushed ourselves to up the ante on our own designs, such as the Curiosity Cabinet and the credenza that separates the dining room from the living room, atop which we placed his bookcase. We've already celebrated Gregory Madzio for his exquisite ability to produce exemplary work in the chapter presenting the private elevator entrance. When he examined Hays's work, he was astounded by the quality. Hearing one aesthete say this about another says it all.

The New York Times quotes Hays as saying about his drive: "It's all based on the idea of making everything I touch." He adds that the foundation of his process is science, materials, and craft; but as the realization of pieces progress, he is observing the alchemy and poetry of each object as he coaxes it into its final form. He sees BDDW as an enigmatic brand. We couldn't have said it better ourselves.

Aria Stone Gallery
Stone Specimens

If you've ever wondered whether the earth has fingerprints, wander through the Aria Stone Gallery showrooms in Houston or Dallas and marvel at the meandering patterns on the fine specimens of stone they curate. Only then will you glean the answer. There are three areas in the penthouse in which the exquisite markings on the surfaces of the slabs are vibrant focal points—the wine niche, the study, and her dressing room and bath. Also from Aria, the Panda stone in the lobby areas of Arabella forms a spirited backdrop that creates a magnifying journey through the spaces.

The stones the company sources are so remarkable because each of the slabs is hand-selected by a visionary whose convictions are profound, the company's founder Vinny Tavares. Born near São Paulo, Brazil, he initially pursued a path in finance until he stumbled upon the stone industry after working with a friend whom he had met at the University of Texas at Austin. It didn't take long for him to realize he was looking at more than just stone, as he felt that finding the next perfect slab was akin to listening to a song for the first time, keeping his senses peeled in order to catch every color and every note. His appreciation for music and art suddenly intermingled in his psyche and led him to develop his vision for what was to become Aria Stone Gallery.

"This is just one of the reasons Aria Stone Gallery stands apart in the industry," says April Graves, COO and partner at the firm since 2014. She comes to the company with a broad knowledge of textiles. After attaining her master's degree in design from Central Saint Martins in London, she decided to concentrate on both textiles and design as she carved out her niche in the home décor market. Having a unique skillset

of being business-minded, along with her strong sense of design, she felt that helping to foster the special environment and the brand that Aria Stone Gallery encompasses was a powerful opportunity.

Her background in design was the solid foundation that enabled her to seamlessly transition into the stone industry. "As partner and COO at Aria Stone Gallery, I have grown by opening a new showroom in Houston and further refining the revolutionary online shopping experience," she says. "One of my primary goals has been to bring the company into the forefront of the industry worldwide, making it an international brand. We've had great success in this and we have so much more potential for growth to come."

Tavares's point of view that stone is slow art runs deep, his *aha* moment taking place in the National Museum in Stockholm during an exhibition called "Slow Art," which explored the origin and history of materials used in artwork. "I was intrigued by the concept of appreciating the beauty of slowly and carefully developed art," he says, "and started to wonder how we could apply those concepts to the stone industry and design world." He believes that a truly remarkable piece of stone will stop people in their tracks, even those who would normally zoom by, as the patterns beckon the senses for a deep dive.

He and Graves travel the globe to hand-select natural stone directly from the most prestigious quarries. They make selections based on the uniqueness of each slab and only purchase stone with deep-rooted history. This is history with a capital H, as the pieces of art they source

were created so very slowly over centuries. "We pride ourselves in collaborating with the most talented designers throughout the United States and beyond," Graves notes. "212box projects are always refreshing because the envelope is always pushed as far as installation concepts and selection of the most rare and unique slabs are concerned, along with technical execution in fabrication."

As to the advice the pair would give others longing to create a distinctive niche for themselves in any industry: "Don't compromise on your ideals and standards. If you want to be different then you have to think outside the box and you need to take some chances." Graves adds, "The constant pursuit of the perfect slab is what sets Aria's collection apart as a unique stone boutique. Instead of trying to fulfill a predetermined stock list of standard materials, selections are made based on the individuality of each stone. Much like buying a diamond, materials are evaluated for their color, content, clarity, and consistency, with a consideration as to how the vein structures lend to book-match veining."

You can see for yourself how the specimens we chose for the Arabella lobby areas and the three spaces in the penthouse are stunningly exclusive in their own DNA. Our appreciation for the talent and the eye of these visionaries has gone beyond a mere business relationship since we completed the penthouse. "Though I met Eric in the Houston gallery when he was working on the Arabella project, I didn't meet Eun until later when I visited their New York office," Graves notes. "Over the years my relationship with 212box has blossomed beyond being merely collaborators into a friendship."

Undulations and drifts; talismans and circular cues. Are they indecipherable symbols and geometries? Only for the uninitiated who've never heard the story of a quintessentially Texan family. These conundrums exist in a mixed-media work of art that hangs singularly on one wall in this public elevator entrance, a composition we commissioned for the penthouse. You will meet its creator, Canadian artist Cybèle Young, after we take a moment to highlight the artisanal design elements in this space.

Serving as a luminous contrast to the warmth of the private elevator entrance, the experience of stepping through the doorway to this hallway entered from the public elevator is a calming confrontation of ethereal brightness. The incandescence of white draws one across the pale marble floor that contrasts with the plank wood terrazzo expanses and breaks the plane of the Curiosity Cabinet ahead. Furnishings in this area include a mirror with a perimeter of exquisite lacquered resin that looks like marble; the surface so convincing, it illustrates the artisanal aspects of the painterly talent it requires to produce a finish that reads like stone.

Including the dark circular element on the wall and placing a vintage bench that has dark and warm tones beneath the mirror were important moves to add depth to this space. The blacks and browns serve as anchors to what is otherwise pale and pristine in color. The mirror also creates a layered experience by reflecting Cybèle's artwork, which is itself such a complex composition built of intricacies. Shadow boxes holding mementos play along the reflective glass and colors drift across the disc that replicates them to echo the artfulness on the opposite wall. There are two classic sconces on either side of the mirror, which are also vintage—all sourced from 1stDibs.

You will see this online purveyor mentioned in several chapters in this book because we source from them often. We respect the company for helping us locate everything from priceless antiques and classic vintage pieces to edgy modern works of art. The profiles posted on the artists and designers they represent help educate us about historical provenance and broaden our awareness of makers we may not have found otherwise. One of the broader intentions of this book is to illustrate how we go out of our way to support artists and artisans. This includes searching for their work in physical venues, some of which are out of the way, and looking online for unknown or regionally known talent not previously on our radar.

At the apex of the wall above the bench, we created a subtle scoop that forms a light trough. This creates a nuanced detail on that side of the space as it sparks the illusion that the wall peels down from the ceiling. When the lights are switched on, an illuminated datum hidden there warms the hallway, as does the mellow gleam emanating from the glamorous sconces. When the sun filters into this space from the windows in the living room and dining room, the tones grow mellow and Cybèle's creation takes on added texture. Walking from this entryway into the main living spaces, pastels are left behind to be embraced by warmth. The foundation is the plank wood terrazzo floor that sets the tone for the new experience that awaits—guests being welcomed as they are heartily greeted and introduced to all the artistry they will take in as they flow through each space.

Contemporary INI Daybed below Maison Jansen marbled
lacquer mirror and Spacek wall sconces by Matthew Fairbank—
all procured from 1stDibs.

Cybèle Young

Mixed-Media Works

Pulsing through the veins of the most creatively driven human beings is a cocktail of motivations: a love of experimentation, a passion for investigation, and a commitment to refinement. Cybèle Young, a Canadian artist living and working in Toronto, has proven her mettle where these ideals are concerned as she has exhibited her works internationally, taken on complex commissions, and published award-winning children's books.

For the first twenty-five years of her career, Young devoted her time in her studio exclusively to creating miniature worlds from fine Japanese papers. "I had studied sculptural installations and had been making larger-scaled works in metal and wood at art school," she explains. "When I became a mom just after leaving my studies, I found myself at home with a baby and with limited space, limited time, and limited funds." Segueing to miniature and to a pliable material after having devoted her studies to welding metal brought her a great deal of satisfaction. "I fell in love with Japanese paper through printmaking because it took to print in a way that no other paper had," she says. "There was a sculptural feel to the etchings in intaglio, which I could create at home."

When she had the idea to manipulate the material into sculptural shapes, Young found that working with the paper was even more rewarding. "It's like having a collaboration with the material—you keep pushing it and it keeps challenging you. It's both delicate and very strong." Though she calls the building blocks to her artistic creations basic—paper wrapped around needles and dowels, and ubiquitous shapes like the cube and the pyramid, she describes the process of discovery as she honed her techniques over the years as "an organic journey to a new way of working."

We commissioned Young to create a work for a previous project in 2016—a composition depicting the manufacturing process involved in producing cashmere for the 1436 / Erdos flagship store in Beijing. That project and the commissions for this Houston residence meant she was creating on a grander scale than she had in the past. This ushered in an entirely new way of fabricating. "For these works, my need to up the production with trained assistants was essential," she explains. "I created the sketches and would oversee the sculptural fabrication, production, and assembling the composition."

By the time Young worked with us on the Houston project, she felt confident that moving into larger-scaled projects would not be overly challenging. "After so many years, I intimately understand the aspects of this process: creating with the paper has become second nature for me," she adds. We were introduced to Young by a friend when she was in Paris during a four-month Canada Council studio residency. "It was very serendipitous," she explains. "We shared a mutual respect, and I was so refreshed by the playful approach to curating and collaboration that Eric and Eun seemed to embody." She described our perspective as freeing, and the Erdos project as a holistic experience where she was able to learn about an entire environment being built from the ground up and to become part of the process.

"We flew to Mongolia and experienced the factory firsthand," she says. "I'd never been involved in such an organic way—not only did it fit so well with my own creative process, even though it was a commercial project, it was very stimulating for me." That experience brought us a comfort level that made tapping Young for the Houston project an easy choice. Young created two pieces of art for the penthouse. *You'll Find Far Away Out Back*, which hangs in the foyer, symbolizes stories that relate to the family's history. *To Understand Better* is installed above the desk in the guest suite. For *You'll Find Far Away Out Back*, Young worked with the homeowners to find out which things stood out for them in their own lives and what elements about their history were important to them.

"I played with those ideas and some of the things I learned about Texas and Houston to create components for the piece," she explains. "It's like putting all the ingredients in a big stewpot and seeing what flavors come out." She adds that this wasn't a linear story; it was more about the feelings, the sounds, and the shapes she discovered during a trip to meet the homeowners. "We were walking through another property they own and the jasmines were blooming everywhere, and they said it was one of their favorite scents," she explains. "What I set out to do was to help them return to their childhood dreams and then continue dreaming through their own children with the symbology of this piece." She says at first, she was experimenting with the topography of the space created by the artwork's dimensions as she was positioning the disparate elements that the homeowners saw as significant in their lives.

"I built in components, putting pieces together like I was playing in a playground, each new introduction exciting me," she notes. "As is the case with most of my pieces, for whatever reason at first, I rarely know how they relate. It is only after I create the components that I see how they interact and which ones work together. It's always surprising what comes out because stories really do emerge." About *To Understand Better*, a larger version of a piece we had seen and liked, she says, "Science and botany have been pretty influential in my practice. The elaborate flower is so much larger than the tiny scissors and pencil I juxtaposed it against. I was trying to create something larger than life out of materials while playing with the motivations behind scientific research, and the absurdity behind that."

Young says the titles always come at the very end, usually as she is about to frame each piece. "I sit with the compositions and allow a conversation to take place in my head, which is when the title will usually emerge." With *You'll Find Far Away Out Back*, the name was inspired from that initial walk around the property with the homeowners. With *To Understand Better*, she says, "It's like a snippet of conversation, like the one we're having now—we're trying to make sense out of something 'so to better understand' it."

One of the reasons Young's work appealed to us so strongly was because we had been working with origami in brass when we were designing shoe boutiques in Japan. In Young's work, we saw the same craftsmanship down to the tiniest detail. We appreciate the microscopic scale that takes so much patience to achieve, which is evidenced in elements like the rotary phone the size of her thumb. Beyond her aesthetic, a dynamic aspect in working with Young was that she was a terrific listener. She was able to observe, absorb, and manifest her experiences with the homeowners in a brief time. With this project, it was a more personal story to tell than the Erdos narrative. It became apparent that she is this huge filter and a true artist because she creates poetry from nothing.

About seeing her art in the rooms of the penthouse, she says the pieces feel rich because everything is so carefully considered in such a four-dimensional way and because there is a sense of history to each element surrounding her pieces. Young calls the project remarkably satisfying both professionally and personally: "Eric is like a magical creature—he's always got a twinkle in his eye! He's like an alchemist who is mixing things or opening things up in some way, whether it's fantastic dining experiences or traveling to some faraway place." She called working with us an eye-opening adventure. "Eun is the perfect foil for that because she's a stabilizer and allows for the magic to happen by making all the bits and pieces around it fit," she adds. "It's a unique partnership." Having her horizons expand was another aspect of this project she enjoyed. "With Eric and Eun, I'm always taken to a place beyond what I expected creatively or intellectually … holistically."

What's on the horizon for Young as she continues to push into new territory? In 2020, she began experimenting in order to incorporate time-based media within her sculpture, such as projected images of tiles on a wall or miniature screens partially obscured within the sculptural paper tableaux. "I am developing these to peer deeper into the works, enhancing them with unexpected forms of storytelling," she explains. "I feel the objects are not actually static to begin with so when aspects are set into filmic motion, it seems to be a natural progression."

Young's past successes since graduating from the Ontario College of Art and Design in 1995 include being featured in gallery exhibitions around the world and she has received numerous accolades, including the Governor General's award in Canada. She has also received critical acclaim in publications, such as the *Globe and Mail* and the *New York Times*; and her work resides in major collections around the world. Young has also written and illustrated over a dozen children's books.

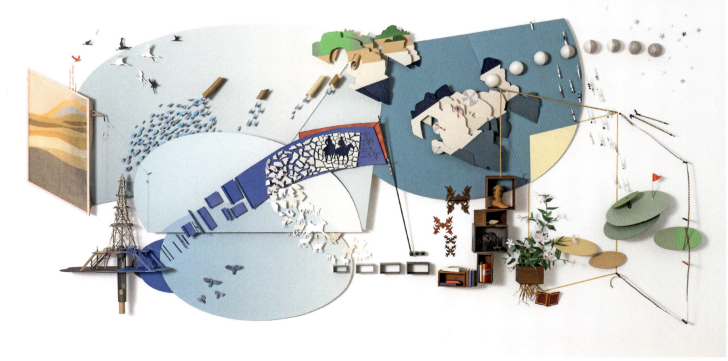

Special thanks for the metal and glass work, coordinated by Kiran Bhavsar and Chelliah Mohan of Sonoma Custom Millwork. Fluted metal panels by Axolotl; colored glass by Rudy Art Glass; fluted glass by Nathan Allan Glass Studios. All installed by Kurt Snell and his incredible team.

Step into the Jazz Age, time travelers. Hear the mellow music while your eyes feast on the tailored grids of fluted, frosted, and bronzed glass in patterns that could have been thoroughfares crisscrossing a bustling city. Listen to the clink of metal as skyscrapers rise in tiered formations, some staggering heights fitted with needling appendages that gleam in the morning light. Follow the throngs of flappers as they prance through lobbies bathed in bold marbles, the patterns echoing the meandering melodies of the Roaring Twenties scene.

Though merely a space that doubles as a guest bedroom and a study, this room, which sits across the private elevator entrance from the Curiosity Cabinet, illustrates how design can transport. References here harken back to a time when fashion was becoming pared down and shimmery, the low-waist shifts ornamented with rhinestones, fur, and fringe defining a new era of elegance. Design details that would have swirled around the gadabouts were geometrically rich, like the steel structure dissecting the "walls" in this room. The grids hold sections of clear, textured, and colored panes of glass by Rudy Art Glass on the foyer-facing screens, and mirrored glass on the wall surrounding the bed. In designing the custom crisscrossing display, we staggered the arrangement and sizes of the different glasses to create a symmetrical rhythm.

This room came together at the very end of the project. We had always intended to include a small office in the interiors but we also needed an additional guest suite. At one point, we were considering simply folding a Murphy bed into the twenty-five-foot Curiosity Cabinet, extending it around the corner by the powder room. As we sketched it a number of ways, the move didn't feel right so we combined the spaces for those times when the penthouse is brimming with overnight guests. A fourteen-foot-long desk and gorgeous antique leather chairs we found at the Paul Bert Serpette Marché in Paris provide a place to read or work. We couldn't believe our luck in finding two identical chairs given their age and the excellent condition they are in, which is so rare.

The hammered hardware pulls on the desk, from E.R. Butler, are linear elements that keep the profile of the cabinetry clean, as does the fact that we tucked the outlets into a fold-down panel in the top. We bought a turntable for the space that sits atop the desk, the music it emits covering many more decades than the tuxedo- and fringe-clad pleasure-seekers of the early twentieth-century would have heard. A special piece of art standing across the hall from the room like a "watchful eye," a theme in this artist's work, is a sculpture by Helena Starcevic, whose art we found on 1stDibs. We share this talented ceramicist's point of view on her work and on her journey to actualizing it in this chapter.

A banquette nestled into a corner on the same wall as the bed is a custom design that feels very much at home with the small dining table with a pear-shaped base and the two antique cane chairs we also sourced from 1stDibs tucked under it. We found the exquisitely articulated glass and copper chandelier through their platform, as well. The vinyl collection in the study illustrates how we pay close attention to all the senses when we turn a completed project over to homeowners who ask us to create a residence that will enthrall. While Eric and his wife Kate Fenner, who's a recording artist, were traveling down Highway 1 in California, they would take detours into small towns so she could purchase albums for the study and he could comb small art studios for works to place in the interiors.

Kate curated a varied selection of records, and Eric came away with works by two artists that are included in this space: sculptures by Riccardo Spizzamiglio and paintings by Patrick Dennis. Eric describes Spizzamiglio, whose profile follows this presentation, as a fun and vibrant man. He purchased several of his studies, which we placed on the desk. Dennis's wonderful paintings appealed to him because they are abstracts that remind him of the ever-changing skies in California.

The initial aesthetics of the room were inspired by the pastel blue marble with its ochre and gray veining that clads the inset into which the Murphy bed folds. We were attracted to the stone, which we also sourced from Aria Stone Gallery, because its colors felt like an exquisite slice of Tuscany when we first saw it. But when we placed it in this room with its modernist feel, its personality copped the perfect art deco attitude. We fitted a matching marble shelf into the alcove to cap the top edge of the bed when it is enveloped by the bookcase and clad bedside niches in the same stone.

The metal hardware on these, which read like boxy drawer pulls, become elegant night-lights when they reflect illumination from inside these recesses. When the bed is tucked into the alcove, the walnut panel cladding its front—fluted to echo other design elements in the space—appears to be a pair of cabinets with two brass handles, though these become the legs as the bed is unfolded, supporting it as they touch the floor. The movement is controlled by a gas piston system so that it raises and lowers with a slight touch of the hand, slowly and gently. The powder room across the foyer serves as a full bath for the bedroom any time it is occupied.

When Eric was visiting the penthouse soon after the room was completed, he sat in the space as he drew a detail that would become a gift for the owner. Van Morrison's soulful voice was wafting through the room from the record player as he reclined on the banquette, sketching for hours and feeling very at home in the sophisticated space. It remains one of his favorite spots each time he visits for its refined reflection of a modernity during which the bobbed hair favored by la garçonne, as the flappers were known, and the sumptuous gowns preferred by Hollywood starlets stood at either end of the style spectrum.

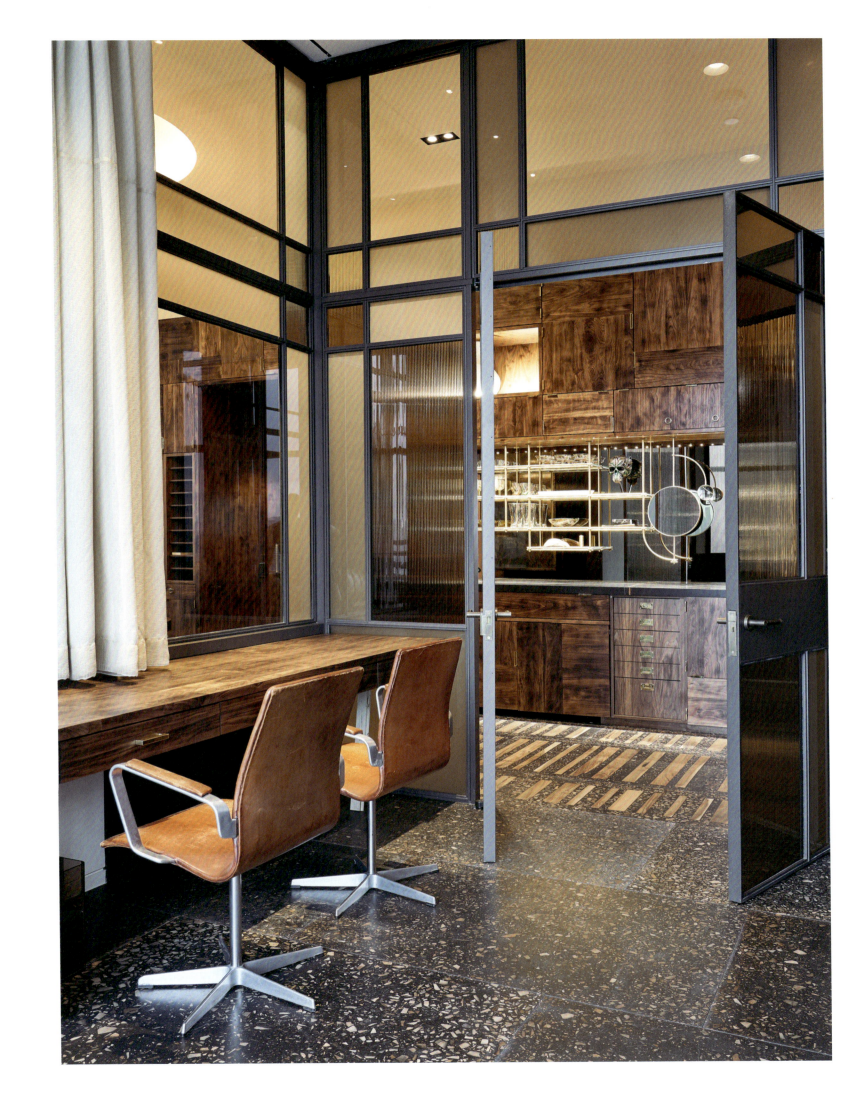

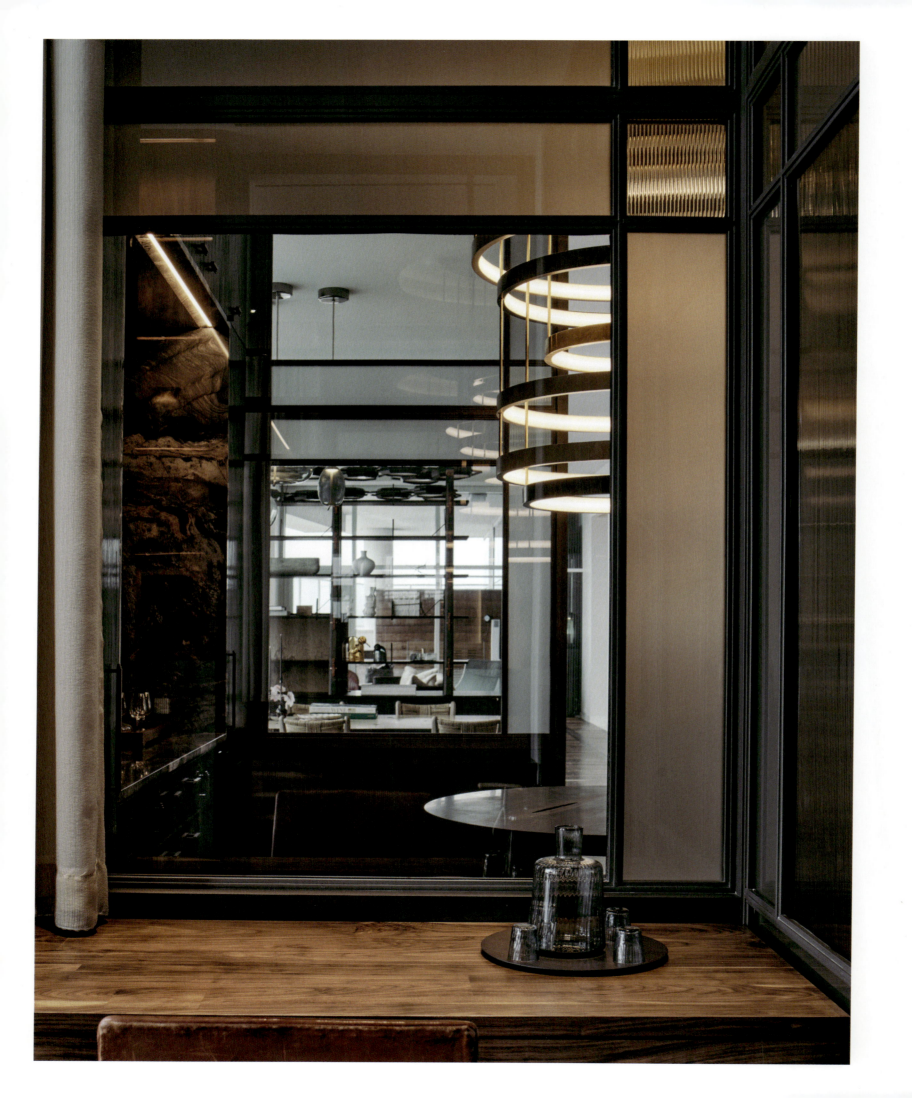

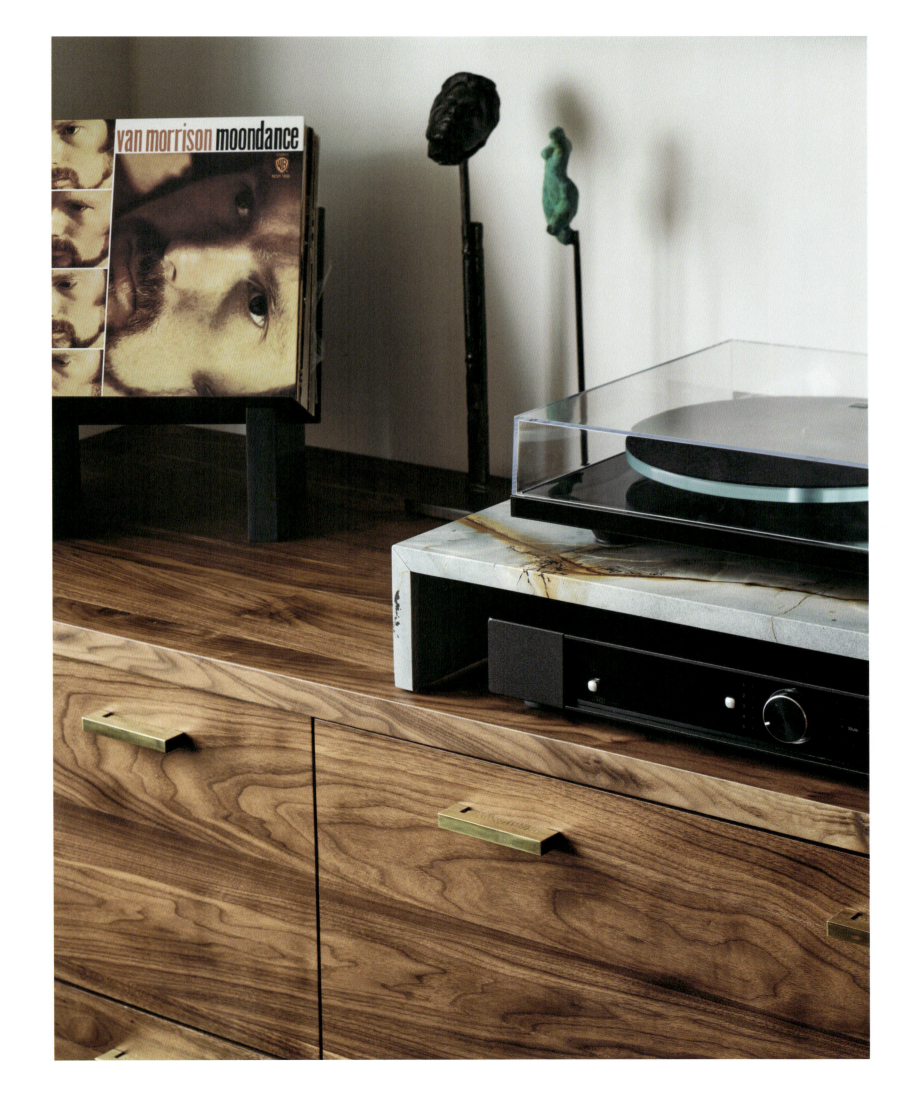

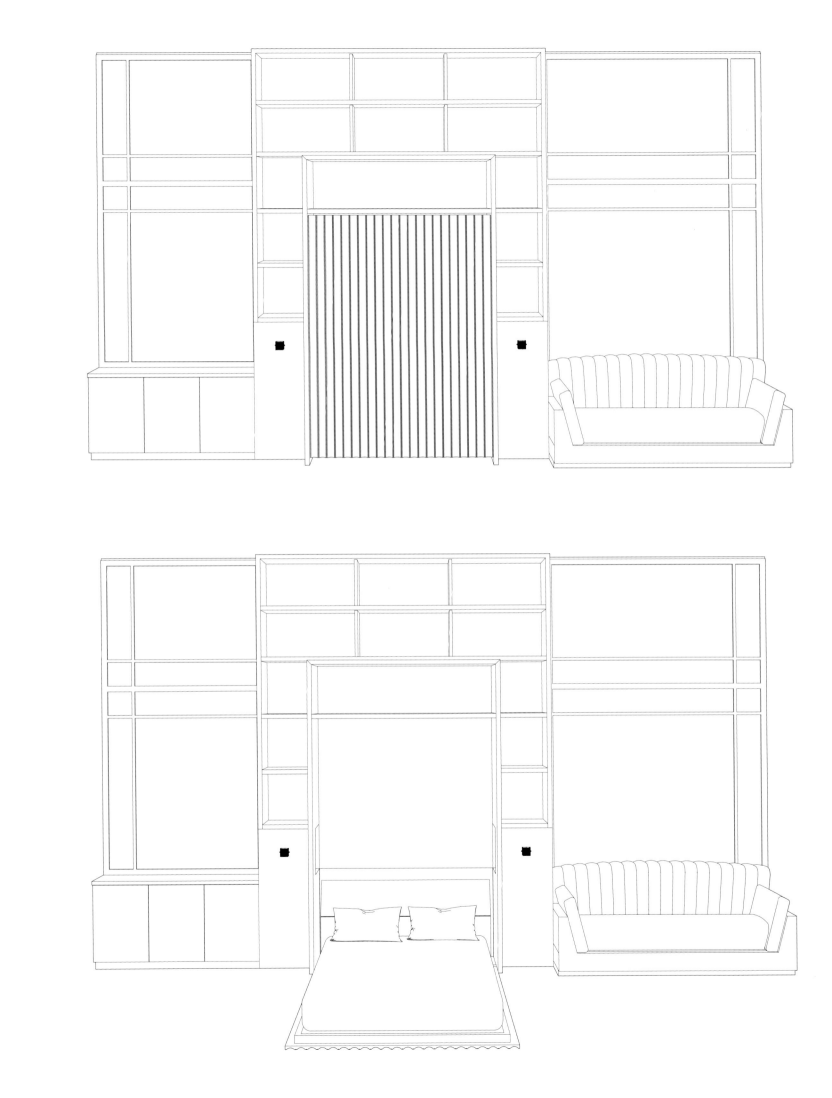

Helena Starcevic

Custos Sculpture

Symbology deeply imbues Helena Starcevic's art with meaning, the forms cascading with personality that make them seem they will walk toward the observer at any moment. She says of the piece she created for the penthouse, a sculpture titled *Custos*, "It stands for something; power, presence, a watchful eye." The muscular profile consisting of three rounded rectangular parts on curved legs illustrates this artist's draw to soft-edged squares and rectangles, standing forms, and work that references the spine. She revisits the patterns she creates like a visual mantra.

"The surfaces of my work are monochromatic and unadorned, which is intentional because I don't want the pieces to be decorative—it's all about the form," she explains. "I believe it is all the better to allow the viewer to project what they want to see. I want my work to contain beauty and grace, and to inspire peace and contemplation." She adds that it is natural for her to work in multiples, an inclination which she describes as "probably the most important subtext guiding my work." So strongly felt is her philosophy, it is as if her past joins her in the studio: "One of six children, and a student of social systems at university, I am always interested in how people interact." A question that draws introspection from her is, "Can everyone keep their personal identity and still be a productive and cohesive part of the whole?"

She has regularly revisited the totemic form throughout the years as a way of exploring these ideas. "When I construct a totem, or a totemic 'family,' I am intent on imbuing each with a symbolic, ritualistic aspect that gives it its own identity, strength, and purpose," she explains. "I may include a secret mark so that each piece has a unique identity and strength on its own, while it stays a cohesive member of the community when exhibited in groups."

Starcevic says her creative process is simple: "I go to the studio and relax. Perhaps I have music on. Sometimes I draw.

Then I take an idea and start to play in clay." As these simple moments of inspiration play out, they provoke insights into new ideas. "This part is so fun and exhilarating, as it is full of possibility and impossible to make a mistake," she adds. "Since I often work in multiples, I will form several related elements to combine later, playing with scale, balance, and proportion. It is much easier to visualize in 3D-form than on paper."

Her process has brought her layers of important awareness over the years: "Once I mastered the technique, I quickly realized that a structured and meticulous approach was not the feel I wanted in clay. Though I take pride in making well-constructed objects, I want them to reveal the hand, the individual, and to be unique through my personal exploration." Though she has always worked with her hands, she waited for the opportunity to work in clay as she began creating both functional and sculptural ceramics. She strives for simplicity in the form, and a calmness on the surface, looking to create a paradoxical presence that is both quiet and strong.

"I love a beautiful bowl, a large platter, or a perfect vase; yet it is in my sculptures that my ideas enjoy their greatest freedom," she notes. "I love how I will take inspiration from a seemingly unrelated source to, later, find it abstracted and revealed in my work. These influences include architecture, midcentury furniture, and, of course, Mother Nature. This doesn't necessarily mean a building or a tree; I am more drawn to the nuances in the twisted trunk of the tree, the silhouette of the building, or two boulders leaning a certain way in the sand."

Starcevic came to ceramics via a circuitous route: "I studied fashion and textiles at the Fashion Institute of Technology, and jewelry design. Studying anatomy and massage therapy brought me to the spine and the skeletal system, as well as the movement of muscle over bone (so clay-like!). My extensive

travels in Mexico and Guatemala, visiting ancient sites and cultures, embedded certain symbols in my mind and inspired the totemic forms which would come later."

For over seventeen years she studied clay, served as resident artist, and was invited to teach at the preeminent Greenwich House Pottery, the oldest ceramic school in the East. By the time she began to show her work, her aesthetic was fully formed and the messages clear. At this point, the transition to working in her own studio was an extremely important step. "Several residency programs were especially impactful to my growth," she adds, "particularly the three months I spent as artist in residence at the Museum of Arts and Design in New York City." Since then, her work has been featured in a number of prestigious publications around the world.

We asked Starcevic if she had always known she wanted to be a maker/artisan and her answer was unequivocal, as there is always something creative coming out of her hands. "The idea of commerciality goes against my personal ideals and desires for how humans can live well together on the same planet," she says. "OK, if commercial success happens, wonderful. But not if it dilutes the creative integrity. The push for makers to create a brand seems a bit hollow because the shell becomes more important than the work itself and any semblance of integrity is lost."

The advice she would give others who are just beginning to explore their artistic sides: "I straddle the line between art and design. Both are important to me, one for the personal expression and the other for the accessibility. I have always told myself to make what I feel is important, what I feel compelled to make, never with regard to the market. I realize this is not everyone's goal, so my advice is to master your craft, learn everything you can, have integrity in your work, and stay true to yourself." Finally, she advises, "Stay open to evolving your practice."

Movement, frozen in time in lyrical lines, is the foundation of Riccardo Spizzamiglio's sculptures. Taut muscles command; arms implore; torsos dance, though they are resolutely still; fingers grasp; and hair entwined with fabric forms capricious quivers. Working from his studio in Cambria, California, his heart remains open to the muse as he captures every gesture to bring motion to its greatest heights. "I vowed to the arts when I was twenty-four," he says. "My evolution has been from jewelry to sculpture—it was when I cast my first piece in bronze that I knew it was a game changer: I haven't been able to stop since!"

He was drawn to the property where he built his studio and gallery space naturally, calling the land a sacred spot where he enjoyed camping before making it his full-time residence. Of Spanish-Italian descent, he was born in the United States to parents who came to the country to take hold of the American dream. He describes his journey through art as a genuine time of triumph filled with liberating encounters. "I find myself in harmony, feeling a zen-like experience when I allow myself to simply be a vessel," he explains. "I see myself as a translator of the transcendental and I consider myself to be very fortunate to be able to live my life as an artist."

Once his love for bronze was established and his sensibilities soared when capturing the flowing forms he envisioned, Spizzamiglio pushed into even freer territory: "I started playing around with bearings, cylinders, and weights," he says. "The vision I had is of lovely forms turning and spinning while moving up and down, like butterflies." He's drawn in and fascinated when these twirling shapes move to the beat of the classical music he often plays as he's working, marveling that they are so alive. Because they are, he doesn't see the sculpted silhouettes as kinetic; he sees them as pure emotion. "I have a pair of sculptures called *The Couple*, for instance. They may sometimes kiss or just miss each other as they move," he explains. "Some people who visit my studio will cry when they see them in motion; others will have a difficult time verbalizing what they are feeling. When something is made from human hands, and with thought and emotion—whether it be love or hate—people can feel it."

Spizzamiglio welcomes those who bring him new insight into how his work makes an impact on them when they visit. As they become lost in the movement they are seeing, it is confirmation that his work is music in concrete form: "As I'm creating, I'll follow the rhythm and pretend I'm playing music through an instrument, lost in the strains, chords, and tones, even though my instruments are clay, liquid metal, pencil and paper, or brush and canvas."

He is acutely aware of his place on the timeline of art history—da Vinci's wings, Rodin's hands, and Michelangelo's Pietà some of the forms that have particularly moved him. "They taught me by their examples," he explains. "I believe if we don't venture back in time, we risk losing the inspiration that comes from recognizing the talents of the former masters. But there is something that history can't give an artist, and this is the drive to create. Being a maker is in my DNA. My ancestry in northern Spain includes carpenters, builders, and masons; once I welcomed them to flow through me, boom—here I was troweling and sculpting."

About the two studies that Eric purchased for the penthouse, he says he enjoys the freedom of creating in the early stages because the results tend to be a fusion of complexity and simplicity. The fluorescent green finish on one of the sculptures was an unusual choice for the artist: "I tend to stay away from flashy patinas because I want each piece to feel as if it was found in an archeological dig. That said, I also want them to feel modern. It's a bit of a dichotomy because I'm trying to create a fresh take on tradition while reminding those who see my work to view it through a lens of history."

To those who are craving a life in the arts, he advises, "Early on, keep your work private—don't show it to any friends or family members you think may discourage you because you are just finding your way. No matter what type of aesthetic develops, if it feels right, continue it because there will always be someone who will appreciate it. The trick is to find that audience and to draw it to the work." He unapologetically uses his own pieces as examples when he admits the art he creates is not for everyone, nor should it be: "My work is not meant to be comfortable, it's emotional."

To newcomers to the daily routine of creation, he notes how crucial it is to go with the flow: "It's important that an artist follow his or her muse; and by follow, I mean surrender to the inspirations that flow. No matter how hard artists try, they'll never be able to trap it, so it's important to let go; to resist the urge to control the process." He adds that the existence will be rigorous but it will be worth it: "The career of an artist is not a job to punch in and punch out; I'm constantly using my mind, day and night."

Spizzamiglio celebrates that he has created a life for himself that allows him to walk a short distance into his studios when he wakes up every morning. The ease leaves his imagination free to guide him as he is propelled toward the tools that will give form to his expressions on any given day—the textures of the peaks and valleys he forms possibly resulting from pen on paper, brushstrokes on canvas, a knife running along the surface of clay, or ridges pressed into a bronze mold. When he's not striating, sculpting, scoring, or casting, you will find him letting it all go during a drive along California's coast road or setting up camp surrounded by nature.

Projectile veining ricochets in every direction in the powder room. The beige and green marble was chosen by the homeowner because he saw the rolling hills of the Cotswolds in the slabs. We book-matched every piece and placed the heaviest veined sections at a low level so the horizontal waves feel like a country landscape disappearing over a hilly horizon when seated. This space is entered through a door tucked into one end of the Curiosity Cabinet. As soon as the plane from the cabinet is traversed through the remarkably elaborate door produced by Madzio and his team, the artistry of Dino Figliomeni swirls in its dynamic complexity.

The owner of Crystal Tile & Marble, Ltd., a Toronto-based fabricator and distributor with a curated gallery of fine stones, Figliomeni views each slab as a painting. This makes it stimulating to move through the variety of specimens gathered there. Visiting with the homeowner, given his deep knowledge of how stone develops, brought us a more vigorous experience than we would have had if we'd gone on our own. The process of book-matching this room absorbed painstaking hours of arranging the marble to make sure the stone wrapped perfectly around every corner.

We decided to make the sink and its pedestal, and the waste-basket from the same material to keep the landscape alive. Once the wide marble threshold is traversed, it feels like a wonderland is beckoning. We kept the playful theme alive in several concepts we developed here, such as the medicine chest that also serves as a candy bar. The back of the bookcase door has storage for extra toilet paper and candy for restocking the medicine cabinet. The inlays in this room were all inspired by the artistry of Tyler Hays, whom you've already met. The puzzled walnut planks with Dutch inlays are exquisite in the textural deep-toned wood that we chose to amp up the energy in the space. It also brings warmth into the room with all the cool marble surrounding it.

We were able to place a large bench in the space, made of the same marble, because the powder room is generous in size. This was important, as it also serves as a full bathroom for the study across the foyer. Though there is a full shower, we did not enclose it in glass because it isn't used very often and because it is completely surrounded by natural material that can withstand water. Instead, we placed a truncated piece of marble at its opening that serves as an implied screen.

This is one of the rooms in the penthouse in which the design was set by marble. We love building an entire space around the coloring and veining in sumptuous stones. The finishing touch in this space is the circular brass logo we inset into the wood wall, which is seen when someone first enters. It is our signature, and how we put our stamp on the overall design of this project.

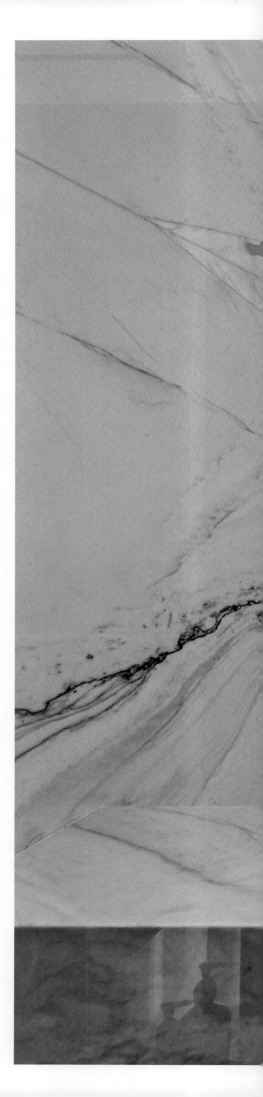

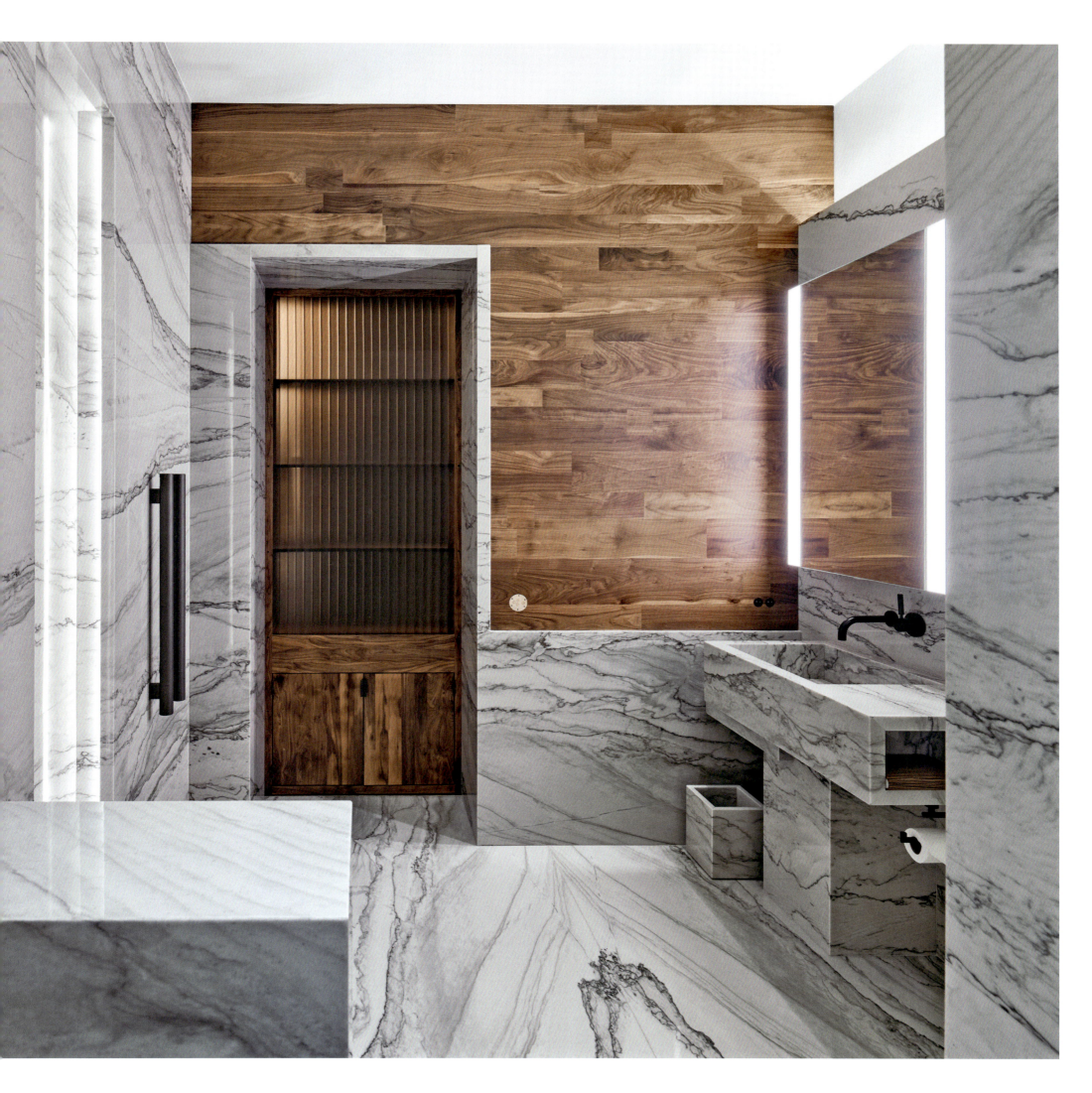

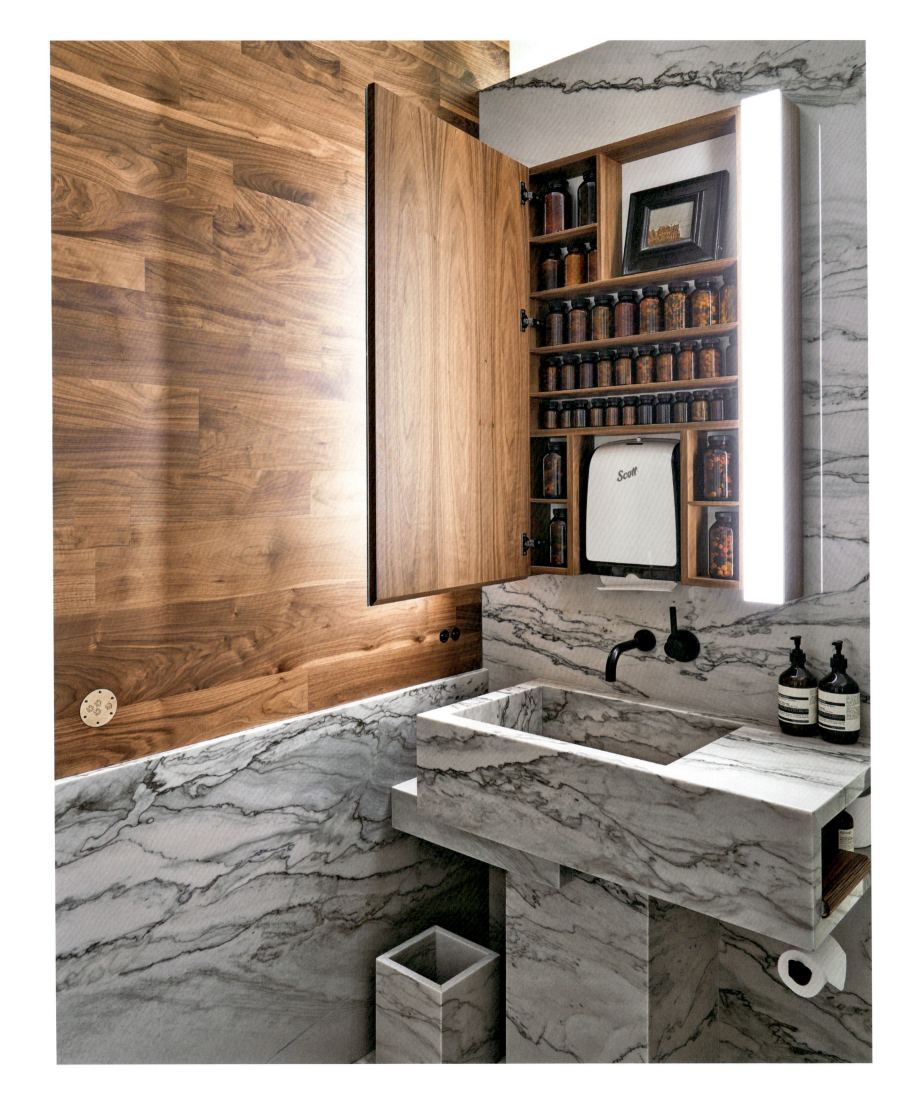

Meandering shadows play across the smoking terrace whether it is daylight or dark; the shades, with their organic shapes, bringing this outdoor space its charm. Carved from the exterior of the building between the study and the dining room, it is a spot for enjoying coffee in the morning, a cocktail and a hearty cigar in the evening, or a nightcap before bedtime.

The Dedon chairs on the terrace have unobtrusive profiles but they are roomy and comfortable. We salute this company that employs great artistry where wood and metalwork meet, which is evident in the details on these chairs. The brand is fearless in melding materials for the outdoors, illustrated by the wood inlays on the tops of the arm rests. The chairs and the other elements were chosen for their ability to withstand the intense sun of Texas.

Among the shapeshifters we mentioned here are concrete occasional tables sourced from 1stDibs that have amoeba-like profiles. Because the area is flooded with so much light during the day, we knew the contours they would cast on the terrace floor would create an interesting range of formations as the sun progressed. The moody nighttime penumbra is a cubist-inspired wall light that brings the interplay of light and shadow to the penthouse after sunset.

It was important to connect this lighting element with the other lit feature in the interiors. When looking right from the spine of the penthouse facing the dining room and living room, illuminated eggs become a wonderful lit element that serve as night-lights for the interiors. When switched on, the terrace light answers these as an exterior night-light hovering above the powerful downtown landscape, the view of which it diminishes slightly with its glow. In order to create the shape we envisioned, we melded two fixtures into one, playing around with the arrangement in order to create this zigzagging focal point.

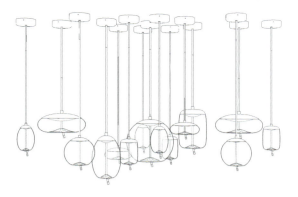

The vistas beyond the windows of the dining room concoct the ruse that guests who are gathered around the long live-edge table are floating above Houston, eclipsing the skyscrapers in the distance awash in mists. The most commanding feature in the space is this table made of interjoined slabs of maple with lovely butterfly detailing, which was designed by Tyler Hays and handcrafted by BDDW as part of the Art Basel Miami Beach lounge in 2017. Choosing a bleached table was an unusual move for us but a stealthy one, as it contributed to the success of the room with its reflective surface that reacts to the changing personality of the light, natural and humanmade.

We spent months organizing a crane to be on-site for six hours to lift the seventeen-foot table into place because it was too large to fit into the elevator. On the first attempt, the crane's arm was six inches shy of being able to reach the penthouse so we had to give it a second try—such are the joys of installation day! Hanging above the table is a meandering pattern of dramatic blown-glass pendants we composed to form a chandelier. The morphing shapes in the Knot Collection were designed by Alfredo Chiaramonte and Marco Marin, founders of the Italian design studio Chiaramonte Marin; and manufactured by Brokis Lighting, a Czech company known for its innovations in glass. We present the company's profile after the tour of this space.

Arranging the cluster of delicate globes was a joy as we envisioned the grouping superimposed on the distant cityscape. The pale blue color we chose reflects the hues of the sky dominating the views, though only in certain light; the pendants constantly change their personalities as the natural illumination ebbs and flows into and out of the room. Once switched on, each of the orbs becomes a luminous bubble of creamy light perfect in its own universe.

The dining chairs by Bruno Moinard Éditions are made of white oak, brass, fabric, and recycled paper that is woven to the chairbacks like rattan. What a find! We fell in love with his work: his sofa shapes are so playful and the dining room chairs combine materials in a way we would never have envisioned, especially the hand-rolled parchment on their backs. The strands are made when the paper is twisted into long ropes that are wound around the frame. The brass details are impeccable; the thickness of the wood is stunning; the ergonomics of the experience of sitting in them is supreme—there couldn't have been a better chair to pair with the BDDW table. We weren't sure the client would go for them so our office erupted in cheers when we learned they were approved!

Every project has its challenges, including occasional surprises. When lifting the crate of the seventeen-foot solid wood dining room tabletop, we fell six inches short from making it to the thirtieth floor, despite maximizing the crane's reach (including the thirty-six-inch safety threshold). How to solve? Note the two top middle photographs showing the angle of the cage supports. After changing the lengths of the cables, we successfully hovered two inches above the finished floor!

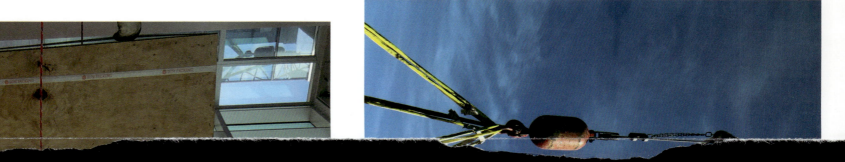

To add a layer of refinement to the delicious dinners we imagined would take place, we designed placemats that are stitched with outlines showing the position of each item in a single place setting. We turned to the discerning team at Maison Jean Rousseau to manufacture the handsome foundations from which plates and bowls designed by Kaneko Kohyo, which we sourced through RW Guild, would sprout like flowers when the table is set. These are accompanied by cutlery by the Portuguese brand Cutipol that Eric spotted in a luxury boutique in Dubai.

It was how the utensils were packaged that first caught his eye, as the presentation reminded him of the gorgeous pieces of cutlery in his mother's pristine cases when he was growing up in Belgium. "I had always wanted to be able to design drawer dividers that kept the cutlery neatly arranged," Eric explains. "Having all the pieces smashing into each other drives me crazy! Being able to work with Foresso to create the intricate trays that were carved from

their terrazzo material with a CNC machine was my perfect Marie Kondo moment."

The effort to trace each of the pieces of cutlery and nestle them into beautiful drawer inserts took many hours but it was well worth it. Rather than echo the color of the terrazzo floor, we chose a white resin to hold the walnut chips to produce a nice contrast to the floors when the drawers are open. We showed the glasses and dishware the same respect by having Madzio, who handcrafted the credenza that separates the dining room from the living room, finish out the drawers with dividers into which each item nestles perfectly. To complement the playfulness of the blossoming dishes on the table, we created a centerpiece composed of beautifully thin metal candlesticks designed by Ted Muehling, which we purchased at E.R. Butler. We arranged them so that they read like a cityscape of silhouettes to echo the urban oasis in the distance.

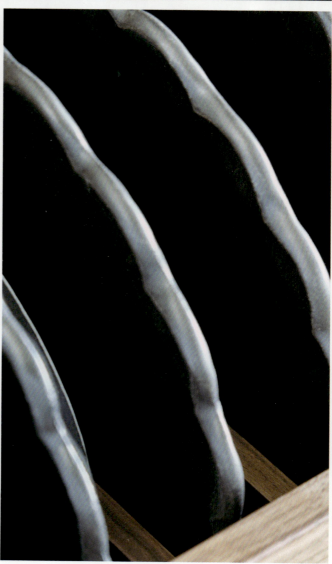

The bar cart against one wall, which we also sourced through RW Guild, has a frame in a darker wood that contrasts with the surface of the dining table and complements the deeper tone in its undulant live-edge. We are serious fans of Robin Standefer and Stephen Alesch, the founders of this company, for the artistry they bring to everything they do. Their profile follows this walkthrough of the space. We watched with great interest when they founded the Guild, which was during an intensive fourteen-year period when we were traveling the world designing Christian Louboutin boutiques. Once the center of our design universe returned to New York City, we decided it was time to create special surroundings for our offices so we put an equal amount of forethought into designing these as they had for the Guild showroom.

While the Guild holds its fêtes to promote the brand and products, similarly we have been inviting our past and current clients into our office for magical, secret nine-course dinners so they can personally encounter an experience we are driven to provide with each project we undertake. This is particularly helpful for new clients we are introducing to our brand. For existing clients, entertaining them is a way to thank them for trusting us with their projects, like the one we're celebrating in this book.

As we finish the tour of the dining room, we approach wood shelves with four ladder-like supports fastened by expressive leather strapping. This commanding construct sits atop the long credenza holding the dinnerware on the dining-room side and the penthouse's only television on the living-room side. The commanding creation, also from BDDW, is peppered with a treasure trove of decorative accessories and works of art, including a marble ashtray by Greg Natale that contains a brass bullet from Fort Standard for holding matches; and Christopher Kurtz's *Meridian (1205)* sculpture, a needle-like composition machined in brass, which we also found at E.R. Butler.

With the floor-to-ceiling windows that infuse the conjoined rooms with natural light during the day and illumination from Houston's ambient light at night, the chandeliers and the tall element formed by the pairing of the credenza and shelf help to ground the long space. Everything else forms a low datum line, which was intentional because we didn't want to interfere with the visual expansiveness experienced through the tall windows. Having a shelf on which to showcase works like Kurtz's sculpture also gave the homeowners the opportunity to support a greater number of artists. We share the Hudson Valley–based maker's story after the narrative featuring the French brand Maison Jean Rousseau, which is renowned for its fine leather goods.

Maison Jean Rousseau
Luxury Leather Placemats

A stitch in rhyme creates poetry. Case in point are the custom-sewn placemats created for the penthouse by the French leather house Maison Jean Rousseau. The bespoke mats have serious manners, as there is no doubt where you should put the knives, the forks, or the spoons! No one would expect anything less from an artisanal manufacturer with a passion for beautiful materials and cultural heritage that has earned the brand the Entreprise du Patrimoine Vivant (EPV) designation. The manufacturer has proudly been a Living Heritage Company since 2007, the designation signaling that a company combines tradition and innovation, know-how and creation, work and passion, heritage and future.

These tablemats represent the perfect collaboration: the leather house took our design, which hinged on the Cutipol cutlery we chose, and utilized fine French craftsmanship to create the placemats with a contrasting saddle stitch. Each is the result of the fine leatherwork for which Maison Jean Rousseau is renowned. The firm is passionate about the creativity involved in realizing its custom leather pieces. Hand in hand with collaborators like us, its master craftspeople bring envisioned ideas and dreams into reality.

We first came to know this company during Meet French Art de Vivre, a design show organized in New York by Business France, a French Government agency promoting French exports and the country's image. Pierre Louis Follet, the United States general manager for the firm, says he appreciated the richness of our initial talks and enjoyed the exchanges we had early on because it allowed both of our teams to contribute different points of expertise in crafts-making, design, and architecture. "Our New York atelier supervised this project, then our headquarters in Besançon, in the heart of the Watch Valley in France, handmade the prototypes and produced the final pieces," Follet explains.

The history of the company dates to 1954 when Monsieur Jean Rousseau founded his atelier (known as Manufacture Jean Rouseau) in Besançon, its proximity to Switzerland driving the company's initial offerings: leather watch straps. The expertise the atelier achieved in making finely crafted straps led to key business partnerships with luxury Swiss watch brands. "In 1999, Jacques Bordier bought the company," says Follet, "and Maison Jean Rousseau has since been a family-owned company with Jacques Bordier, general manager Pascal Dupenloup, and Anaïs Bordier at the helm."

The brand is quite proud of the expertise for which it is known, and one of the goals the company holds dear is to share the French savvy its craftspeople have perfected as they create contemporary design pieces. Growing far beyond its initial purpose of producing luxury watchbands, Maison Jean Rousseau has expanded over the decades into tableware and decorative arts. Among their popular offerings are a leather-covered box that preserves exceptional wines and champagnes, and a leather holder for carrying wine bottles. The brand has created leather covers for titanium phones; and has contributed to the luxury cosmetics industry with scented leather bracelets and leather cases designed for niche fragrance bottles.

About receiving the EPV designation, Jacques Bordier says, "This label rewards national firms for the excellence of their traditional approach and industrial know-how. We were proud to receive this recognition, as we are deeply involved in the preservation of our craft-arts. Our skill is indeed the base of our work and philosophy. Being awarded the EPV is a confirmation that our company masters rare, if not unique, expertise in the creation of extremely high-quality products. It also certifies that we are able to creatively respond to even the most unusual requests from our customers."

As is illustrated by the placemats we designed, a hallmark of this brand is simple, sleek, and pure design realized with traditional techniques. This is evident in the stitching used to outline where the cutlery perfectly rests. "In keeping with our attachment to authenticity and tradition, we bring our best to the execution of each product, from the original leather to the final article," Jacques Bordier explains. "It is the 'Made in France' spirit in our workshops, in the heart of the Franche-Comté region, that has cemented the loyalty of our demanding international clientele with a particular appreciation of French culture."

He notes how deeply the "Made in France" passion runs through the company's DNA: "We like to see ourselves as ambassadors for French heritage and culture across national and international markets, so we are grateful to each member of our incredible team who has helped us earn the EPV label." Anaïs Bordier, the company's Global Brand Manager, adds, "From sewing, assembling, and dyeing, each creation is single-handedly brought to life by one artisan. There is no assembly-line work within Jean Rousseau. This is another of our special characteristics. Though we are proud to meld traditional know-how with great modernity, technology is never used to replace the work of the human hand. A motivation to always be pushing beyond our boundaries serves our ambitions and makes our role crystal clear."

The fact that the company continues to innovate while staying true to the authenticity of their handmade products is one of the aspects of this brand that made us eager to collaborate with them. "It is a great responsibility and we must stay very mindful of preserving this reputation," Jacques Bordier says. "When anyone orders a Jean Rousseau product thousands of miles away from us, he or she acquires an article of perfect quality that was created by the close attention it receives from our team, and the mindset of our culture at its best."

He goes on to say, "We are so attached to this value of authenticity that it has become our signature. Custom-made items, colored and stitched by hand, are at the heart of our identity. They distinguish us from the rest. When our creations are labeled 'Made in France' or 'Handmade,' we are proud to say just how truthful this is." The suppleness of the leather and the precision with which each utensil's profile is stitched illustrates his point perfectly, the placemats adding a luxurious touch to the finely arranged place settings for which they serve as a foundation.

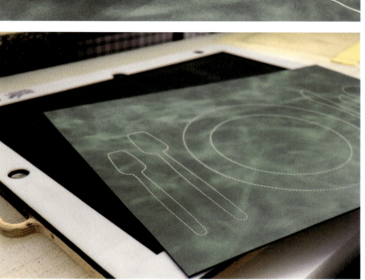

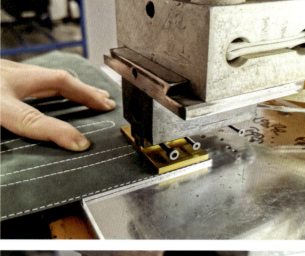

Mystery. Contradiction. Enigma. Its needle-like extensions put the air on notice. *Barbed* is a strong word. It expresses the idea of sharp by its clipped ending, the mouth opening wide only to close quickly as it is pronounced. *Thin* is far from fulsome: the lips barely parting as the word is uttered. *Airy*, so soft and subtle to say. These are just a few of the paradoxical traits Christopher Kurtz created when he carved his Meridian sculptures.

"One of the things I've always appreciated about the pieces in this series is they are equally threatening and vulnerable at the same time—just as human beings are both fragile and strong," he explains. "The sculpture looks like something that can kill you while at the same time its lines are so delicate you don't want to breathe on it too hard because it feels as if you could destroy it." The sculpture we chose for this Houston penthouse is made of metal but its earliest predecessors were realized in wood, the idea coming to Kurtz during an artists' residency in New Mexico that began in 2004.

Kurtz signed on to participate in the residency because he felt the need to stir things up a bit. He had worked as an assistant to Martin Puryear, a well-respected American artist, for five years by that time, refining his woodworking skills and maturing as a maker. As he evolved through this experience, it became clear he wanted to find his way with his own art. "The residency was far away from Martin's shadow and I was trying to figure out what I was about," Kurtz explains. "I love him but when you work under someone who is so powerful, you have to find your own strength."

After his time in New Mexico, Kurtz set up his studio in New York State's Hudson Valley and began crafting new work, including the Meridian series of sculptures. Looking back, he believes the shift in atmosphere, light, and vegetation that he found in the desert had stirred something in him: "Having gone from the landscape of the Hudson Valley to the high plains of New Mexico was such a radical shift. There was something about how light traveled through space—that shift of going from a mountainous landscape with rivers to UFO-land. I believe the inspiration grew out of the reaction I was having to my surroundings."

From this visceral response came sculptures with attenuating lines that point toward infinity. "It dawned on me in New Mexico that I could make material express something immaterial," he explains. "It had never occurred to me that I could use material to talk about something immaterial." His experimentations in wood expanded from sculpture to furniture as time wore on. Though the process between each of these has its differences, it also has similarities. "I think the two are more similar than different," he explains. "There are certain things I do that are more technical with furniture—a chair has more practical aspects than a sculpture—but there is some cross-pollination. The way it's one big epic story that's unfolding all the time is I use the same tools, the same studio, and the same flow-state mentally for all the projects I'm working on."

A dictum from John Cage's list "Ten Rules for Students and Teachers" has remained top of mind with Kurtz each time he begins the creative process with new work. It's rule number eight: "Don't try to create and analyze at the same time. They're different processes." Kurtz explains, "Self-critiquing and creating are separate elements and they shouldn't be happening at the same time. At the beginning, I'm not

judging what it is. Afterwards, I ask, 'Is it a one-off design or could it go into production, by which I mean handmade batch production, or does it just live as a sculpture?'"

The exhaustive part of the process comes once he is involved in the serious editing that brings refinement to his work as he continues to carve away mass. He likes wood because it gives him just the right amount of push-back as he is working with it: "The process of making wood furniture comes with many rules—grain direction and seasonal changes that make it contract or swell, for instance—but when I'm sculpting, it's malleable enough that I can push up against its parameters and get a little cheeky with it." We were curious to know if wood had been a favorite medium for him from the start. "I've always been drawn to structural materials like wood or steel fabrication," he says. "During my undergraduate years, my training was not material-based; it was far more conceptual. I studied in the 1990s, and everything had to be smart work—we had to be aware and ironic. After leaving art school, I had the confidence to go back to what I had always wanted to do, which was to make refinement the aim. Being an assistant for Puryear, who is known for his virtuosity in wood, also furthered this, as I found the material suited me: it gives resistance and I like materials that have friction but that eventually yield."

When choosing the species of wood he will use for a piece of art or a product, his decision is driven by the structural demands: "I don't get seduced by grain or figure—sometimes wood pieces are just showing off their wild features like bird's-eye maple does. This goes back to my rigorous training. I often paint wood because I want the personality of the wood to take a back seat to the purpose I'm imposing on it." The idea for the limited-edition Meridian sculptures in metal that we chose for the penthouse from E.R. Butler came about when Rhett Butler, one of the visionaries behind the brand, approached Kurtz.

"When I was first showing my work, I was included in an exhibition in New York City with one of my mobiles on display," Kurtz explains. "Rhett Butler saw it in the show and contacted me because it piqued his interest. He was wondering how he could make the attenuated spikes in metal." Butler, who Kurtz calls a person of deep curiosity, asked him if he thought they could make them in brass. "Because I felt all the pieces I had been making were intimate and intuitive, I was concerned the pieces might lose something in the machining," Kurtz told him, though he admits he knew at the time that if there was anyone in the world who could do it, Butler could. Plus, he really wanted to work with this insightful man.

"To maintain the fidelity of my wood sculptures," Kurtz says, "Rhett digitized it and made a computer file. He then figured out a way to construct one, which was technically challenging and incredibly impractical." How impractical? There are only a handful of machines in the world that can achieve the delicacy and precision the sculpture would demand, and Butler located one. It was originally designed to make needles for endoscopic surgeons. Kurtz calls this project one of the most special collaborations he's had to date.

Kurtz also salutes Butler's dedication to refinement. "His medium was in metal so it's no surprise he could figure it out; it's just that on my own I would never have thought to

do what we did," Kurtz explains. "Rhett brought something to the table that made this possible when he helped me make something in metal that performed at the same spiritual level as the wooden sculptures do." The otherworldly presence of *Meridian (1205)* in the penthouse, which is one of a limited edition of twenty, is evident as it gestures from the bookcase between the living room and the dining room.

This iteration of the *Meridian* is small, whereas an exhibition that took place in the United Kingdom in 2019, "The Traveler cannot see North but knows the Needle can," features monumental specimens. Arranged in a fourteenth-century monastic tithe barn sixteen miles from Stonehenge, the spiked sculptures in white were ethereal surrounded by the weathered stone of the medieval building that is now the Messums Wiltshire gallery. Assembled in an array of formations, Kurtz likened the entwined profiles that cast sharp shadows onto the monastery floor to druid tools. Given the meticulousness of the pieces that needled in all directions, we wondered if it was craftsmanship that drove his discipline. "I think craft is the sticky area," he answers. "Though it is certainly at the heart of my practice, it can only take equal space or, in some cases, a back seat to the idea. Sometimes technique can be a crutch so I try to keep the craftsmanship at the service of the concept."

This devotion to creativity has had its rewards for the artist, who grew up in Excelsior Springs, Missouri, and studied sculpture at the Kansas City Art Institute, landscape architecture at the GSD at Harvard University in the Career Discovery Program, and received a BFA in sculpture from The New York State College of Ceramics at Alfred University in Alfred, New York. Proof is the international attention he has received with his art and his furniture designs, which are included in a number of public and private collections. Kurtz has received numerous grants and awards, including the prestigious Louis Comfort Tiffany Award and a Loewe Craft Prize.

Having reached this level of actualization in his career, we asked him if there were always signs he would be an artist. "There was never a time when having a career in the arts wasn't the plan," he tells us. "My father was a professor at the Kansas City Art Institute and I was always on campus so when I was growing up, it seemed normal that students were making full-body casts of their second selves, throwing molten metal at the wall, or crawling across the floor in broken glass as performance art!"

By the time he'd landed in art school, he'd also had a hefty education in the practical aspects of making things thanks to the aged Victorian house in which he grew up, assisting his father in all manner of fixes. His flair for manipulating materials into sculptural things showed itself by the time he was ten when he canvased the construction site of a renovation of the home for rubble he could use to make objects. We asked Kurtz if he has any advice for others who see these signs and are just beginning to launch into their careers.

"I always feel like I'm asking myself that question," he says. "This doesn't seem to change no matter what I achieve. I'm reminded of one of the most important bits of wisdom one of my professors gave me when I was a freshman: don't try to be original; try to be good at what you do. If you stay on that track, the originality will evolve from there. If you try to will the originality to happen, you'll end up chasing the trends and losing your way. Try to be competent and try to be good."

RW Guild
Furniture and Tableware

A plumb line dropped into the course of history has an endless cord that disappears into the mists of time. Traditions exist at every length of the thread that binds us to antiquity as we follow the strand into the present day. The earliest guilds are believed to have been formed as early as 3800 B.C., a mind-numbing number given how many centuries it represents from where we sit as we explore nuance in modernity. Roman & Williams Guild (RW Guild) has infused its existence with the same time-honored processes that makers have employed for generations—simple tools, hands that caress a product through the process of creation, and a commitment to elements that endure.

Founded by Robin Standefer and Stephen Alesch, the company opened its doors in December 2017 in New York City. As principals of the award-winning design firm Roman and Williams Buildings and Interiors at the time, their aim was to create a vehicle through which they could sell their own designs of furniture, lighting, and accessories, as well as to bring together a highly curated selection of goods from all over the world. But the production and sourcing of furnishings was just the start, as the duo was determined to make the effort a collective vision for our modern times.

They accomplished this by carving out space for a gallery in which exhibitions would be presented, and invited Chef Marie-Aude Rose to open La Mercerie inside their Soho location as a respite for visitors to enjoy fine French cuisine. Rose's oeuvre balances her classical training and avant-garde practices in a thoughtful reimagining of dishes from the country famous for extraordinary gastronomical offerings. The restaurant and store are seamless—diners sit on the furniture Standefer and Alesch produce and their lighting designs illuminate each space; the café banquettes are versions of the Catalpa Sofa we purchased, and food is served on the dishes RW Guild sells.

By melding these experiences with a boutique from which benchmade and artisanal furnishings can be purchased, they created a mecca for firms like ours obsessed with sourcing the finest elements available for our projects. The exemplary offerings made by this team are at the top of our list because the production practices at RW Guild are in lockstep with the most inventive traditions through the ages—each form, shape, and idea underpinning every piece they create furthers the narrative of a cohesive story we aim to tell in our interiors.

They describe their construction quality as stubbornly uncompromising because it is foundationally built upon natural materials, and it celebrates the master craftsmen and artisans who have dedicated their lives to the proven, ancient techniques and methods through which their products are realized. RW Guild Original Designs are so resolutely steeped in the concept of endurance, the furnishings by Standefer and Alesch are made to last for generations, which makes them immediate heirlooms.

This is one of the reasons we chose pieces of furniture that were handcrafted by the team at RW Guild for the dining room and living room of the penthouse. We tapped the Bachelor Bar Cart for the dining room, and the Catalpa Sofas, the Hub Stone Coffee Table, and the Rex Throw for the living room. We also chose tableware by artisans they discovered. In these, we also feel their "hand" in the aesthetics of a number of the pieces. This is because not only do they scour the globe for remarkable offerings made by talented individuals who connect the dots between ancient techniques and contemporary sensibilities, they collaborate with the artisans and artisanal brands to create unique products that are available only through RW Guild.

The different pieces of tableware we chose by the three virtuosos we feature below are examples: these include Yoshihiro Nishiyama's Octagonal Glasses and Kaneko Kohyo Pottery Company's dinnerware that grace the dining room table, and Yuki Osako's glassware that was chosen for the wet bar tucked into the Curiosity Cabinet. The Octagonal Glasses by Yoshihiro Nishiyama, a glassblower in Ishikawa, Japan, are placed on the dining room table as water glasses when it is set. He has been deeply influenced by glassware from the Edo, Meiji and Taisho periods; and is a master of *katabuki*, a technique that results in extremely light and thin glass with a characteristically expressive surface. He says about his medium, "Although glass is usually considered cold, in reality it also has warmth and softness, which I try to express." It's brilliant how Nishiyama equates looking into the surfaces of his glasses with the experience of floating on the surface of a lake.

The artisans at Kaneko Kohyo Pottery Company in Gifu, Japan, created the dishes for the dining room that bloom along the surface of the table. The company was founded on a mountaintop near Toki City in 1921. The team there is known for their passion for modernizing ancient techniques and updating styles to create their own designs that are grounded in history while also being very comfortable in terms of present-day aesthetics. They were originally renowned in their own country for making Shinto and Buddhist altar pieces, and sake bottles. The company began producing handmade earthenware for the table in 1995. RW Guild is the exclusive carrier of Kaneko Kohyo's Rinka line in North America, and over the years Standefer and Alesch have brought them to New York City and co-designed several unique pieces that have been added to the collection. As a symbol of their ongoing partnership, the dishes are imprinted with both the pottery company's insignia and the RW symbol.

Yuki Osako, who produced the facet glasses we chose for the Curiosity Cabinet bar, practices the alchemy of glass from her studio in Kanazawa, Japan. Inspired by her surroundings, she aims to infuse her creations with the feelings evoked by an array of sensory reactions. These include glimpses of fresh-fallen snow blanketing rice fields or the mood created when winter light filters through a window. Walking the tightrope that melds form and function, Osako handcrafts her glassworks in phases that progress from blowing to grinding to cutting, and then to burning the glass in a kiln. RW Guild is also the exclusive global carrier of her larger glasses, designs that resulted from conversations Standefer and Alesch had with her on how to bring the art of ceremonial sake glasses to a broader audience. She is the sole maker of them and can only produce a few dozen a year, which means there are relatively very few of them in existence. In fact, we understand that the Houston residence likely has one of the larger collections of them on the planet!

"We often say that we are bound by an ethos, not a style," Standefer and Alesch say about the culture they have nurtured. They often encourage people to "master the mix" and create spaces that are unique to them as individuals by breaking down the conventional boundaries of traditional/modern, old/new, and plain/fancy. You can see why we can't get enough of this company's philosophy and offerings; we will certainly be eagerly sourcing from RW Guild as we create new environments into the future.

A poem unfolds as the sun rises to frolic within the globes that hang above the dining room. Its protagonist is drawn in because these small universes are the very color in which the blazing orb is accustomed to traveling. At day's end, the earth's brightest star must depart, making way for the moon to create a softer glow like a fairy tale. This poetry is a luminous handblown composition of glass shapes that bubble above the long undulant table. The translucent spherical bodies dangle from the ceiling on ropes that take on a new seriousness given they are combined with such a refined artisanal material.

These are tied as the fixtures culminate at their bottom-most points, seeming to pull the underside of the glass inward to create the ruse that they are pliable. The sophisticated design treatment gave the Knot Collection its name. The Czech manufacturer who produced them calls the gentle curves of the handblown glass against the austerity of coarse rope "striking, forthright, and dignified." During those evenings when the new moon leaves the inky sky to its brooding, the globes themselves become the heavenly bodies through which luminescence effervesces.

They are lit by LED panels mounted beneath elegant hoods made of stamped metal and muted ever so slightly by handblown triplex opal diffusors. As you have read in the presentation of the dining room, these lustrous lights were envisioned by Alfredo Chiaramonte and Marco Marin, who founded the award-winning Chiaramonte Marin Design Studio in Venice. Brokis is equally celebrated in the design arena for the fact that the company is preserving Bohemian glassblowing traditions. Czech entrepreneur and engineer Jan Rabell founded the brand in 2006, determined to create a platform to enliven and elevate Bohemian glassmaking to new heights. He was also keen to preserve knowledge and craftsmanship that extends back generations.

The foundation for his efforts was his acquisition of Janštejn Glassworks in 1997, a company that had been on the scene since the beginning of the nineteenth century. Located in a bucolic setting southeast of Prague in the Vysočina Region, the manufacturer was foundering because demand for traditional products had declined significantly, and many of the glassmakers were growing old and leaving. But Rabell knew that the time-honored technologies and techniques were at risk of being lost so his vision was to restore the factory to its former prestige and to ensure that the ages-old Bohemian glassmaking tradition endured into the twenty-first century by bringing a fresh, modernized style to product designs.

Keeping the storied Janštejn Glassworks name, Rabell accomplished his goal by making forward-thinking changes in the production process, which included building several Italian-style furnaces, and discontinuing grinding and glass painting to revive glassblowing using optic molds and traditional hot-shop techniques. Nearly-forgotten formulas for manufacturing colored glass were reinstated and became mainstays in the company's portfolio. In 2006, he founded Brokis to push the envelope of creating finely crafted, artisanal glass even further. Illustrating his pioneering spirit is this quote: "Nothing's impossible; never say it can't be done."

With the success of Brokis, design talent from around the world was drawn in, including Chiaramonte Marin Design Studio, already known for projects that widely vary—from interiors and graphics, to industrial and lighting design. Not only has the duo behind the atelier created products and projects for some of the world's most sophisticated producers of luxury home décor products, they teach at the European Center for Preservation of Architectural Heritage in Venice, fostering new generations of talent.

The roster of designers that Rabell has tapped to design for Brokis are from all corners of the globe—Italy, in the case of Chiaramonte Marin Design Studio; Japan; Israel; and Slovakia. He has also chosen collaborators from his own backyard, as there is major design talent in the Czech Republic. It's not surprising he would have a multicultural view, as he was born in Prague to a Puerto Rican father and Czech mother; and would grow up in his father's country, returning to Prague only when it was time to pursue a master's degree in economics.

The playfulness involved in arranging the Knot Collection kept us absorbed for hours on end, the final composition we achieved remarkably satisfying in the beauty the orbs bring to the dining room and the complexity they introduce to the open spaces over which they hover. This is one of the moments in the penthouse that reminded us how remarkable it is that poetry can be the result of engineered precision.

Hazy afternoons bring a softness to the hard edges of the buildings that rise in a clot beyond the living room windows. The ethereal transparency of the hand-stitched *ombré* curtains in this space (and the dining room) are misty creations themselves. Graduating from pale chocolate brown to beige and then cream as the eye rises toward the ceiling, the panels feel like beautiful lace gowns unearthed in a vault where history's finest haute couture is preserved.

The richness of this room is pleasing—the neutral color palette complemented by soft shades of rose, and the studied choices of inviting vintage and contemporary elements work in harmony. Furniture in this space was sourced from our favorite brands or found at the flea markets in Paris, where we bought the curved Brazilian bench from AK galerie at Paul Bert. The leather and wood sofas, and the wood and marble coffee table were purchased from RW Guild. Given the freed-from-the-wall attention the sofas receive, we chose a pair with walnut backs that are as beautifully actualized as the upholstered fronts. A mix of leather and textile upholstery brings sophistication to the classically rounded sofas, and the tones in the wood echo the colors in the terrazzo floor.

Serving as an anchor for the seating area, which also includes a pair of burgundy Oyster Chairs from Avenue Road, is a silk rug. The stitching and craftsmanship on the chairs impressed us, as did the ergonomics and the striking color of the leather. Behind these occasional chairs is a credenza from BDDW. This is another piece that would be viewed from all sides since it sits away from walls. We never have to worry about

this with Tyler Hays's work because he treats everything he produces like objects to be seen from all sides. The Iris Table Lamp placed on it is a bronze and handblown glass piece of artistry we found at Holly Hunt.

Dangling from the ceiling in a slim line behind the credenza is a chain-like light fixture by Viabizzuno called the Sempre Mia Suspension Lamp 3000. We chose it because it reads like a Japanese rain chain (*kusari-toi*), embedded with square prisms of light. When it reflects against the wall in the corner, it activates the area in a nuanced way. We've studied Viabizzuno's work for quite some time, and what draws us to the brand is how esoteric their designs are but in an authentic 80s/90s-Italian way. We see their pieces as timeless; and we always think of them when we are going to be using lighting as an artistic conceit rather than a utilitarian necessity. This fixture is perfect in the corner as an art piece because it is reflective regardless of the position in the room from which it is viewed and it throws dynamic shadows on the walls.

The airplane sculpture in front of the light fixture was a vintage find from the Marché aux Puces. You'll see us mention this Paris flea market several times in the book because it is one of our favorite places to find unusual furnishings that we know will be personable elements in projects. There are times, as is the case with this sculpture, when we see a special piece and purchase it without knowing where it will live. These are often the last statement pieces to be placed, and each time we include them, they become the little surprises that sing.

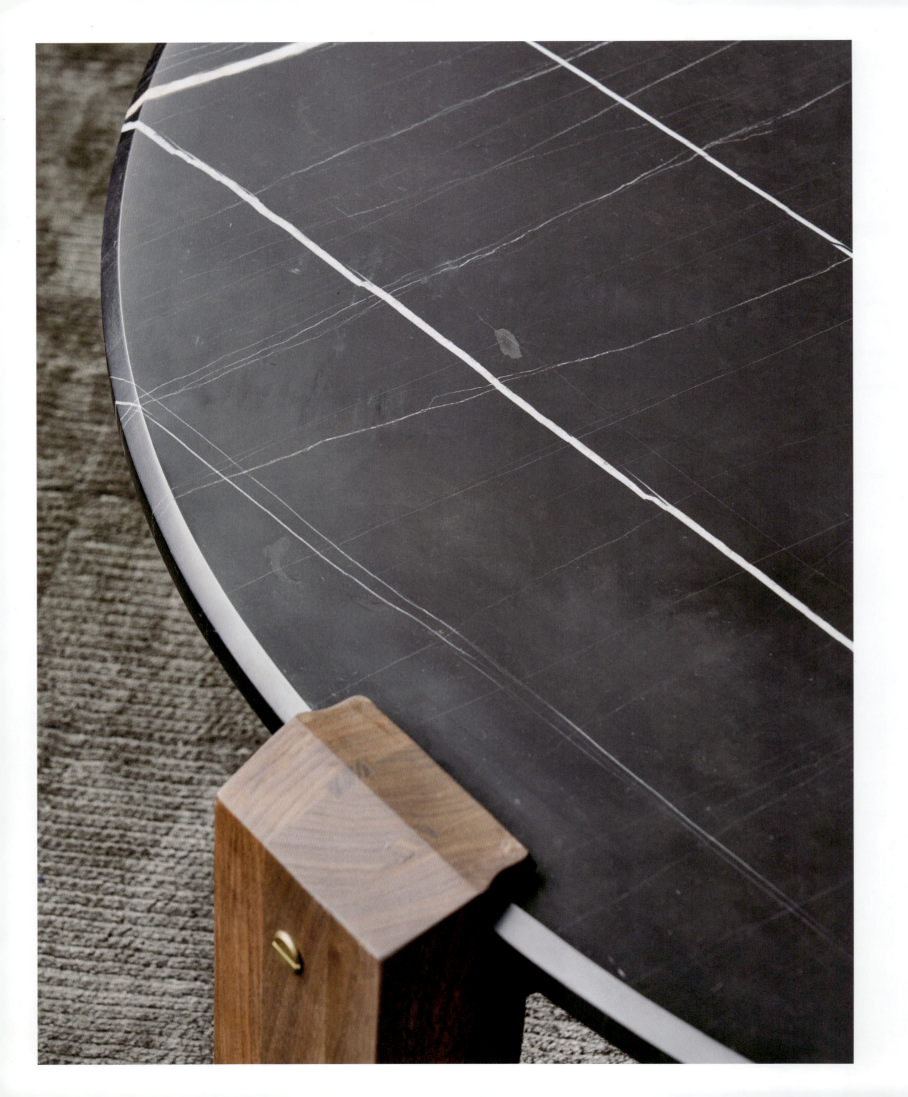

A bit removed from the seating area is a bench from BDDW placed in front of the windows dividing the living room from the pool terrace. A decorative element that rests beside this clean-lined bench illustrates how our collaborations inform projects like this penthouse. We chose the same Sahara Noir marble that forms the top of the coffee table for the countertops on the Curiosity Cabinet and the pedestals for the eggs that serve as night-lights, one of which glows beside the bench even when it isn't lit because it absorbs the natural light spilling into the space. A second is seen through the fluted glass in the corner of the guest suite, which rises a bit higher than the one in the living room to create greater visual interest. We also sourced these translucent shimmering eggs from AK galerie at Paul Bert Serpette Marché.

Two of the cleverest elements in the penthouse are nesting stools by Yoshiaki Ito. The Yosegi Nesting Stools are fabricated like puzzles in graduating segments, a concept that Ito first developed when he was making cube animals and trays with us. We hired him as a featured product designer for three-and-a-half years so he could develop the stools. Along with tapping into his talent as an industrial designer, we gave him the task of connecting us with craftspeople in Japan who produce *kumiko* screens so we could use the concept to create the ceiling in the kitchen, which you'll see when we tour that space.

It is to Ito's credit that we were able to experiment with this ancient art form. We've been so fortunate to actualize a great deal of architectural work in Japan over the past two decades, but Ito was a perfect bridge for us to connect architecture and product design. Our 212box Hearth Collection spawned a "Designed in NYC, made in Japan" mantra as a branding tagline. The two stools in the living room are the first prototypes we developed with Ito. They are made of Hinoki wood, a Japanese cypress. The original ones we manufactured are darker than the fresh-cut wood in its golden yellow hue because they were cut from logs that had been soaked in a swamp for a substantial length of time.

This method to darken wood is a long-standing tradition in Japan. Creating the geometry of the stool with Ito is another example of seizing the opportunity to collaborate with artisans and designers to develop unique products. We share more of Ito's journey in this chapter after we've toured the space. This corner of the living room with the stools and the rouge swivel chairs is one of our favorites in the penthouse. The spot simply beckons with the jewelry-like string light, the comfortable chairs, and the dexterous stools.

Illuminating the larger volume of the sumptuous living room are two oversized honeycomb fixtures by Dimore Studio Lighting. They are incredibly heavy in scale but with the twelve-foot ceilings, we knew we could get away with sourcing something vigorous. Fixtures this large will often overwhelm a space but if everything else in the room is chosen wisely, there is a balancing act that transpires. The openness of the room and the serenity of the furnishings in it allows these sculptural ceiling lights to breathe; leaves them free to do their own thing in the space, which is magnetic.

Yoshiaki Ito

Yosegi Nesting Stools

Academicians will tell you that mathematics is an art and a science. Illustrating a model that joins the two as forcefully as we've ever seen is Yoshiaki Ito. Though he dreamed of being an artist when he grew up in Japan, the home furnishings industry gained a brilliant thinker when he decided he wanted to work with his hands as an adult. As he explored traditional techniques that hail from his homeland while living in New York City, he grew increasingly fascinated with paradox. This manifested in works in wood with minimal profiles that had within their creations complicated mathematical systems he developed. From this intricacy of joinery, he was able to create profiles that are quintessentially Japanese.

"I really like wooden puzzles," the product designer notes, "especially traditional Japanese Shintō *kumiki* puzzles." He was manipulating one when the idea of producing furniture struck. "I kept sliding the pieces many times," he explains, "and I began to think about how cool it would be if I could make furniture with the same method." From this moment, the pair of Yosegi Nesting Stools in the penthouse living room were born. "My true passion is creating exquisite patterns using inlaid wood," he goes on to say. "With this pair of stools that merge seamlessly and are easily separated, I employed the *tsugite* technique—*tsugite* means 'joined' in my native language—with geometric wooden joints and twelve diamond-shaped columns."

The beginning of the process during which the stools were realized was highly calculated as he extruded one facet after another in CAD. After a few days of working to simplify all the possible parts, the puzzle morphed into the pair of stools. Though a snap to manipulate once made, the adroitness is hard-won during the design process. At the heart of the meaning of Yosegi is *yose*, which means "gather together," and *gi*, which means "wood" in Japanese. The tradition that brought the method into being is ancient, as it dates back to the first ages in which human beings began living in wooden buildings.

When a column or a board on a façade would rot or be damaged in some way, the craftsmen developed a method to repair the wood so that no viable material was ever wasted. "It is very complicated joinery," Ito remarks. "By using this method, they don't have to take a building or a gate apart. This is ironic because my stools are meant to come apart, even though they are seamless looking when joined."

Ito lived in New York City for over twenty years, eventually joining the team at David Weeks Studio in 2008 where he developed a toy called the Cubebot for Areaware. As he became more immersed in the world of interior and product design, he witnessed how much Americans in his field were drawn to Japanese aesthetics. "I was the only Japanese designer with the company," he explains. "I care about contemporary design, whether it is Japanese or American; the only rule is the pieces have to be very carefully made, which is why *tsugite* appeals to me." After leaving David Weeks Studio and a stint as a freelancer, Ito connected with Eric and came on board with 212box as a product designer from 2016 to 2019.

By this time, he had become an established professional in his own right and we were drawn to his aesthetic. We collaborated with Ito on many things, appreciating how he fulfilled our desires to use traditional Japanese woodworking techniques to realize a new age of three-dimensional modern objects. He was our much-needed link to Japanese manufacturing, which gave us the opportunity to produce the wood *kumiko* ceiling in the kitchen.

We were able to produce the stools that reside in the living room because Ito was able to find a fabricator who could manufacture them. "It took me two years to find one," Ito says. "Everyone said they could do it, but I had to find a traditional craftsman who used digital machines so that we could achieve a 0.3 millimeter accuracy. It's this precision, which is impossible for the human hand to achieve, that makes them so seamless. Traditional craftsmen will argue but I can tell you that it can't be done without a machine."

The physical creation of the nesting stools takes place in this order: three types of diamond-shaped columns are made: short, long, and bias; one short, one long, and two bias. These are glued together to create a large diamond, which becomes one leg; the three parts of the leg in the previous step are repeated, then they are rotated and glued into a hexagon shape, resulting in one stool. Repeat the process to make the second stool and slide them together. The fact that it requires such precise machining means it is expensive to make, but we feel it's worth the added cost given what a remarkable design it is conceptually.

"I originally didn't intend to make a stool that fits within a Japanese aesthetic, but as circumstance would have it, it is what I did," he remarks. "I enjoy so much the idea of continuing to simplify until only the fundamental parts remain. This naturally creates a beautiful object born from a similar idea as Bauhaus." While working with us, Ito and Eric collaborated to design a chair inspired by the *kumiko* method of woodworking, which until then had only been employed to create two-dimensional screens. "Eric wanted to use the screen like a three-dimensional puzzle so we set out to turn the screen patterning into a chair," Ito explains. "Once I managed to make the shape, Eric asked if he could sit on it and the answer was, 'No.'"

Ito kept at it, struggling to make it sit-able, a process that is ongoing. "I am still looking for a solution," he notes. "I have been reaching out to different fabricators, one in metal, to see if we can put an armature inside it to strengthen it while maintaining the aesthetics we want. I did a CAD drawing and made a replica of the chair in 1/20th scale on a 3D printer. I took this to a *kumiko* screen fabricator but we've yet to find a solution. The prototype is in the 212box office." It was always meant to be a non-functioning art piece, though it did tempt us many times to question the idea of an implied chair so we christened it the "Ghost Chair."

When the pandemic began in 2020, Ito decided to move back to Japan where he has been living on his family's rice farm since. "Creatively it has been good to be here," he says.

"There is no COVID where I am living and it's a relief to not be stressed from paying high rents, working by myself, and dealing with fabricators from Asia, which were halfway around the world when I was in the city. Working in the countryside is a relief, and after being away from Japan for twenty-one years, I am now networking with fabricators of high-end traditional furniture here, which I hope will result in more collaborations with 212box."

We asked Ito if he had any advice for struggling artisans or craftspeople who are dreaming of actualizing a career path that would support their creativity. "I am an example of how someone can achieve success even without an education or money at first," he answers. "When I moved to New York, I worked in a kitchen as a dishwasher, then I moved up to being a busboy, then a waiter, so it was a leap to become an assistant designer. I'm fortunate that a company invested in me, especially because I was an immigrant and from a rural area."

While Ito was employed by David Weeks he put himself through school at Hunter College in Brooklyn. "I paid for my education and my living expenses with my salary," he says. "But because I was working full time while going to class, everything was pretty dramatic!" The drama is beginning to pay off with one significant success during the past several years of which he's quite proud: he has licensed his newest project, Morphits, a series of transforming animals that put a new spin on the wooden puzzle toy, with MoMA. He has also won a number of awards for his design work, including several Golden A'Design Awards in the toy category in Italy; and a Special Mention in a competition for furniture design in Germany.

He says he values the time he spent in America because he learned how important fabrication, special machining, computer skills, and knowledge of CAD are. He also benefitted from looking at traditional Japanese design work from a New York perspective. "In Japan, we are quite far behind in this sense. So many craftspeople have never used a CNC machine or designed a product with CAD," he says. "In New York City, there are many layers of skills, from high-tech to low-tech, that exist in one marketplace. I feel this is knowledge I can use to help others in my country understand how to expand their skills."

But he still gives traditional Japanese craftsmanship the credit for his current path. "The world of design I experienced in New York elevates certain names as giants in the industry, which is appropriate," he explains. "But when a temple is made in Japan, there is no named carpenter. This is a fact that I believe instills the soulfulness in the humble makers in my country, whose talents are obvious in everything they create. It is this world I revere."

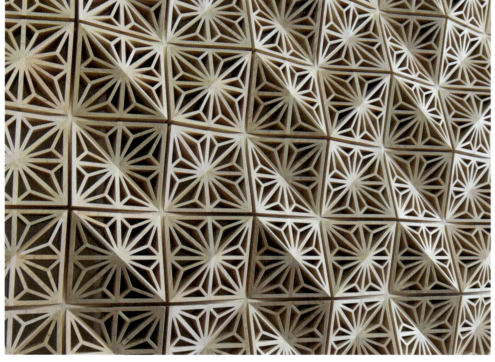

Amber waves of undulant planes. We haven't left the penthouse for the prairie but it is a fascinating slight-of-hand we've employed to call this anthemic-sounding phrase to mind. To witness it, there are only two simple steps: walk into the kitchen and look up! The design of the entire open room revolved around what is now a glorious wood ceiling handmade in Japan by craftspeople using ancient traditions we have already described in the chapter on the living room and in Yoshiaki Ito's profile. The company that achieved the delicately dynamic plane is Tanihata Kumiko.

We were originally going to specify rough planks chosen from the stockpiles of the client's reclaimed timber business, but as the aesthetics of the spaces surrounding the open kitchen grew more sophisticated, we knew we had to introduce a surface that was more polished. We showed the homeowner six other ceiling treatments, two of them being our three-dimensional *kumiko* wood studies and our geometric wood tiles. When the client picked those two as his favorites and couldn't decide which was better, we suggested combining the two treatments. Once this was agreed upon, we set about designing what soon became a meticulous study on symmetry and balance.

This space was, without exaggeration, a relentless pursuit of seam alignments, beginning with the ceiling, which was manufactured in a very unforgiving four-inch grid. There could be no deviations because every wood tile is an assemblage of twenty hand-cut pieces that are hand-assembled and glued to fit. This was one of our most rewarding collaborations to date given Tanihata is one of the oldest *kumiko* manufacturers in Japan. They have endless flat patterns suitable for wall and ceiling applications, and doorways; and we were thrilled they were willing to work with us when we approached them in 2018.

Once they said they were up to the task, we set about designing three different tiers within one pattern of wood tiles. The design emerged only after we undertook a number of studies, carving into the wood to see how we could alter their lattice-style pieces. We were finally able to give them

enough data that they could interpret their flat designs with undulations. The result is a rising and falling surface made from concave and convex tiles, a wavy effect that is stunning to experience.

We designed it in a diamond grid on a sixteen-tile pattern, the repeat being four tiles by four tiles. This was a mind-bender for sure but once we accomplished the manipulation, we see how there are endless patterns that can be realized—in herringbone or cube shapes, for instance. With the ceiling conquered, our next challenge was the overhead lighting. Because we had to work within such a strict grid, we had to have a chandelier with small canopies that could be installed in four-inch increments. The chandelier we created highlights another collaboration we had been hoping we could undertake for years—designing a custom product with Astropol.

We saw the French company's lighting at one of the Maison et Objet shows in Paris, and when we looked at the website to choose options for this project, we were drawn to a fixture with a beautiful maze of circuitry in horizontal and vertical lights. We completed a number of configurations to discover how the customization of the canopies would have to be tweaked and then asked them if they could build the chandelier in the arrangement we required. Fortunately, the fixture was made up of set pieces they were already interchanging between a number of designs so they were able to work within their own system to give us the configuration we needed.

The metal work of the frame was the only element that would have to be manufactured as a new variable; otherwise, the placement of the glass tubes was similar to the other chandeliers they produced. On our end, we had to replace the *kumiko* tiles with solid, flat tiles at the points where the fixture was mounted. The result is asymmetrically lovely when you see the fixture in person. What's incredible about this room is how it juxtaposes ancient techniques of woodworking with avant-garde custom lighting within one collaborative process.

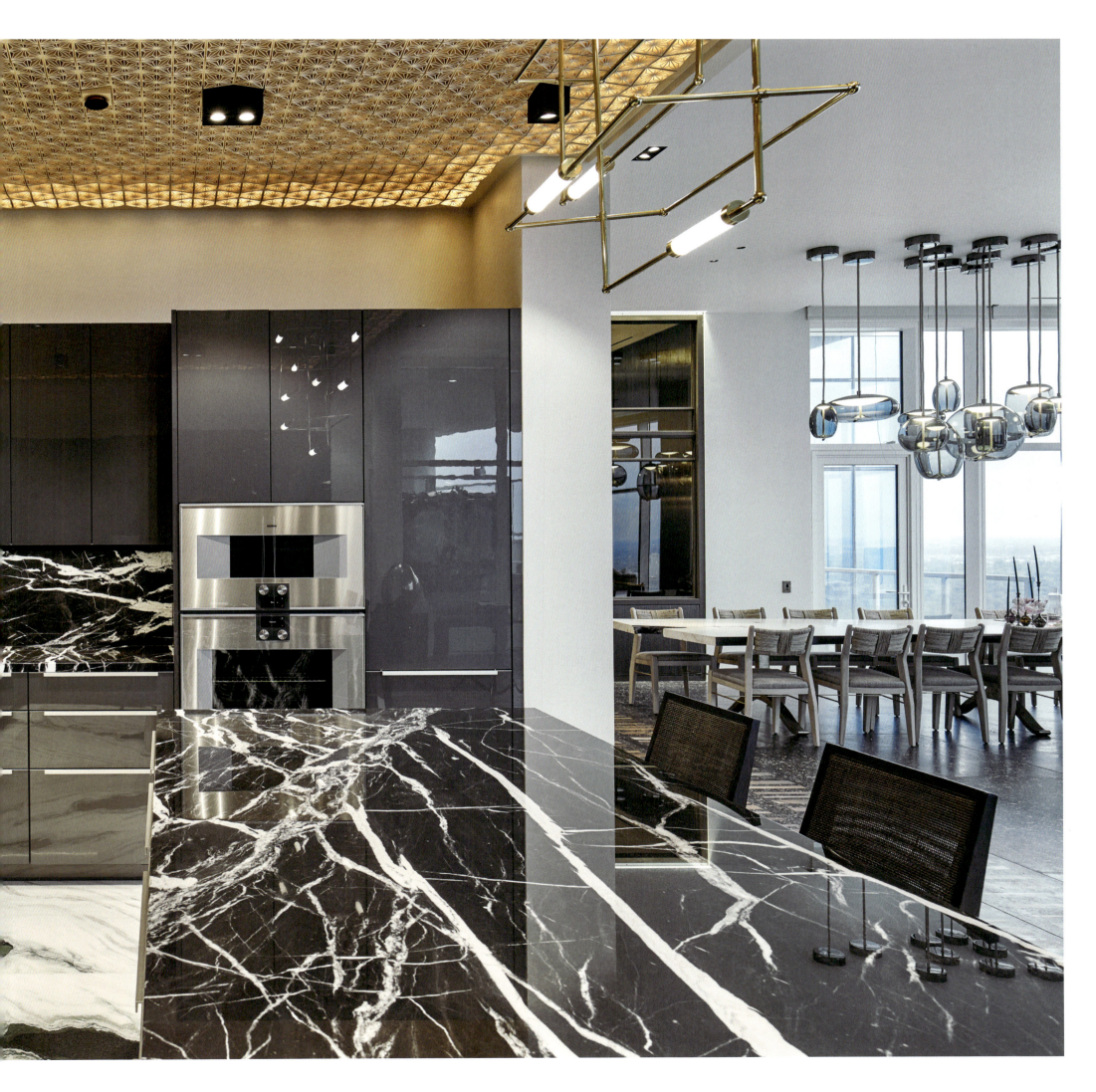

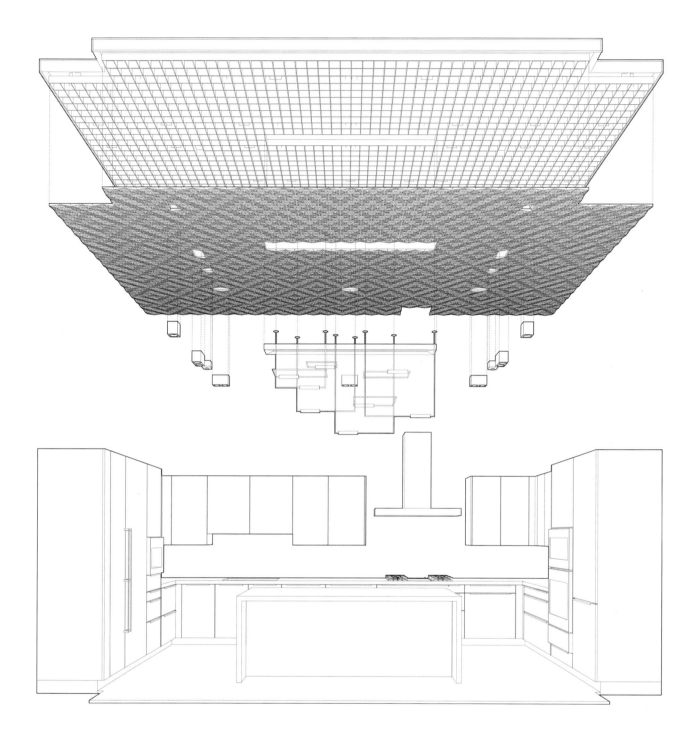

Because a kitchen is one of the rooms that demands task lighting, we illuminated the space between the solid ceiling and the screen, which bathes the room in a nuanced glow. The ceiling is one of the aspects of the penthouse that we know will spur collaborations in the future. Before working with the Japanese craftspeople, we visited the factory in the village of Tanihata. Now that we have produced a product with them, we are excited about continuing the relationship. This aspect of the penthouse project satisfies one of our passions, which is to take traditional artisanal treatments and create new applications with them.

Another stunning design aspect of the space is how we adapted the marble patterns. The walls are clad in an incredible black lighting marble, each piece handpicked by Dino Figliomeni of Crystal Tile & Marble, Ltd. We laid it out meticulously and book-matched it throughout the entire kitchen, as we did with the white Dalmata marble on the floors. We stayed with the original kitchen cabinetry company because Arabella had chosen an excellent vendor in Eggersmann Kitchen & Home Living. We elevated the line that had been chosen for each residence in the building by adding inlays and requesting upscale finishes like the black lacquer on the upper cabinets that has a tremendous sheen to it.

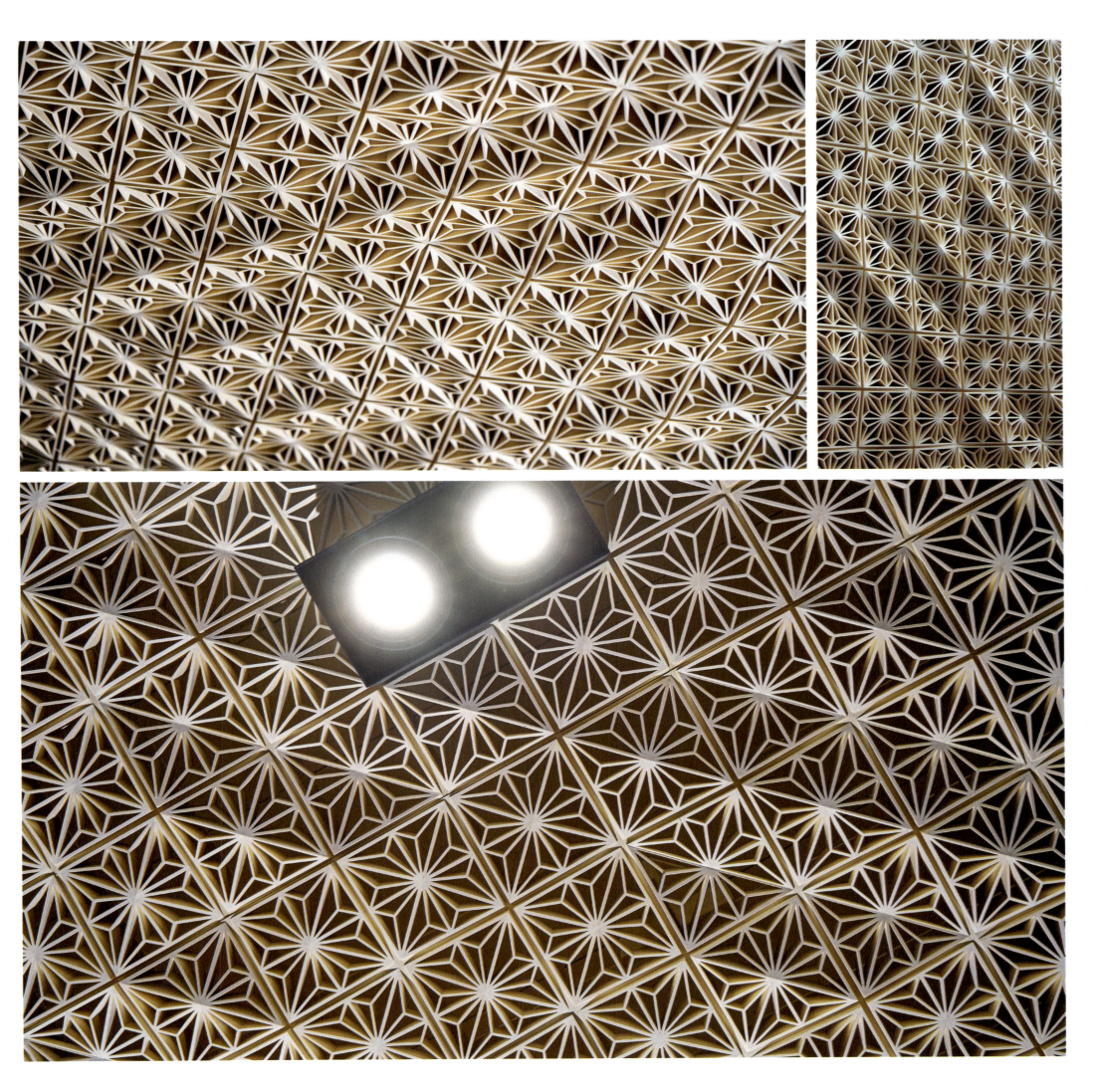

Monolithic steel and glass skyscrapers in modern times could not exist without grand volumes. Along with clean lines and contemporary materials, the lexicon spoken by these stalwarts that reach toward the heavens is a language of strength. The Arabella bellows its resoluteness, as can be seen from the pool terrace, which is the last of the public spaces in the penthouse before moving into the bedroom suites. It sits at the end of the long living room/dining room space so its position in the views of the penthouse demanded that it be carefully nuanced.

This is because the original design was seriously lacking given it was as utilitarian as the living room is sophisticated. The steps were awkwardly placed, and the first thing that came into view was a wall of unattractive access doors to the pool equipment. There was no way we were going to create an elegant living room with a view of unadorned walls and service doors!

Our solution was to create a substantial cabinet that we worked into the stairs. It serves as storage for towels,

glassware, and accoutrements required for alfresco dining, sunbathing, or swimming. We retiled the pool in a deep blue; and chose a pale marble for the pavers on the stairs, the pool deck, and the top and sides of the teak cabinet into which we carved a modern shelf detail. On the lounge-side of the deck, we placed a silk flower arrangement on the back of the cabinet to add a nature-inspired visual feature that is seen from the living room and the lounge area on the terrace.

In this niche, Dedon's MBRACE chairs with quilted fiber cushions, designed by Studio Sebastian Herkner, are comfortable spots from which to enjoy the fall and spring breezes, summer mornings, and the occasional winter afternoons because they embrace the body as their names imply. The oversized pillow beside the pool, by the United Kingdom brand SHORE that we found via The Future Perfect, is grandly sized. Its *ombré* blue tones echo the sky that is reflected in the windows, the tiled pool, and the slick surface of its water. The story of the birth of this company, founded by two dynamos of design, follows.

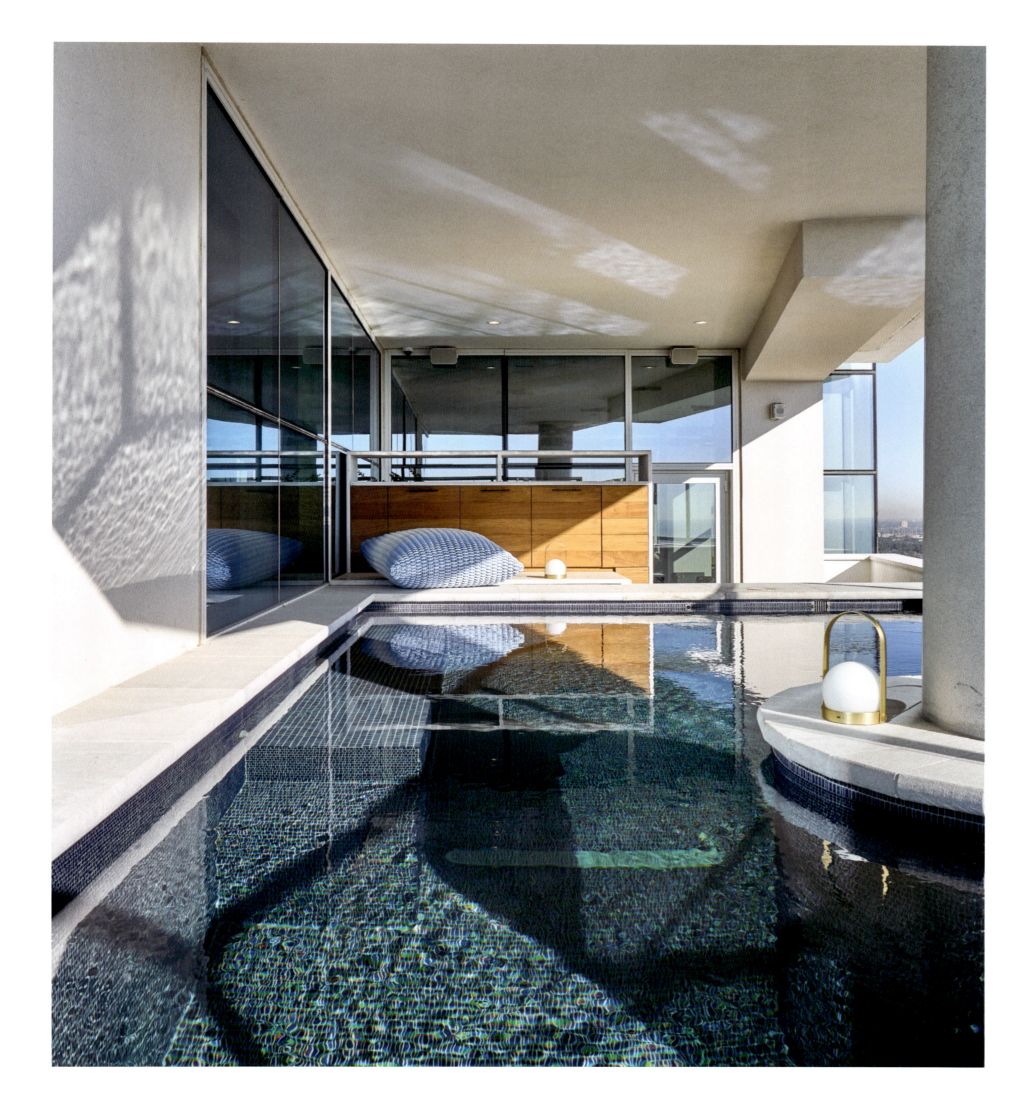

Poolside Pillow

Monumental architecture has its demands, and only distinctive furnishings will live up to the muscle. Nestled into the massive volume of the pool terrace surrounded by swaths of masonry and glass, an unassuming contender quietly resides. It is paradoxical: as soft as the linear lines telescoping around it are hard, it is also resolutely strong. Beckoning from its corner, the pillow is an innovative construct that sprang from the minds of Louie Rigano and Gil Muller. The pair teamed up to found SHORE just after they graduated from their master's degrees at the Royal College of Art in London. Both studied industrial design, and Rigano graduated with distinction.

The innovative pillow we chose for this project illustrates a feat that only the most talented designers manage to achieve—taking a mundane material and turning it into a finely designed, beautiful product. The silicone cord that is woven to create the covering of SHORE's pillows was originally invented to make gasket seals for engines and other mechanized constructs that require cushioning where the metal elements meet. The fact that it can become so lovely in the hands of Rigano, Muller, and their team is the coup. The life the material brings to the pillow is one of its charms when the human body eases into it—tightly packed with foam, the cord is wrapped around it with a high level of tension that makes it supportive while it's cupping the body and makes it spring back to its perfect form when it is vacated.

The *ombré* effect that flows along its surface meets the eye with its own embodiment of softness. "The pillow has a gradient to it, which we achieve when we feed multiple colors into the material as it is being extruded," explains Rigano. "Then, we weave the material after the cord is fully formed to create the *ombré* patterns the client has specified." Choosing blue hues for the pool terrace, we sought to reflect the rippling water close at hand and the expanses of sky farther afield. The playful scale and durability of the material from which the pillow is made was another attribute that caught our eye and made this a perfectly comfortable accent for the pool's edge.

How did Rigano and Muller hit upon taking this prosaic concoction to create products that are so attractive and weather-worthy? "We began looking at the health industry when we graduated from school and found that so many products in that category are not designed to be beautiful," Rigano explained. "Take antifatigue mats, for example,

which was my favorite. We were interested in taking a product like that, preserving the functional qualities, and constructing it in a way that made it a luxury offering." They concentrated solely on rugs at first, taking them from sizes that worked well in front of the kitchen sink and bathroom vanity to a scale that would accommodate pool decks and yachts.

Having solidified their manufacturing technique, the design duo felt compelled to create offerings that eclipsed the floor, but always with an eye to merging health and design as they created products that would have similar energizing qualities. "This led us to custom products like the one for the Houston penthouse," Muller notes. "We launched our pillows in 2020 and we introduced a collection of furniture that includes ottomans and chairs in 2021. The idea is to produce every element required when creating an outdoor lounge." The inspiration for the ottomans came to them when they were asked to design poofs that are now sailing the globe on the decks of ships in the Virgin Voyages cruise line.

"I was excited about the commission from the cruise line because I always knew our products would have an indoor/outdoor strength," Rigano explains. "If you think about the deck of a cruise ship, it's a rigorous environment where weather is concerned, from intense sun to salt water, so a product has to be extremely durable." Given the success they are seeing, it may surprise you to know that neither of the designers had any experience in weaving or textiles when they set their sights on creating their own product line. Rigano's disciplines were woodworking and ceramics, and Muller concentrated on jewelry and metalwork.

The idea that the designers could do things their way created a freedom that led the duo to the material they chose. "We had to find ways to do the weaving that made the most sense to us," Muller explains. "It took us a while to refine our techniques; now that we have, our proprietary products are all made in-house; and our tools, like our frame looms, are all bespoke." Craftsmanship is extremely important to the pair because they know the luxury design customer has a demanding sense of aesthetics.

"There was no precedent for what we were doing so there was nothing we could emulate," Rigano says. "We were able to use the same principles of weaving threads but with our products there are no loose cord ends or knots: every

strand merges back into itself." Since they founded SHORE, Rigano and Muller have assembled a team of five people, each of whom is just as eager to continue to break new ground. Everything SHORE does is highly customized, as each product is woven and each color is mixed by hand. Though this puts the business in the same category as ones that rely upon the handmade aspects of their products to earn the distinction of being luxury brands, Rigano and Muller realized during the early design shows that positioning their brand was going to take as much innovation as the production of their products required.

This occurred to the duo when they set up booths next to large rug manufacturers whose products are woven of refined materials in South Asia. "If you look at a major rug company's website and read about the traditional craft they are executing in places like Nepal, the rug's origin will be its value proposition," Rigano explains. "Because we had to invent our product, we didn't have this built into our messaging so we had to wrap our minds around how to position a rug as valuable when it's not manufactured in this traditionally valued way. To put a rubber mat next to a rug woven of silk created such a stark contrast!"

It is not surprising that Rigano and Muller continued undeterred because from the very beginning they were driven to experiment. This began when the pair borrowed a broken loom at university and repaired it to understand how to create their own tools. Their grit has produced offerings with a long list of pluses that include being ergonomic, UV resistant, heatproof, waterproof, easy to clean, hypoallergenic, vegan, and exceptionally durable. "We value health and freedom above all else," says Muller. "That's why we're challenging the traditional hierarchy of luxury that's based on rarity, provenance, and hype—because you shouldn't have to choose between something luxurious and something good for you." Rigano adds, "We believe true luxury is not only about what something is, but how it makes you feel."

What would the duo say to young designers/artists hoping to build their own unique brand? "It's important to clearly define your values, whether as a designer or as a brand, way before even thinking of a final product," Rigano says. "We've always found that a core set of beliefs will guide and propel the design process and ensure that whatever you create will resonate on a personal level." Muller adds, "It's essential to love and believe in what you do and make."

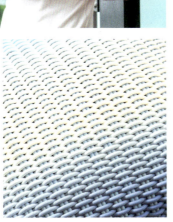

A marvelous music awaits in the hallway that connects the main living spaces with the bedroom suites. The passageway represents a journey of emotion and intensity by way of a sculpture that reveals how powerful design can be when its fragments have meaning. When we walked into Galerie Géraldine Banier on rue Jacob in Paris, where we found the colorful skull in the Curiosity Cabinet by Laurence Le Constant, we noticed the client standing spellbound in front of an arrangement of hands created by Eline Dussart.

When the gallerist told her the motions mimic the first six hand gestures for Debussy's "Clair de Lune," she was moved because this was one of the first pieces of music her daughter learned to play when she began taking piano lessons. The personal nature of the attachment the work of art drew between the past and the present was such a powerful encounter for her, we placed it in the intimately scaled space that leads to her inner sanctum so she could enjoy the memory each time she passes it.

By stepping into this hallway, we have left the rhythm of the Foresso planks behind for other melodious notes as the paleness of the white Dolomite marble floor with its whispery black veining ushers in a moment of transition. We chose a textured cream wallcovering for this space because we knew when illumination washed over it, the striations would gleam. The pastel crispness also draws out the lighter tones in the framed piece of artwork by Elisa Strozyk.

We include the profile on this remarkable artist in the chapter on the primary bedroom suite, which we will soon tour. It includes details about this wooden textile of seamlessly fitted triangles she hand-dyed and composed into a cloud-like explosion. Close up, the composition is a pattern-on-pattern and texture-on-texture study; from far away, the piece is fluid, as if the triangles of wood are rearranging themselves as the onlooker marvels.

Also in the hallway is a gleaming console table by French furniture maker and artist Anasthasia Millot, whose profile follows this presentation of the space. Her creations exist at an intersection where Santiago Calatrava and Tim Burton collide, as their profiles engage observers in a mythological narrative that spans architectonic elegance and quirky posturing. Eric reveres her pieces, which he found in the Marché aux Puces. He was so enamored with her work, he bought seven pieces in half an hour, but only after an internal struggle brought on by the power the baroque-meets-brutalist pieces unleashed.

"I was so overwhelmed that I walked to several other booths and circled back around to make sure my initial instincts weren't whims," he explains. "Once I saw them again, I knew I had to buy as many of them as possible." Every piece Millot makes is a masterpiece of shape, some crafted in one resolute material and others layered, like the bronze and leather table you will see in the guest suite. The table in the hallway space, in solid brass, has svelte flowing lines that are as intriguing as the sculpture placed above it.

Sitting atop the Millot console in the hallway is the Germes de Lux Table Lamp by Thierry Toutin, which we sourced from 1stDibs. Once the client told us the story about her daughter, we wanted to place an element on the table that felt melodious and Toutin's lamps read like little vibrating musical notes encapsulated in a glass dome. There is something so playful in his one-off pieces that also feel mysterious. To us, the three special elements in this hallway strike chords in a design musicality that could only be composed of the finest notes.

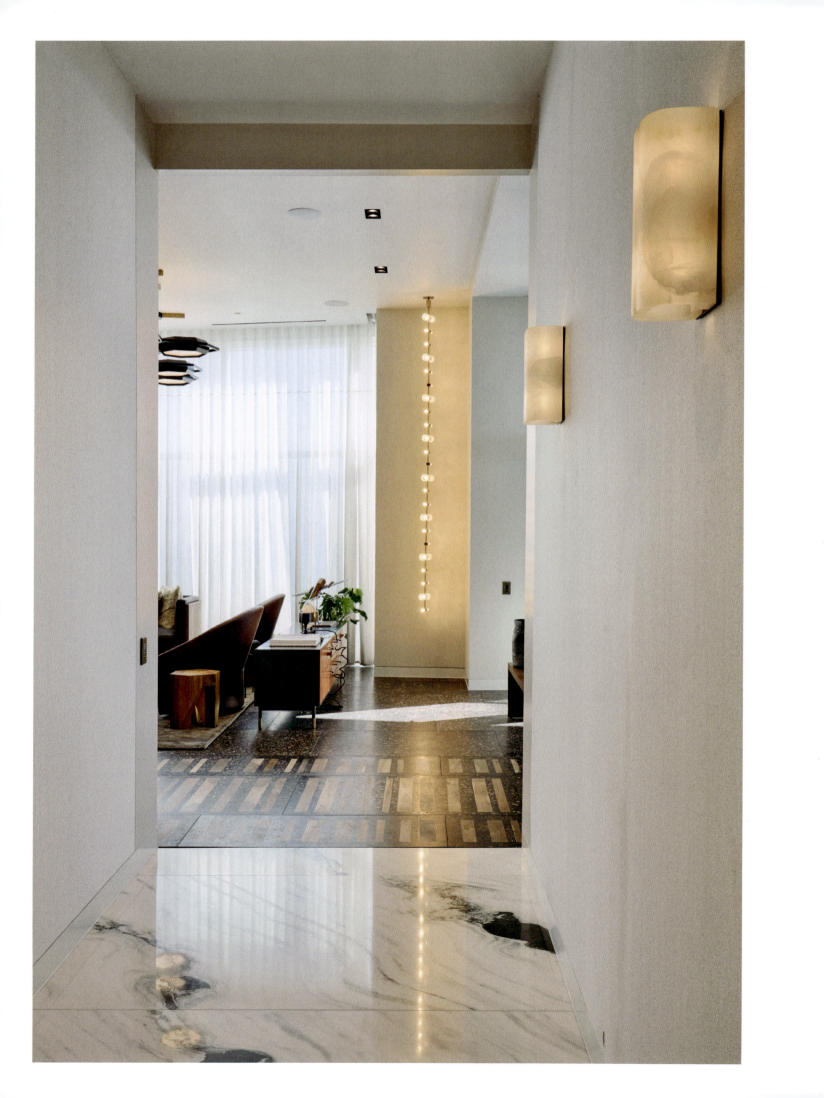

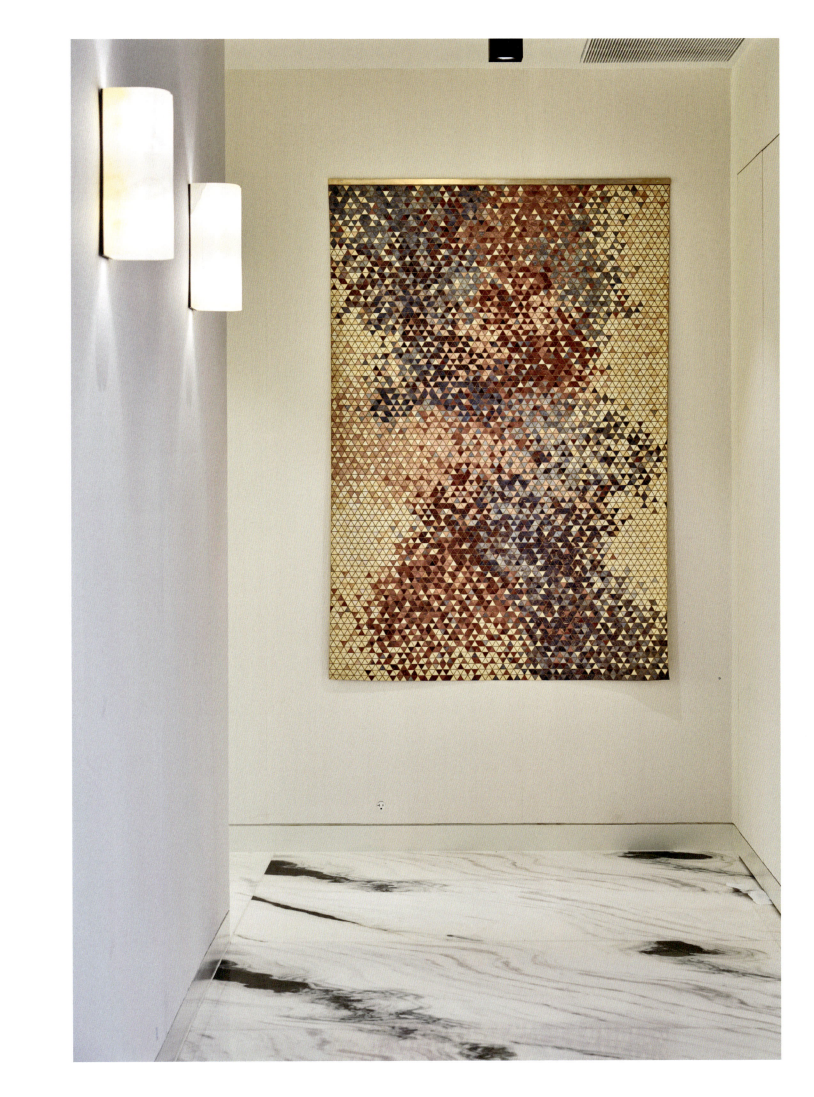

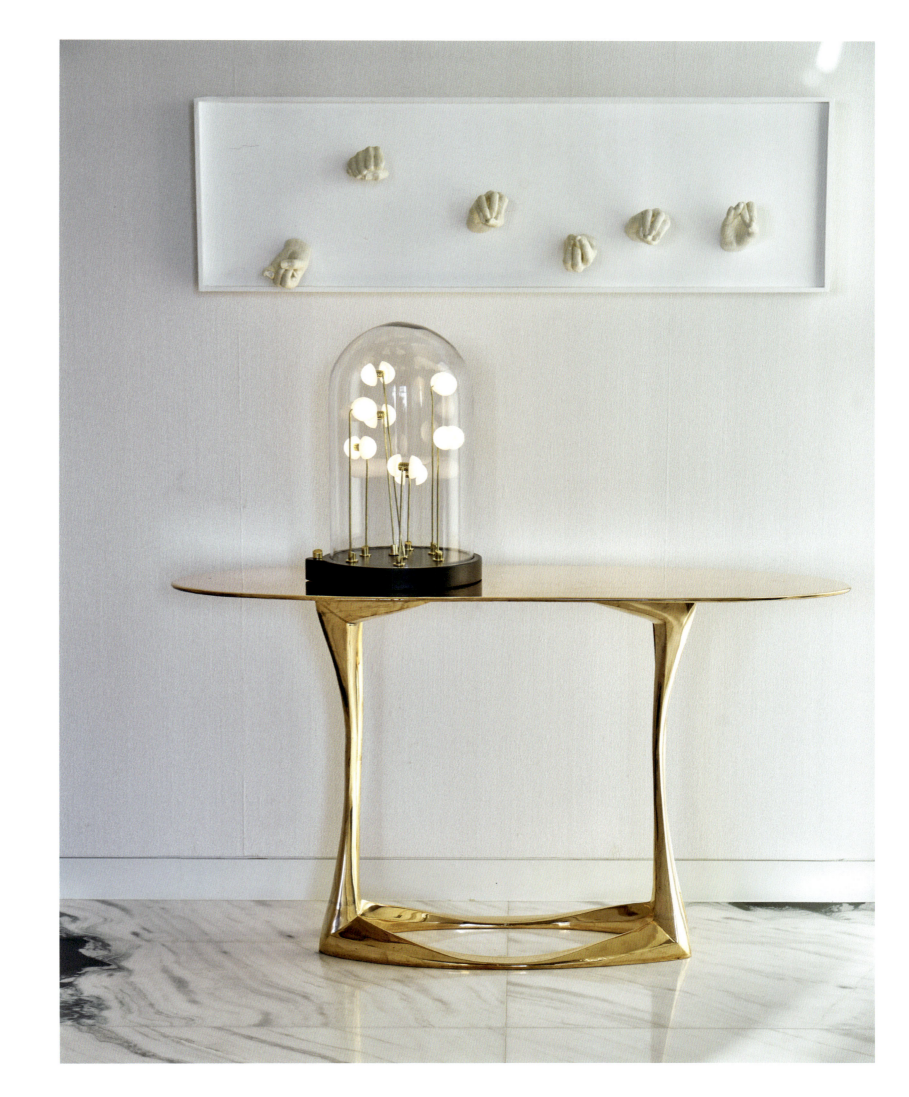

Anasthasia Millot

Stardust Console Table
Gueridon Kimira Side Table

As we enter the paradoxical world of angular and poetic, legs thicken, then thin; arc, but ever so slightly; and link in inextricable solidarity. Coaxing them from reverie to reality, Anasthasia Millot brought these artful attributes to life in the Stardust Console Table and the Gueridon Kimira Side Table. Firmly placed atop the Stardust is a blade-thin oval of gold metal; the Gueridon Kimira culminates with a leather-wrapped disc except where sophisticated rectangles of bronze win out. As we have already shared, Eric was smitten with Millot's designs when he first spotted them at the Marché aux Puces in Paris.

The talented furniture designer worked in luxury ready-to-wear before leaving the fashion industry to join the universe of foundry art. Her ambition was to translate her fascination with fabric to this field of craftmanship, and we would say she has achieved this with remarkable verve! Her methodology included spending many hours in the workshops to which she had access, the experiences instilling in her a deep desire to emulate the heavy fall and fluidity of cloth in bronze. As her acumen grew, Millot began producing bronze furniture with these characteristics. When she had amassed a selection of pieces, the Galerie Avant-Scène à Paris tapped her work to be shown at the esteemed design fair PAD Paris in 2010.

It was also in 2010 when the Foundry Art Fodor that she had chosen as her artisanal home was distinguished with an Entreprise du Patrimoine Vivant (EPV) designation, which represents excellence and industrial expertise in manufacturing in France. As she continued to explore her visions for her work, she stayed true to her instincts, which were to give the impression of lightness and to mimic rippling lines: "This may seem so simple to a layman's eye, implying it would be nothing out of the ordinary," she says; "but it is the multitude of details, which may seem useless afterwards, that are indispensable for the construction of a piece."

Illustrating how she sees the flowing profiles that make her tables in the penthouse so special, she says, "Textile is never far from bronze in the way I use it; the metal reminds me of those heavy jerseys that are so elegant without adding any superfluous details." The Foundry Art Fodor was born in 1967 when her husband's father Claude Redoutey began making elements like decorative hardware. When her husband, Didier Redoutey, took the helm of the company, he began producing bronze furniture for designers. Millot's collection, which she calls a true boost for her career, is the latest evolution of this. "It is not only rewarding for me," she explains; "but also for my husband and for the team assisting me during the different phases of the production process."

She is continually inspired, even by the smallest objects she sees, always asking herself how a shape would look when cast in bronze—these include ribbons, cotton strings, and stones. "I really love using plaster on ribbons to accomplish curved shapes," she explains; "waxed thin plates are also my favorites when I explore different textures. I never think of bronze first; I am looking for a shape. This is what seduces me. I keep all of the first drawings of a new piece together for reference, and most of the time these will be filled with short, uncompleted lines that splay in different directions."

She calls the Kimira table a tricky piece: "I wanted to create a side table that seemed classical but was definitely not. I worked with the cabinetmaker, the chiseler, and the leather artisan in order to accomplish it," she says, "folding the leather around the top-plate so that it was flush with the edge, which was one of the most demanding aspects of the design and was a lengthy process. After the Kimira table, I eventually returned to the scene of the crime, so to speak, and produced the Gueridon Kimira, which was chosen for the Le Mobilier National Collection in Paris in 2021."

The Stardust console was another challenge, which she admits flummoxed her coworkers because there were so many angles and so many details on the legs, which is exactly what attracted Eric to this piece. "I eventually continued the work in wax with my colleagues, and it took months more to achieve the exact shape, though the word exact gives me pause because each piece I produce seems to be a never-ending story," she explains. "It is difficult for me to ever be completely satisfied."

This passion for exploration appeared early in her life. "As far back as I can remember, I have always loved making things," she says. "For me, my creative aspirations do not end with the creation of bronze furniture; there are many fields I want to try. I really love it when I have the opportunity to visit artisanal companies, and luckily France still encourages its patrimony. In fact, so many people who visit the foundry are amazed at the way we work, which has changed only slightly through the years. I also enjoy visiting companies whose craftspeople have perpetuated the know-how of their trades over centuries. It is always inspiring, and those moments make me realize there are so many things I could do."

Her advice for others who have a similar drive toward spending their lives expressing themselves creatively is straightforward: "Everyone's way is so different, but you must never cease to believe in your work. I could spend years in a bubble reading—I have the ability to easily tune out everything and focus on visionary pursuits. I love books, especially art books, and everything related to furniture and fashion during the 1930s and 1940s—these decades were really fabulous!" She sees these examples of immersion as excellent tools to help young artists and artisans learn about what draws them in and what will be satisfying enough to keep them engaged.

Her vigilance has paid big dividends, as she has been represented by Valerie Goodman Gallery in New York since 2013 and is one of the artisans whose works are sold through the Invisible Collection, an online platform with a motto that is very apropos for her work: "Design is Art."

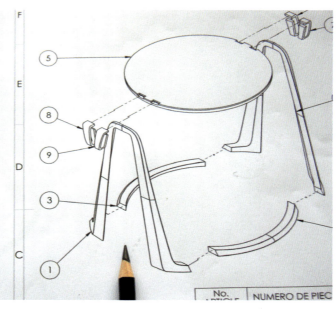

The far shore is beckoning—smudged blots of filigree from a distance grow more concrete with every stroke of the oar. Soon, jagged scallops become shallows below and a canopy of trees above the horizon line. This moody tone in the guest bedroom suite was set by painter Nanci Yermakoff, whose dusky mural produced from an original painting depicts a sunset over Lake Kabekona. The abstracted scene of the body of water at the edge of which her studio stands is a point of fascination in this room. The elaborate straightforwardness of the scene is mysterious and compelling.

The composition fosters a more spirited experience than could have been due to the way the room is situated. While guests enjoy the natural beauty it evokes from any spot in the room except in bed, someone lounging on the pool deck soaks it in from there. This is important because booth "spaces" are tucked into the opposite side of the building from where the dramatic twilights take place over the city. Having the wallcovering behind the bed means a permanent interpretation of a sunset can be enjoyed from both. The mural was manufactured by Area Environments, a conscientious company we feature in a full profile, along with a look at this artist's techniques, after we tour this space.

As the room came together, the mural significantly influenced the color palette here. The wall treatment disappears beneath a sophisticated shelving unit that serves as a vanity. On the opposite side of the built-in is a thin sliver of ribbed glass by Nathan Allan Glass Studios that effervesces at night as illumination from the night-light washes it and during the day when touched by natural light from the adjacent windows. The ricocheting veins on the marble wainscoting behind the bed introduce a dynamic element; the tension created by its gray, rouge, and rusty orange pillowed clouds is exquisite.

The movement is echoed in a reclaimed tin panel we placed on the ceiling to act as a textural plane and knock down the volume of the room. The darker wood tones in the floor and cabinetry, along with a long leather bench at the foot of the bed, draw out the moments of natural decay on the textured pieces of reclaimed tin panels that we found in New England.

The rhythm of the Foresso planks extend from the main living spaces into this room beneath the sculptural egg lamp to act as a textural border along the windowed wall. Beneath the bed is a rug that contrasts the terrazzo floor and cements the color/texture story in such a lovely way. Designed by Stéphane Parmentier, it was produced by La Manufacture Cogolin, whose profile we also feature in this chapter. This room is a dynamic study in color, though one that maintains a subtle, classic feeling of elegance.

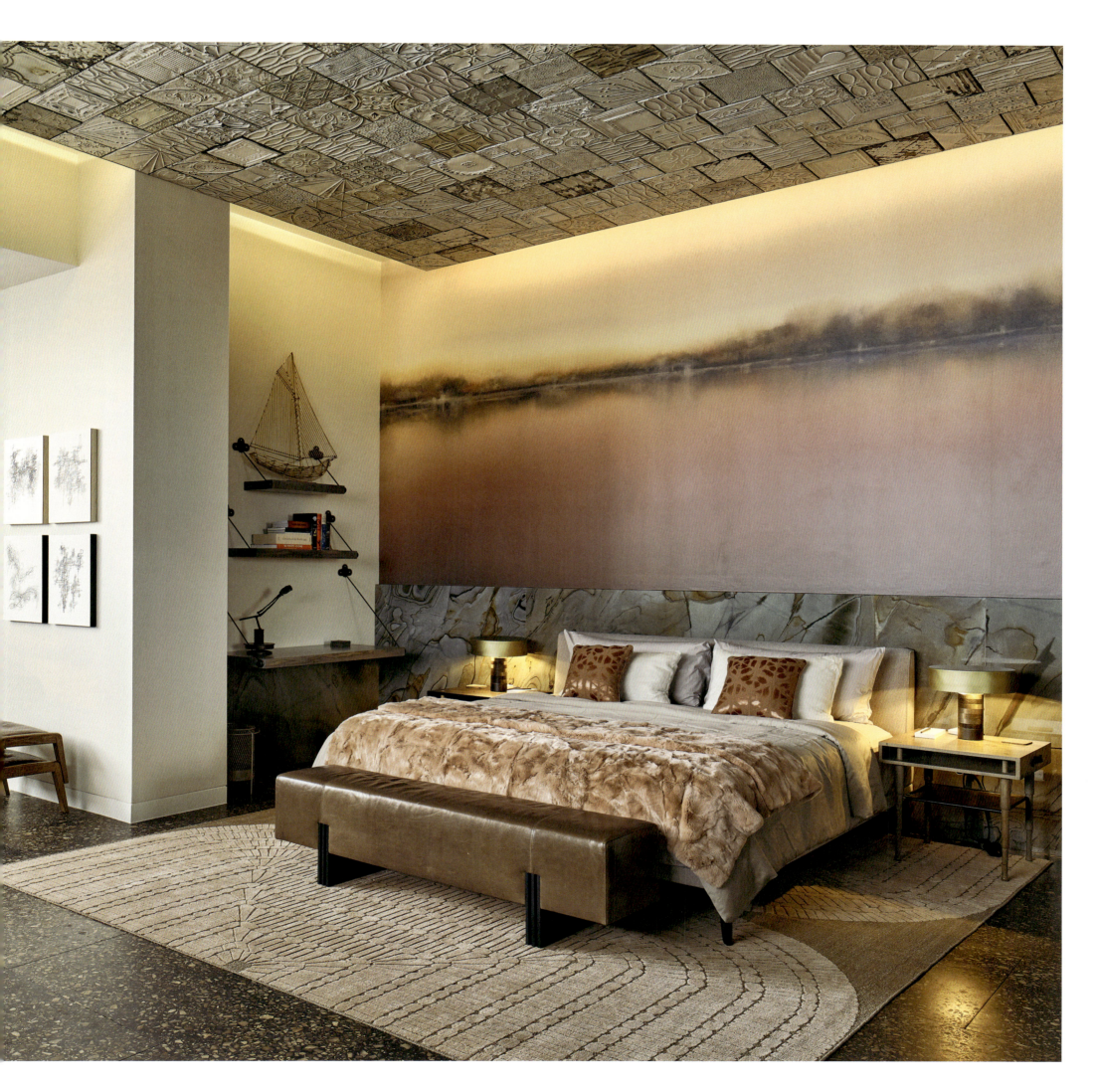

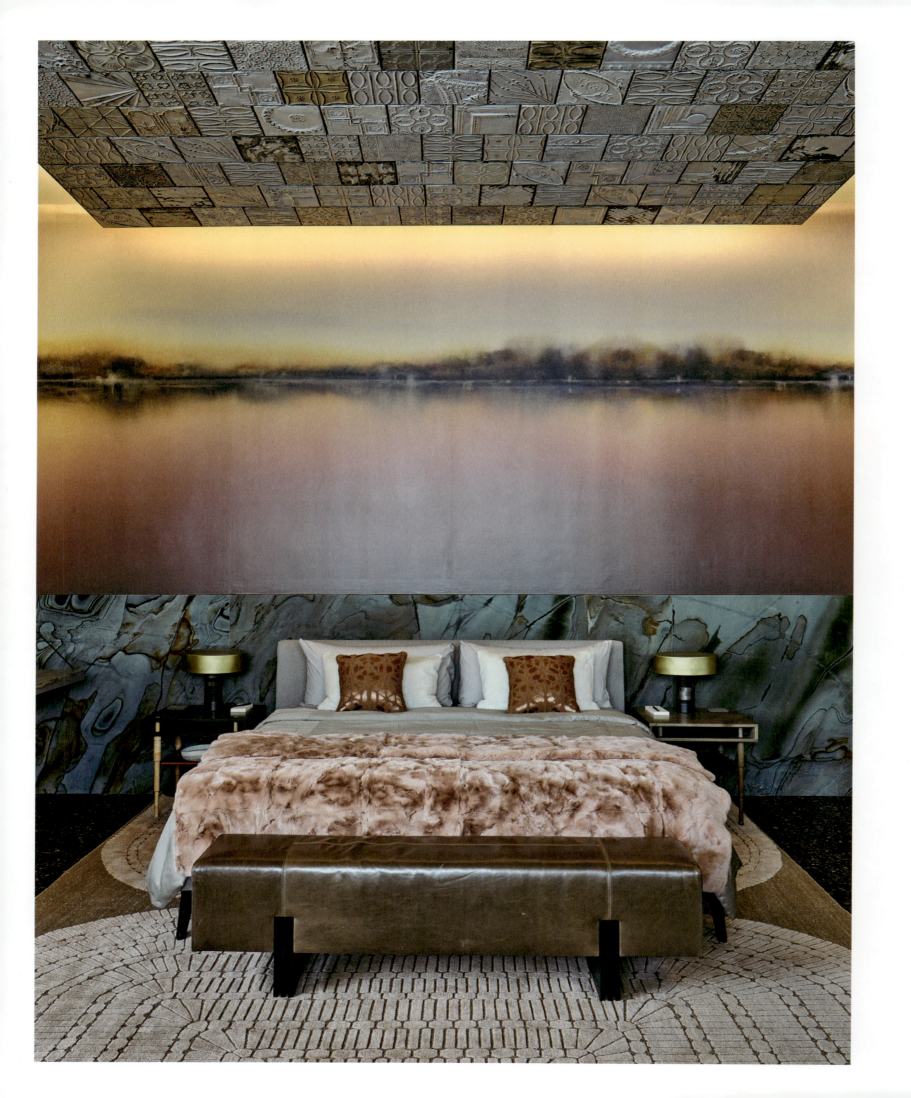

The generous size of the space—it was originally the primary suite in the real estate plan—brought us some significant challenges. The enormity of the volume and the intense light from the floor-to-ceiling windows were hurdles, as was the fact that the lower windows are blocked by the structure of the pool, which is raised about four feet above floor level on the terrace. This created an awkward exterior partition blocking the lower windows, which made it impossible to see out when lying in bed. To erase this design flaw, we installed a horizontal panel of millwork made of the same wood as the vanity surround. The move also gave us a place by the windows to include a seating area that anchors that section of the room and makes the space feel less intimidating.

The client loved the two bedside tables we bought during a BDDW live auction, which were prototypes by Hays that he decided not to manufacture. Along with the comfortable area for sleeping that these flank, the guest suite includes a bath and a desk lounge, which is a calm addition to the room perfect for reading and relaxing. The banquette adjoining the desk in this area creates cohesion in the space. The panels into which it is built are at the same height and made from the same walnut as the partial wall we created for the seating area opposite the bed. The two join to create a datum line that ties the large alcove to the main volume. Above the desk and

banquette hangs a David Weeks wall lamp that illuminates both; and Anasthasia Millot's bronze occasional table with an orange leather top sits beside the chaise lounge.

When the desk drawers are pulled open, brass paper clips, pens, and other office supplies have niches to keep everything orderly. The elegant desk chair, by Studio Sebastian Herkner, has a lightness to its profile that adds to the alcove's glamor. Suspended above it and the desk is a remarkable work of art by Cybèle Young, whose profile is featured in the public elevator entrance. Titled *To Understand Better*, she describes the philosophy behind her mixed-media piece in her written portrait.

Another artist featured in the desk lounge is John Hovig, whose quartet of single-line drawings graces one wall. You'll read about his work in greater detail as we present the full profiles shortly. Herkner also contributed tiles in the guest suite bathroom. We enjoy working with this talented product designer whose creations are so far-reaching. The fact that he works with a large number of companies to produce a mind-boggling array of products, we see him as a true master of product design. The breadth of his work reminds us of the trailblazers during the 1950s when everyone was designing incredible midcentury modern pieces, the variety of products they produced only limited by their boundless imaginations.

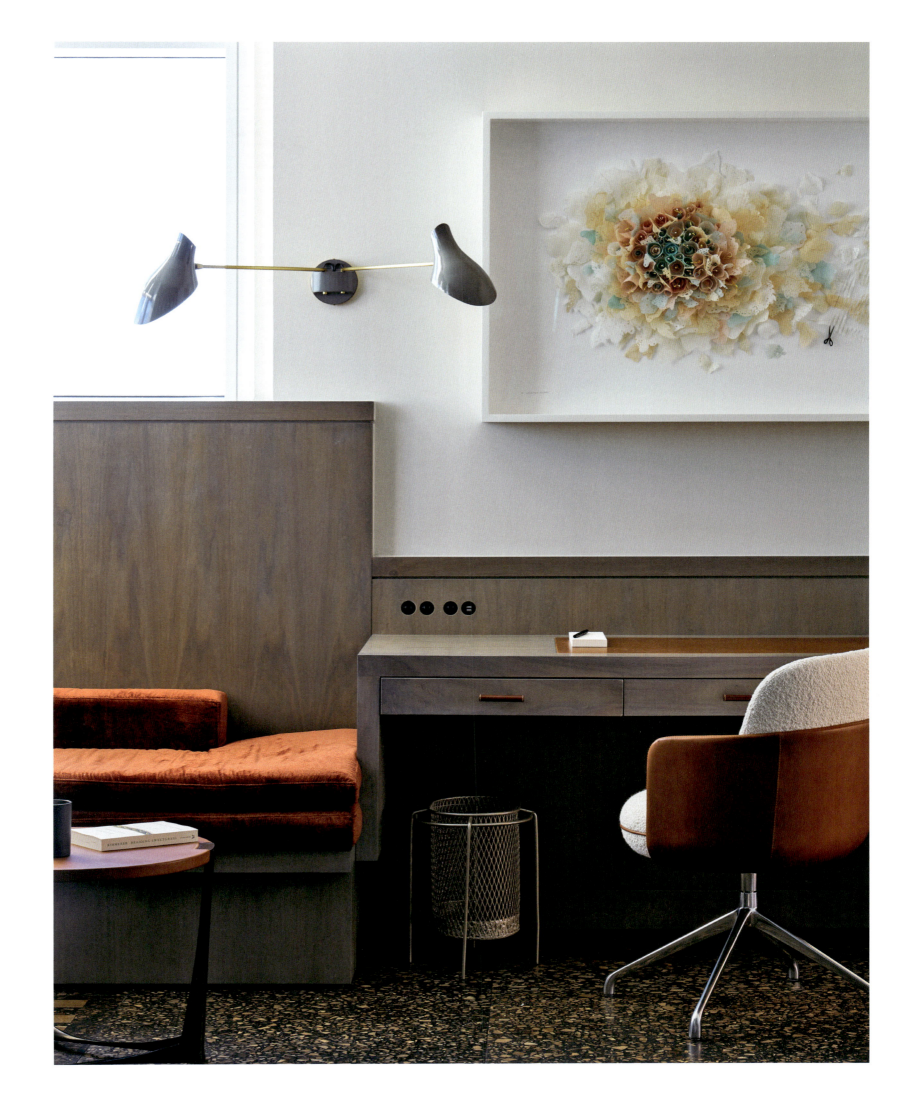

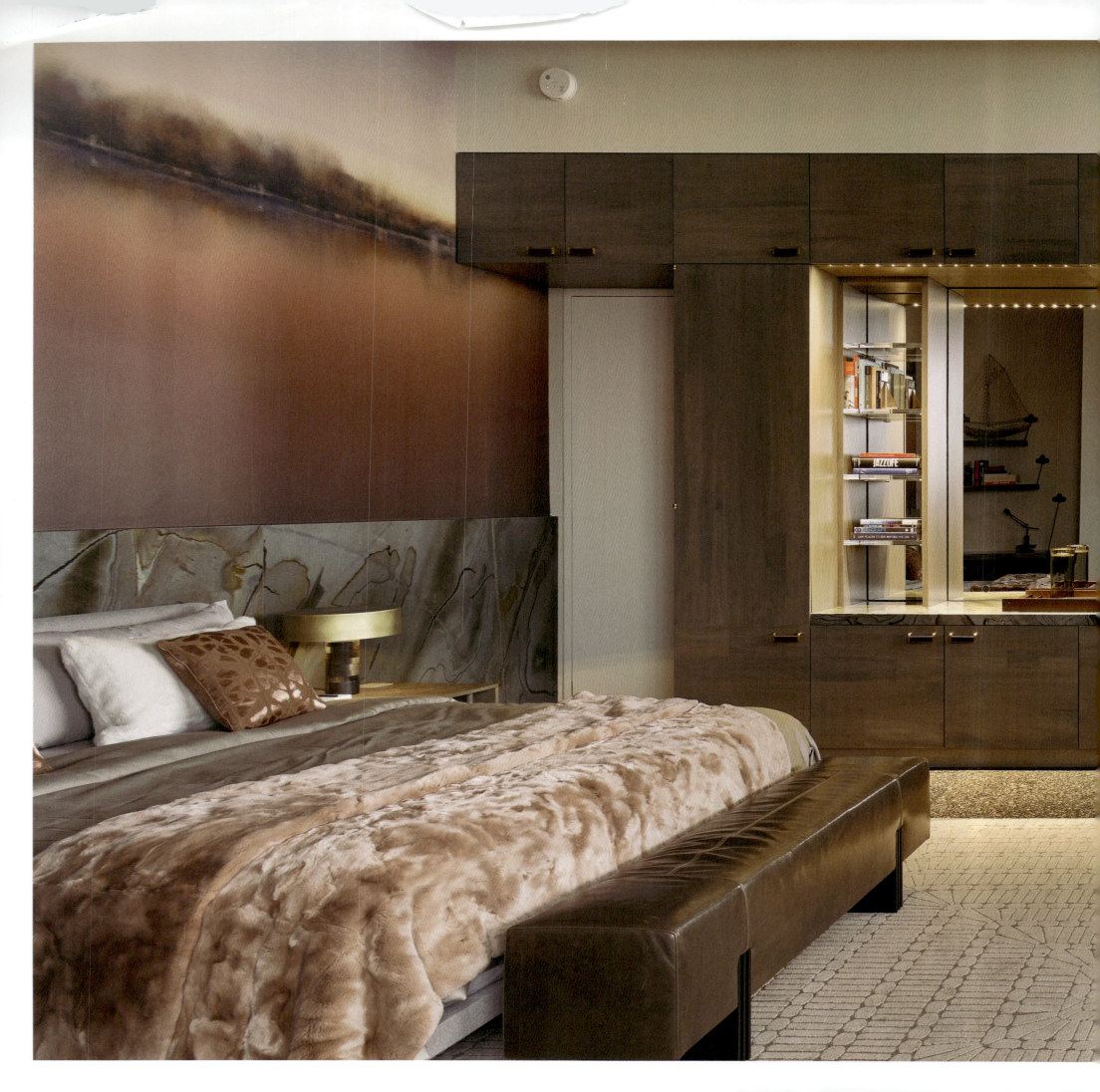

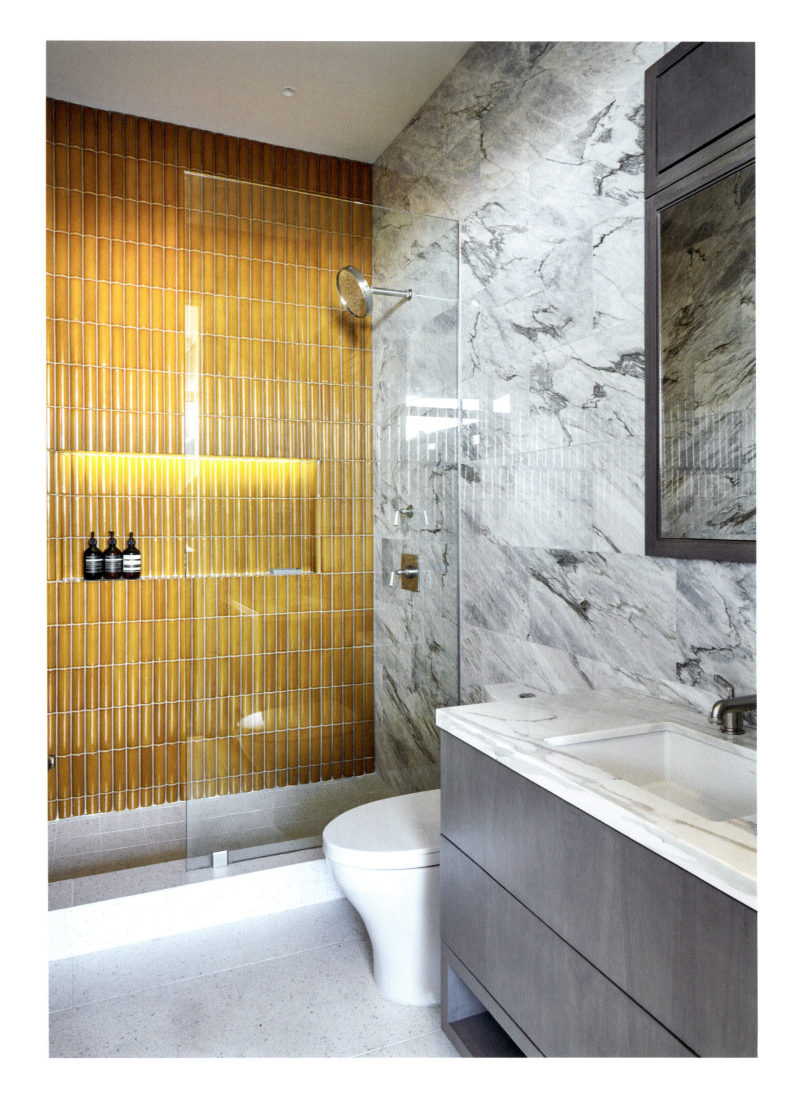

The daily movement of the sun from sunrise to sunset—when captured over a large expanse of water, the surface takes on the plum personality of one and the peachy persona of the other. Created in abstract as the eye moves from the water toward the shoreline, the psyche has to ask, "Does this smearing represent the demarcation where solid and liquid meet?" Then perception discerns the subtle shapes of trees as the canopies rising from the flat lakeside froth in the air. It's winter and the absence of leaves heightens the feel that what is seen isn't of this world but of a dimension not known to human experience.

The universe described, which unfolds above the bed in the primary bedroom suite, began as a painting, one of many of Lake Kabekona by Nanci Yermakoff. As she has rendered the moody settings over a number of years, they have grown less specific. Her studio overlooks the lake so it has become a definitive muse. "Early paintings were more representational, depicting a particular time of day, weather condition, or season," she explains. "Over the years my work has become more abstract. It still retains the horizon line and a sense of the landscape/seascape, but in a looser, more evocative way."

The Minnesota artist derives her inspiration from her love of open spaces, particularly when a body of water is part of the scene. "I am definitely a water person: I love to be near it, in it, on it, or painting it," she notes. "My original painting, the first in this series, was of a night sky over the lake where we have a cabin." Fast forward to the luminous lakescape that brings depth and warmth to the primary suite and the evolution of her work in watercolor is powerful. But the large-scale mural wouldn't have been possible had Yermakoff not trusted Area Environments to translate her painting into a wallcovering.

"I love what Area Environments has done with the artwork," she explains. "It has been fun to see my work at a scale I could never have imagined and in such a beautiful space. The bedroom photo is stunning and I'm pleased my piece was chosen to be part of the project." Not only did we choose it because it was a perfect element for the space, we source from Area Environments because we deeply respect their business model of supporting their artists by generating income for creators all over the world.

Diane Perry, who is the president of the creative studio that curates original work from contemporary artists to produce exclusive wallpapers and large-scale murals, is just as psyched about the point of view of the artisanal manufacturer: "I have obtained bliss!" she exclaims. "I am so lucky to be able to work for a really cool company that values art and the creative process." Area Environments was born in 2012 out of a shared adoration its founders have for fine art. The company's approach to creating wallcoverings continues to be fueled by this passion, alongside an obsession with quality, and a desire to challenge the links between art and the environment.

The company sees the artists whose works they transform into interior design elements as partners with wide-ranging artistic voices, stories, and talents. This philosophy has allowed the brand to build consistently compelling collections. Their formula for success is three-fold: a pride in the individuality of each artist they represent; a dedication to maintaining the integrity of their original pieces; and a commitment to compensating each of them with a portion of each sale.

Perry, who is a dynamic influence in gaining the trust of artists, has an impressively multidimensional background of her own. She was a talented photographer and graphic designer who initially studied fashion design. She would go on to found her own photography business while simultaneously working in retail management for two decades. Then she came on board at Area Environments as a graphic design intern, which blossomed into a bold and wonderful career as operations manager, and then as president of the firm beginning in May 2018. It was Perry who spotted Yermakoff's art and knew it would translate into dynamic murals.

"I really fell in love with her work," she explains. "I first came across her paintings at an art show that is a huge, crazy spring event in Minneapolis called Art-A-Whirl. It's the largest open studio tour in Minnesota. I was blown away with how smooth her gradients were and knew these were trending in interiors so I chose her very abstract landscapes." All the products the company produces are custom-printed to the size of the walls they will cover. Perry respects the process that results in artists being signed because it is collaborative and democratic. "Anyone can bring art to the table, which we vote on. If chosen, I reach out to the artists and have a discussion with them," she remarks. "Not all of them are interested but when they are, it feels very much like a partnership." The relationship Area Environments has cemented with Yermakoff is an example.

As for the advice Perry would give to young artists who dream of relationships on par with the support Area Environments provides? "Get off of social media for a while," she proclaims. "It is good to be inspired by others but it is more important to fine-tune your own voice, develop your own process, create the work no-one else is creating. Maintain really good habits for yourself; don't copy anyone else's work; and be kind. You will never regret doing any of those things." Perry offers this advice for anyone wanting to achieve the level of success she has in her career: "Always be ready and work harder than everyone else because eventually the right people will notice. And if they don't, you are working for the wrong company. Can't find that company? Build it yourself. I know this is easier said than done …"

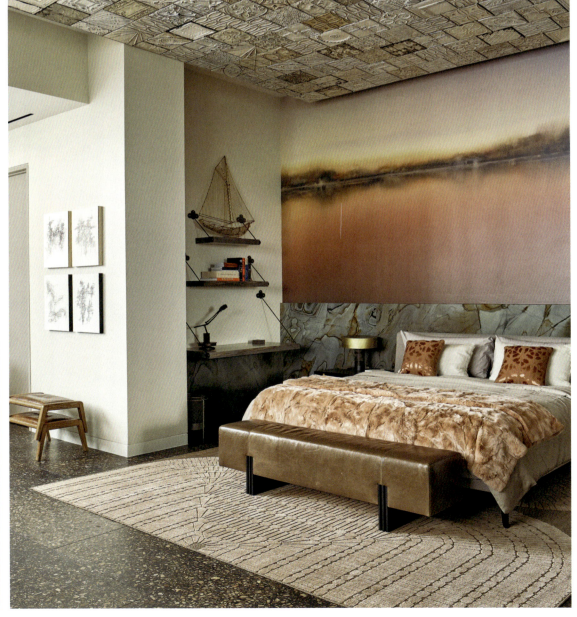

Two toddlers play beneath dining room tables—one in Belgium and one in France. Subtle pings from silver tines caressing the ornamented surfaces of porcelain anoint the air, and gay voices fill the rooms as sumptuous dinners continue well into the evening. These children navigate the maps made by the luxurious carpets underpinning their happy worlds, taking in the patterns, the textures, and the colors. Neither of these boys realize their creativity will intersect once they have become the highly actualized beings they are now, the convergence of their shared devotion to quality and beauty realized within this Houston penthouse.

Our own Eric Clough of 212box would linger beneath that Belgian table as a boy; and Stéphane Parmentier, who designed the carpet made by La Manufacture Cogolin in the guest suite, explored the patterns in the rug in his parents' home in the south of France. Parmentier remembers the backdrops for those evenings spent atop that carpet, which was also manufactured by Cogolin, as similar to films from the late 1960s and early 1970s. "I am originally from Nice and my parents had so many friends who owned rugs from La Manufacture Cogolin," he explains. "For me, Cogolin is intrinsically linked to the image of the south of France of my childhood, reminiscent of a movie set like *Les Biches* by Claude Chabrol."

During Parmentier's early discussions with Sarah Henry, the managing director of Cogolin, he recounted how it felt to be that little boy. "In France, a dinner lasts for hours and hours, so Stéphane's memories included playing with his toys and cars on the carpet," she explains. "The high pile with a low ground imitated traversing over hills and through valleys." It was these recollections of the handloomed carpets of his youth that compelled Parmentier to work with Henry on a line of rugs for Cogolin. "Something was imprinted in him that stayed with him," she says; "it's a very personal collection for him."

When they initially explored his ideas—a system of rugs woven with motifs inspired by paving stones in France—they presented Henry with a challenge. "Stéphane really wanted to do a collection to be produced at the Cogolin workshop, but these designs were not constructed based on a pattern repeat that can be woven on a jacquard loom," she explains. "There are too many curves, so it was technically impossible to produce these designs on our looms in France. I really liked what he had designed and how the rugs could work together, so I proposed to keep the designs, but produce the collection in Nepal with our partner workshop that we use today for hand-knotted rug production."

From this idea, the Nord/Sud Collection was born. "We created the rugs using a hand-knotted technique very much in the spirit of Cogolin with a higher pile for the pattern over a lower woven ground, and in the mixing of materials like linen, silk, and wool with nettle, a more rustic material," she remarks. "Cogolin is known for being sophisticated and elegant but not fussy, and you really get that with these rugs."

Authenticity on so many levels is a hallmark of this line of carpets and of this brand. "Making goods in France means there is much more transparency around how things are realized, so people feel more connected to the pieces they receive," Henry explains. "We're making the rugs in our workshops using the same techniques that were used a hundred years ago. Our electric bill is ridiculously low because everything is created with human power. All the looms are handlooms and the panels are hand-sewn together. The whole point of it is to continue the tradition."

All the carpets in the Nord/Sud Collection were inspired by pavers that edge the country's streets and cover its squares. The carpet we chose for the guest suite is called Albon, designed to resemble paving stones found in its namesake city in southeastern France. "Depending on the color of each particular rug, you are transported either to a picturesque Provençal square or to a busy Parisian Street," Parmentier notes. "In fact, the rugs were named after cities along the Nationale 7 road in France, also called the Holiday Route, that runs between the south of France and Paris."

Henry adds that the collection, under the "Cogolin et les Mains du monde" (Cogolin and the Hands of the World) line, reconnects the manufacturer to its original techniques, as the brand's origins were in making hand-knotted rugs. "Stéphane's experience in the fashion industry has given him an innate sense of materials and colors, as well as the ability to think directly to the construction of a cohesive collection, which was a great asset," she explains. His seventeen-year fashion experience included stints at Lanvin, Karl Lagerfeld, Hervé Léger, and Givenchy—as director of women's ready-to-wear and licenses—and as artistic director of Claude Montana.

Parmentier would go on to launch his own label, the creations distributed in high-end stores like Maria Luisa in Paris, Saks Fifth Avenue in New York, and Isetan in Japan. When he was awarded the contract to revamp the first- and business-class cabins of Singapore Airlines' planes in early 2000, he decided to expand into interior architecture and design, opening his own agency in 2003. Since then, he has created sophisticated interiors for private residences in Paris, London, Ibiza, Geneva, and Miami, on Mauritius, and along the French Riviera. He has also designed numerous collections of products.

In January 2012, Christofle entrusted Parmentier with the redesign of its new Madison Avenue flagship store, an initiative that carried over to stores in other cities, including London, Singapore, Shanghai, Milan, Miami, Lyon, Los Angeles, and Tokyo. From April 2013 to April 2016, Parmentier was the creative director for this celebrated French silversmith, a role that allowed him to guide the maison to hone its identity and to develop new collections, notably in the jewelry category and in a new lifestyle line. In 2017, he realized his desire to design for Cogolin after this impressive breadth of experience.

Like Parmentier, Cogolin was born in the south of France. The manufacturer was founded in 1924 in a tiny French village a stone's throw from Saint-Tropez. When textile engineer Jean Lauer purchased the atelier in 1928, he began transforming his new acquisition from a factory specializing in silkworm culture and hand-knotted rugs into an atelier for innovation. He installed nineteenth-century jacquard handlooms, and imported a host of new techniques for knotting and weaving.

These advances allowed the company to produce a wider variety of rugs and led to Cogolin's increasingly widespread recognition throughout the 1930s as a leading creator of bespoke products. Cogolin creations would soon be found gracing some of the world's most prestigious interiors, from Versailles and the Élysée Palace to luxurious French ocean liners. This acclaim led to collaborations with celebrated artists and decorators across Europe, which included Christian Bérard, Jean Cocteau, Jean-Michel Frank, Jules Leleu, and Sir David Hicks.

As the decade of its centenary approached, La Manufacture Cogolin experienced a rebirth in 2010 when it joined House of Tai Ping, a group of several of the world's leading carpet brands bound together by a shared philosophy, an artisanal expertise, and a commitment to excellence. With the support of this new partnership, Cogolin has been restructured, the looms have been revamped, the buildings have been renovated, the color palette has been reworked, and new materials have been introduced, enabling the workshop to create brand new collections with a more contemporary signature. Simultaneously, Cogolin's time-honored technique of hand-knotting continues to live on in the "Cogolin et les Mains du monde" line that includes the Albon pattern in this Houston penthouse.

Henry says she is proud of the fact that they continue to perpetuate tradition and to bring value to French craftsmanship. "When you are making the product that you sell, you have a very different relationship to it than when your production is outsourced: you look at it differently and you look at the people who are making it differently," she explains. "They're not robots, and the psychology of what's important to people is different when they are makers. It's been an enriching experience for me to manage producers. Everything is much more real and you have complete control over what you're making—the good and bad of that. It's squarely on your shoulders and it's very gratifying."

The skills required to create luxury carpets at the level Cogolin demands are the product of an intricate training process that takes place on the job. "It's cool to see people progress and gain new confidence," Henry explains. "Everyone who comes in has to be trained on-site because no one knows how to do this until they're taught by experienced makers. We're between twenty and twenty-five people, so Cogolin has a family-business feel."

We can vouch for the quality that this manufacturer achieves because we have specified their rugs numerous times—each of these in Albon patterns in the Nord/Sud Collection in varying colors. We have chosen several colorways for different projects, and we're amazed at how the feel of a room changes with the simple variation of tones. It was a significant moment for us when we found this collection while attending an event at the Cogolin showroom when we were in Paris for Maison et Objet because Stéphane's carpets are now solidly among our favorites.

John Hovig
Single-Line Drawings

One line manifesting itself as it leads the artist's pen along the page in wayward movements that clump, whisper, or texturize depending upon the mood of the person wielding the instrument. "I believe that drawing is like writing, and vice versa: primitive acts of mark-making that can nonetheless construct complex, meaningful structures," remarks artist John Hovig. "I think of my single-line drawings as large works of extended calligraphy."

We were thrilled to find the intricate art by this Houstonian because we were keen to include local artists in the penthouse. When we searched through galleries in the city, his pieces stood out because they draw the brain in and keep it fascinated until it is lost on the page. Each time Eric sees them when he visits the penthouse still, he finds himself following along and contemplating each continuous stroke. One of the remarkable aspects of Hovig's work is he doesn't lift the pen from the page until a composition is finished, which is why he calls this collection "Single-Line Drawings."

Because of the sophisticated patterns this method creates, we knew the four works we chose would bring depth to the room. "The result of my careful line-making reads like embroidery on the page," he says of the pieces. "They are my visualization of the conflict between the structured thinking of the mechanical age, and the human struggle to live in a world overpowered by technology."

This is a soulful aspect to his story, as he is one of a group of humans closest to the turbines that turn tech's engine given the field he chose to explore during his career. "I stepped away from my role as a software chief technology officer when my daughters were born, about fifteen years ago," he explains. "I wanted to do this to concentrate on the possibility of communication through imagery."

Though he still uses computers in his practice, this is mainly for planning and for creating software-based artworks, including unique pieces resulting from programs he writes himself. This talent combined with his artistic aptitude are strengths in the visual productions he achieves, but it is his desire to introduce a bit of mystery into his oeuvre that sets him apart. "I prefer stories that leave facts unsaid, reasons vague," he says. "I want viewers to bring their own meanings into my work, and to reflect on the nature of human interactions in the age of ubiquitous machines."

When we asked Hovig whether he had always known he wanted to be an artist, he answered, "I have been a tinkerer for as long as I can remember. This led me into internet development during the 1980s and 1990s. Exposure to fine art in the 1990s awakened in me the understanding that one could 'tinker' in many dimensions, and create understanding in ways that were not necessarily concrete. My practice is inspired by the idea that communication can exist between the lines."

His advice for others hoping to flesh out a creative career like his: "Don't rush, don't cut corners. Make sure everything you create is something you would be proud of, even if it were featured publicly one hundred or one thousand years from now." Knowing the intuitiveness that compelled Hovig to realize these compositions with their hypnotic pull makes us all the happier that we chose his work to include in this project.

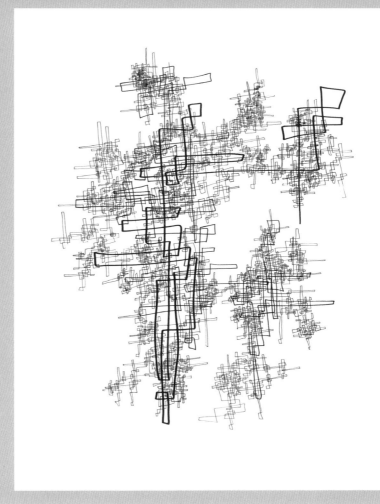

Primary Bedroom Suite

The long primary bedroom suite curves gently toward the end of the penthouse, the narrowing reminiscent of the prow of a boat. The luminous room holds a lounge at the narrow end and a sleeping area at its widest point. Because the long, tall wall behind both areas is so voluminous, we clad it in sections of warm faux leather panels dripping with random cascades of stars in relief, separating them with tall vertical elements made of a tight-grained wenge. Both of these warmly toned elements absorb the intense illumination from the floor-to-ceiling windows when the curtains are open. The smart panels were created by British artisan Helen Amy Murray, whose full profile is featured after we finish the tour of this space.

We chose a mix of pale lavenders and handsome browns for the room to create a feeling of whispery calm, and chose only subtle patterns so that nothing is jarring. The suite is an artisanal wonderland that includes curtains made of intricately cut pieces of wood attached to fabric, which transforms the stiff material into a remarkably fluid textile. When the sun is up, nuanced shadows are cast on surrounding surfaces.

Elisa Strozyk, whose full profile also follows this tour of the primary bedroom suite, created these delicate drapes that read like lace. Placed in front of these are two wood sculptures carved by French artist Thierry Martenon, who is also featured.

Delicate porcelain roses by Maria Moyer, whose profile follows, were purchased as a surprise for the client who was drawn to the delicate floral elements when we walked through BDDW. We knew we would put them in a special place so we purchased five of them—three single roses and two clusters. We found a place for them when we wrapped a column on the window-wall in wenge that left a sliver of a painted surface remaining. We placed the exquisitely delicate flowers on the light-toned wall and lit them so they glow in tone-on-tone shadowy relief. This creates the illusion that they are sprouting from the surface and serves as an example of how much restraint is required to hit upon the idea of placing five tiny flowers on a tall wall. The vignette is one of many moments of fine finessing achieved as a result of great struggle with enormous effect.

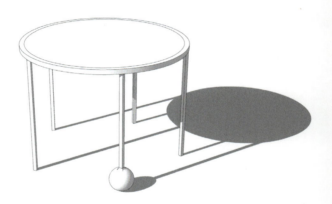

Curving gracefully beneath the wall ornamented with Moyer's roses is the Mobu Bench by Sean O'Hara of O'Hara Studio, whom we feature in this chapter. Its name is short for Mobulidae, which is a species of fish with wide flowing wings like manta rays and devilfishes. The profile on O'Hara Studio follows in this chapter of the book. Though flowers and stingrays in this corner of the room reflect the marvels of nature, both elements are seriously sophisticated in their execution thanks to the talented artists who envisioned and realized them. Across the room is a BDDW hutch in a bleached wood, which satisfied the need for a light, tall, and airy element on that wall. The lounge area is flanked by two remarkable sconces by Markus Haase that we found at Todd Merrill Studio, a dynamic boutique filled with an eclectic and crazy world of light and furniture.

Haase's story, which includes the inspiration for the pale fixtures, follows this presentation. To contrast the lavender faux leather paneling, and the wenge cladding the walls and columns in places, other pastel elements include pale marble

furniture and accessories, soft pink upholstery fabrics, and equally light-toned rugs. The oblong cocktail table we designed and built for the lounge is made from slabs of red, gray, and white marble. On it are arranged three candlestick holders by Anna Torfs, one of which looks like an upside-down wine glass.

This creates a playful detail that glows given there is so much natural light in the space even when the flickering flames from candles are absent. All of Torfs's blown glassware is exquisite. A dark contrast in this corner of the bedroom is an edgy occasional table by J.M. Szymanski, whose surprise at seeing how incredible it looks in such an elegant setting is explained in his profile to follow. Though there are so many other elements in this space that contribute to the overall feeling of serenity and sophistication, we have illustrated the most artful elements produced by some of the most insightful designers and artists with whom we've had the good fortune of collaborating.

Helen Amy Murray

Hand-Sculpted Wall Panels

Stars cascade along faux leather panels to create a smattering of shapes as fluid as the Milky Way. The motifs are balanced in the same random way that nature is a master at achieving—the dripping blossom of the wisteria; a flock of sparrows migrating; a shower of stars in an inky sky. But these winsome ornamentations superimposed on the supple material were created by human beings—first, envisioned by Helen Amy Murray; then, brought to life by the talented craftspeople she employs in her atelier. The globally recognized artist and designer has become well known for enlivening the surfaces of silk, leather, and high-tech materials, creating depth and movement where there was none before.

Since Murray graduated from Chelsea College of Art and Design in 2002, she has been astonishing and delighting the luxury design sector with her unique, hand-sculpted surfaces in relief. In 2003, she founded her atelier, which has grown from a one-woman business into an influential studio. Her commissions have included bespoke, handcrafted pieces for jets, superyachts, flagship stores, hospitality environments, and private residences such as this Houston penthouse.

"The artwork for the Houston primary bedroom suite was a really exciting development," Murray says. "I first created my three-dimensional star design around seventeen years ago and have played over time with different iterations of the motif, experimenting with scale and pattern coverage, but this was the first departure from a uniform shape." The fact that the design is both random and ordered, with the star shapes appearing to be scattered, was intentional. "In the design phase, they are created to be geometric—meaning that the alignment of all motifs is exact," Murray explains. "Then perfection takes on a new meaning through hand craftsmanship. The new distorted motifs allow subtle variations in the relief and pattern to create a complex and unique artwork for the client."

We knew about Murray's work for quite some time but we had to climb to her caliber client-wise to be able to spec her products. We knew the two large walls in this penthouse would be the perfect canvas for her; that her panels would bring a subtle design note that would pack a huge wallop. Her abiding passion for working in surface relief took root during a research trip to India in 2001 when she was captivated by carvings she discovered in wood, marble, and precious stones.

She was compelled from that point on to achieve a similar aesthetic in fabric and has since been involved in a progressive journey of creating intriguing sculptural surfaces in unexpected materials. The evolution of her process that results in her embroidered designs has brought about a wide array of pieces with varied scale and depth. The drifts and dimensions that bring a sense of movement to the reliefs create dramatic and striking surfaces. Given her passion for envisioning exemplary forms, we knew that Murray would be masterful at designing a beautiful adornment for the walls in the primary bedroom suite.

To begin the process, we visited her London atelier so we could understand the full breadth of her work and her talent firsthand. "Eric Clough contacted us out of the blue," Murray explains. "We invited him and Eun to my workshop and studio in Shoreditch to show them where my artwork is handcrafted. Eric seemed to know more about the area than myself and my team, and we have been based in this particular studio for over a decade!" We knew the area so well because we had been visiting the neighborhood for the past twenty years. It has been growing in popularity for some time, and her studio is at this incredible intersection, a roundabout with a tiered park in the middle of it.

It just so happens that this was one of our sets for a film we've been writing. It was wonderful to think about our characters coming to life just outside those doors as we met with her. We actually talked about collaborating with her on a substantial exhibition, but this has yet to come to pass so we were thrilled to be able to bring her work to the penthouse project. "Working with Eric and Eun was great," Murray says of our collaboration. "We were allowed to interpret the artwork freely from the concept stage. We worked closely together to develop a completely custom color for the artworks, the palette driven by the design team at 212box."

About the outcome of this effort, Murray says, "I was delighted when I saw the final photos. The scheme is sophisticated and tactile, and the light-flooded apartment provides a magnificent variety for the subtlety and drama of the sculpture." Over the years, Murray has gained international acclaim and has won prestigious awards that include the Oxo Peugeot Design Award in 2003, the Balvenie Masters of Craft Award in 2013, and a nomination for the Walpole British Luxury Award in 2014. She was subsequently awarded a place in Walpole's Brands of Tomorrow mentoring program in 2017, and since then has been a member of this organization, which champions British luxury brands.

In an interview with Murray, Walpole asked the artist/designer: "When you started out, who was your biggest inspiration? And what did they tell you that helped make you a success?" Her unequivocal answer is what shines through in her works: "My biggest inspiration when I started was not an individual but an aesthetic. I was passionate about surface relief and absolutely driven to create similar sculptural aesthetics using textiles." In 2019, Murray's studio was awarded the coveted Butterfly Mark by Positive Luxury, given to brands that demonstrate a commitment to sustainability.

Site-specific works by Helen Amy Murray are featured in a number of the most prestigious hotels in the world, including The Peninsula in New York and Paris. In the Paris hotel, the paneling in all the guest rooms and suites evokes the architecture and design of the early twentieth century in that city. Her atelier has produced designs for a number of luxury brands. Her most recent collaboration and ongoing partnership is with Rolls-Royce Motor Cars. She is creating one-of-a-kind artworks for The Gallery, a dedicated art space in the new Phantom.

The creation, dubbed "Whispered Muse," was inspired by Charles Robinson Sykes' sculpture, *The Spirit of Ecstasy*, which is the automobile company's famous bonnet ornament on its cars. Alex Innes, a bespoke designer for Rolls-Royce, who worked with Murray on the project, calls her drawings and the works that spring from them "serene landscapes" from which forms begin to appear. "What emerges is," he adds, "the trailing arm of *The Spirit of Ecstasy*."

Murray says of the project, "As a textile designer, I identified straightaway with *The Spirit of Ecstasy*. I love the drapery wing-like effect of her arms and I love that I can connect my sculpted aesthetic with the form itself." She adds, "It feels like a huge privilege to think of my work being inside the flagship car for the leading luxury brand in the world." Alongside commissioned work, Murray creates personal artwork that uses flora and fauna as its inspiration. These pieces are made by her own hand and framed to museum standards, and have been purchased by collectors around the world.

To other artisans who want to create brands around their passions, she advises: "Be inspired and driven to create something unique and unexpected; be willing to work hard with dedication and determination; enter shows and awards in order to win funding and recognition; slowly and steadily create a valued team, as this is instrumental in keeping creativity at the heart of the business; know what your values are—commercial, mass-production is not for me; and continue to hone and refine your skills, and stay creative."

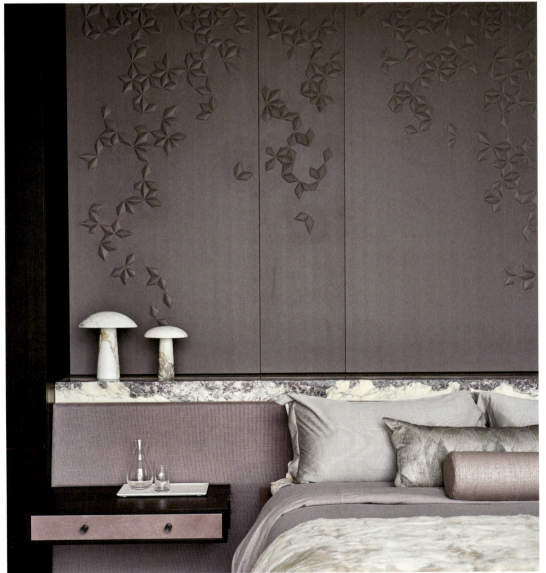

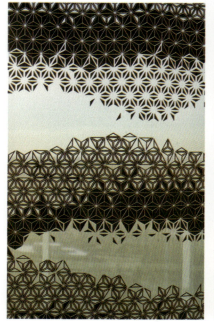
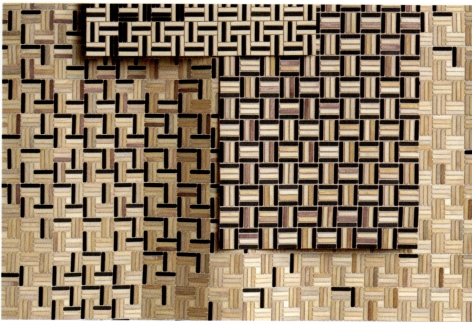

When wood dreams of being free, of being given the gift of fluidity, Elisa Strozyk is at the center of its fantasies. The Berlin-born artist studied textile and surface design at the Weißensee Kunsthochschule Berlin (KBB); the École Nationale Supérieure des Arts Décoratifs (ENSAD) in Paris; and the Central Saint Martins College of Art and Design in London, where she earned her master's degree in Future Textile Design. These years and the experiences she had during them paved the way for her ability to transform wood into the supple sensations her designs create.

We first saw her wood curtain in a publication produced by the Paris fashion boutique Maison Ullens in 2015. When we were in France in 2017, we made a specific trip to the store to see the curtains, but they had been taken down for a seasonal change. The store manager was nice enough to bring them up from the basement and we spoke about the delicate nature of the install. Over the years, we returned to the store to look at the curtains again and desperately wanted to work with Strozyk on a collaboration. After three years of lusting after her work and waiting for a perfect client, we finally found them in the owners of this penthouse.

Strozyk's dyed wooden textile in the hallway through which you enter the guest bedroom suite and the transparent curtains in the primary bedroom suite illustrate her ability to turn the rigidity of trees into lithe objects. About her wooden textiles, Strozyk says, "I invented this unique material in 2009 during my studies in London. It's a hybrid between wood and textile, using the traditional crafting technique of marquetry work with the goal of providing the material the possibility to move."

She achieves this transformation by using textiles as a base material. "The idea was to create a wooden material which mirrors the fact that wood has once been alive," she adds. "My process to design a flexible wooden surface is its deconstruction into small triangles, which are then attached by hand to a textile base." The two pieces she created for our project illustrate how complex her process is. The wooden curtains with transparent, open areas and organic, scattered patterns in the primary bedroom suite add shadow play to the room, the wafting tracings traversing the space with the movement of the sun. In the nearby hallway, it's the colorful wall piece, which she hand-dyed, that enlivens the space. As the triangles were carefully colored in, powdery-hued cloud-like shapes formed on the pattern-on-pattern and texture-on-texture composition.

"Our collaboration has been very trustful and straightforward," Strozyk says. "I felt that Eric and Eun truly understood the intention of my work and this is the best premise for a beautiful and harmonious overall picture." We couldn't agree more. After seeing her work in Maison Ullens, we happened upon her booth during Maison et Objet in 2019. "I was exhibiting my wooden textiles and Eric and Eun found my stand by accident," Strozyk notes. "They were quite excited, as they already planned to include my work in this project. After the fair we began working on the designs."

The process and the results are beyond exciting for us and we knew the pieces she would create, particularly the curtains, would add a layer of surprise to the penthouse. That's because we are all accustomed to experiencing wood as a hard material; seeing the fluidity she creates with her art is a delightful experience that defies what our bodies are hardwired to expect when the word "wood" is mentioned—the feeling of walking across solid floors, of touching a firm tabletop, or of running our hands across the rough surface of tree bark. To see the shadows from the curtains walk slowly across Helen Amy Murray's star pattern is a meditative journey on its own. One of our favorite places in the world is the space and light between Elisa's curtains and Helen's leather relief.

"Wooden textiles convey a new tactile experience," Strozyk says. "This is because we usually don't experience a wooden surface that can be manipulated by touch." She describes the results of her process as "an approach to responsible thinking concerning the lifecycles of products" because she is giving a material with a limited life span an infinite future when she constructs her designs. "The outcome is a material that is half wood/half textile, an interplay between hard and soft, which challenges what is expected from a material or category," she explains. "It looks and smells familiar but feels strange, as it is able to morph in its form in unexpected ways."

The transparent curtains in the primary bedroom suite personify this surreal sensation, and extend beyond mere window dressing: it's the very definition of functional art. Besides continual collaborations with other artists, designers, and companies beyond ours, Strozyk is always pushing the envelope in her own experimental designs. She has received the German Design Award from the German Design Council and the German Ministry of Economics. She participates in Salone del Mobile in Milan, Maison et Objet in Paris, and DesignMiami/ in Miami Beach, and her work is included in the collection at the Victoria & Albert Museum in London.

Strozyk also works in ceramic and glass, producing decorative tables and lighting. She has collaborated on fashion projects as well. Her interior design commissions include the curtains for Maison Ullens, which introduced us to her work; an apartment at the Ritz-Carlton in Almaty, Kazakhstan; and the Technogel Sleeping Experience Center in Berlin.

Thierry Martenon
Wood Sculptures

Thierry Martenon is lost in his art as the blade he holds creates a rhythmic song, the cadence matching the movement of his hands. As the tool chews away the wood to expose the negative space, the surface grows smoother and smoother. Each pass is resolute, yet poetic. "Sometimes the repetition of the same gesture for hours leads me to almost euphoric states that feel like little trances," the French sculptor says of the process. "The tool then becomes the extension of my hand, and I become the gesture." The piece of wood that will soon birth the sculpture is examined: from top to bottom, rotated side to side; Martenon's mind spinning and his creative spirit fully empowered. The beginning of the process, which he calls direct carving, requires tremendous energy and there is no room for mistakes because once an error occurs, there is no going back.

"Every tool-stroke will remain," he adds, "so every stroke is important." This could not be more evident than in the pair of sculptures Martenon created for the primary bedroom suite of this Houston residence. We came across his work during Maison et Objet in Paris but didn't meet him until we returned to the market a few years later. Before we were introduced to him, we knew we wanted to include his art in a project. Not only were we inspired by the sculptures themselves, his beautiful booth with perfect lighting spoke to us—it was mysterious and gorgeous and captured the same spirit we wanted to infuse the rooms of the penthouse. Once we met him and realized he was such a lovely guy, it was a bonus!

The complex surfaces he achieved for the sculptures in the Houston residence illustrate how he employs a textural tempo to create works of art. And yet, Martenon declares, "I don't recognize myself in the word 'artist.' I am a sculptor. My work is not underpinned by commitment or conceptual discourse. I do not seek to condemn or reconcile man and nature; my only commitment is to myself—it is not thought, but gesture that defines me." Though reconciling man and nature is not his aim, his days are spent steeped in the elemental—one man connected passionately to the natural world. As he walks along the hillsides of Entremont-le-Vieux, tall grasses flanking him, he explains, "I was born here; I grew up in these landscapes. I am descended from a lineage of farmers—mountain farmers."

He says his roots reach as deep as those of the trees from which he takes his material. Everyone in his village works with wood, and many of the people living in the valleys over which the Chartreuse Mountains loom have done so for generations. His grandfather was a sawyer. Winter evenings when Martenon was growing up were long—there was no television in his home so he spent the hours tinkering with wood, making little toys and wooden objects. Now that he is an adult, his works range from small to monumental. "I haven't invented anything," he says; "wood is simply my mother tongue." As he moves around his atelier, his range of tools comes into view—from the simplest chisel to the most complex machines.

Sketchbook in hand and the pencil rasping along the paper's surface, Martenon envisions the next piece he will create, his leather apron crackling as he draws. "I've always wanted to stay home and work the wood," he says. "I didn't go to art school but I completed a professional certificate of aptitude in cabinetry. I didn't decide to become a sculptor, but little by little, I turned away from utilitarian constraints—right angles, measurements, dimensions—and allowed myself a freer gesture." The first step in this process toward greater fluidity for Martenon was making unique pieces on the lathe; then he began cutting new shapes directly, which segued to creating abstract shapes eaten into and away from the mass. "Basically, my pleasure is in the act of sculpting, and in the handling of tools, the smells, the material, the workshop," Martenon says. "Some people talk about 'the intelligence of the hand,' and I like that."

Sawdust is his ever-present companion as he works. "In the village, the people didn't really understand what I was making," he says as he draws the outline of the piece he will fabricate. "'Why design something that has no use?' they asked me; 'Why make an object that has no function?' Here, this seems quite absurd." But this questioning is mere curiosity as opposed to rejection, and the people who have watched as he has moved more resolutely toward art respect his work whether they understand his motives or not. "As a child, the sculptures I knew were religious statues, limited to the holy virgins," Martenon says. "Here in the valley, art was seen as something bourgeois."

Just like the village and the chalky-hued limestone mountains that surround it, his atelier has historical relevance and great meaning in his life. The building in which he creates was his grandfather's old barn. Martenon restored and enlarged it. "It's a very important place," he explains. "When I go into the atelier, it's like going back to childhood. I'm in another space-time, in fact, far away from the hustle and bustle of the town." Flipping through his sketchbook, Martenon says that sometimes inspiration springs naturally—a mistake on a sheet of paper or a reflection in the window might bring a shape to mind that he can finesse. Other times, the process will be more complicated. "I may work for whole days cloistered in the atelier, blackening the pages of my sketchbooks," he explains. But even when revelations are elusive, he refuses to hurry and he never does anything by chance.

Everything around him has value, even the scraps of wood from past sculptures, which are precious to him. He stores them away in a section of his atelier to become possible points of inspiration down the road. The shapes of the sculptures in the Houston penthouse were inspired by the rising mountains surrounding his village. To Martenon, the surfaces call to mind a rock-climbing wall—the ascent aided by the pieces of wood that are splintered, remaining jagged in textural felicity. "It's so interesting to see the new life that new interiors bring to my sculptures," he says of the two works of art in wood.

Martenon works mainly with local species that proliferate in his region of France—ash, maple, and spruce among his favorites. "I choose woods that have grown slowly, which makes them very dense," he explains. "The tree is a living thing. It preserves the memory of everything that has happened to it in its rings. You can read in each the abuse it has suffered—injuries, infestations, atmospheric pollution, periods of drought, times of overly wet weather." He says each tree is different, which means he is involved in a new encounter every time he begins a new piece. And he is meticulous in his preparations for these artistic confrontations. "I choose the wood according to the piece to be executed," he explains. "I need dry wood, though wood is never completely dead—it never stops living and moving."

His focus is most intense early on as pieces are shaved away because once a sliver is removed, there is no way to put it back. "Some woods are four- or five-hundred years old—they are exceptional pieces, so it is intimidating," he adds. "I have to work quietly and slowly." Though he is steeped in a centuries-old tradition, there are aspects of his philosophy that run counter to custom: for most who choose wood as their medium, it is normal to work in the same direction as the grain, but he chooses to go against the grain in order to create texture. "It took me years to unlearn all the conventional rules," he explains. "The other fundamental factor is the direction of the cut, which makes it necessary to predict how the artwork will evolve because it is essential to anticipate the way it will twist and to intuit its curvatures."

Martenon is always questioning: "How far should I go; when should I stop?" His answer as a vividly creative human being is, "I don't know. It's complicated to be devoted to the essential." Taking his cues from fashion designers, Martenon presents two "collections" each year. Several notable commissions he has completed include the ceiling in the wine cellar of the Hôtel de Crillon on the Place de la Concorde and *Ours*, a sculpture of a bear that sits in the courtyard of France's National Museum of Natural History—both in Paris.

His works are included in the collections of the Museum of Fine Arts in Boston, the Yale University Art Gallery in New Haven, the Minneapolis Institute of Art, and The Center for Art in Wood in Philadelphia. It was during a residency in Philadelphia many years ago where the trajectory of his professional career began. The international renown he has gained since is illustrated by the cities around the world in which his art has been or is being shown: New York, Shanghai, New Delhi, Jeddah, Honolulu, Sydney, Geneva, Milan, London, and Moscow. He advises anyone who is looking to follow an artistic path: "Don't doubt yourself if you are passionate about a way of working. If you don't know what that is yet, go and search for it."

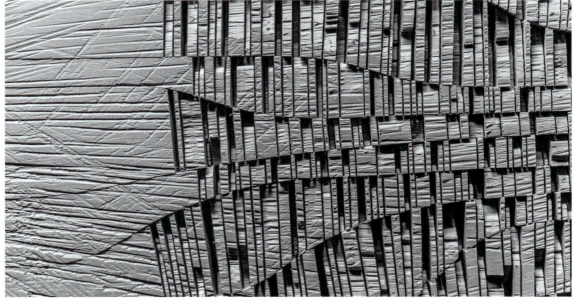

Tough-as-nails meets perfectly pretty in this tale of a brute material hammered into being as it rests in elegant surroundings that are as soft as it is hard. Seeing his Table No. 2 Round in the primary bedroom lounge was a revelation for Jake Szymanski. "Most of the time, our pieces are placed in edgy, hyper-masculine spaces," he explains, "so when I saw that photo of the lounge in the Houston penthouse, I was obsessed with the space because it was more feminine than masculine and our table cut the femininity somewhat when it was placed in it. My pieces have been out in the world and have been published many times, and it's not very often I see a space with one of them in it that pleasantly surprises me. That room was so exciting after being in the industry for fifteen years!"

The concept for this particular table was born during one of Szymanski's first forays into furniture making. "I started with very few resources," he explains. "I worked in the basement of the school of visual arts and made pieces on the side. Though I only had limited materials to work with, I had this cool cast-iron ball and attached the ball to a slim square frame that made the design very dynamic. Since then, it has evolved into different variations, this side table being the round version." Each of the pieces the popular maker realizes feels to him like an object with a story, tales that have vibrant life to them. "This piece has five legs, which is reminiscent of a little spider. I call the pieces I create little beasts or my minions. They do have an animal-like quality to them that gives them the feel they have their own lives."

The first iteration of the forged table was a console table. Szymanski has created coffee tables and myriad shapes since. "Clients have a way of pushing us to experiment," he notes. "They will see a piece and ask us if it can be done a certain way, which results in a new version of the design. With this table, we can play with the geometry of it because the ball can be placed anywhere within the design. We've created others that have flanked a sofa to bring the arrangement a bit of asymmetry. I love symmetry, but it's fun when you can create a slim symmetrical form and then put some asymmetry in the mix."

Many of his metal pieces have geometric twists or off-beat details that enhance their personalities. One leg will stop short of the floor, a pair of tassels dangle off-center, a tabletop rolls to a flourish, frames are dissected, and candlesticks seem to teeter. His brand, J.M. Szymanski, is known for these anomalies, as is his team of makers, and they are deeply respected for the exceptional furniture and objects they realize. His studio has expanded since he founded it in 2016. "I've grown from a one-man show working out of the school of visual arts to employing five people now," he says. "We have a 4,000-square-foot space in the south Bronx, and we're launching new pieces consistently."

Metal has always held a draw for Szymanski. "It was the most exciting material for me so I chose classes on metal over ceramic and wood when I was studying," he explains. "The elements that make up metal are really cool and it takes a certain persistence to work with the material. The vision of the pieces I have in my head seem to translate best in metal, so for the past five years, metal has been my language."

About the alchemical aspects of what he does, he says, "When the material arrives in our studio, it's not by any means a precious material. Steel is industrial and unrefined. The process I've developed is very unique because the steel in the end is gorgeous and rich, and has this beautiful depth to it. It's a time-consuming process because we have to strip the metal down and take off the elements on the outside. This leaves a deteriorated, ruddy surface that turns it into rich blacks that range from blue blacks and red blacks, and caramels. Once we clear-coat and wax it, it becomes this special version of steel that many people don't anticipate when they think of steel. Most people think the richness comes from a bronze or a brass but we take steel and turn it into the best possible version of itself."

His passion for making is obvious. Sparked during his early childhood when his family spent seven years in Nepal, it was strengthened during his early twenties when he moved to Spain. Here, he studied the designs of Antoni Gaudí, visited the Alhambra, and made frequent trips to Morocco. When he returned to the United States to study interior design, he settled in New York City and undertook his training at the Fashion Institute of Technology and at the School of Visual Arts. Before founding his own firm, he worked for the eminent designer William Sofield.

Once he was working in the design field, he had a realization that led him to choose product design hands down. "I always knew I wanted to work for myself, and to build and brand my own vision," he explains. "My background being in interior design, I had always assumed I would have my own firm. But the reality of an architecture/design career today is that 95 percent of the work is set behind a computer screen. With a little pivot, I explored making and I very quickly realized that this is where I could express my vision the best."

When we asked him if he had any advice for other young professionals posing the same questions he considered during his early career, he says, "This table is a good example of what I would advise. It evolved from very limited resources. Looking back, I feel like some of my best and most popular pieces were born from limited resources. You don't need unlimited resources to get going. Use what you can and from limitations, oftentimes come the most unique solutions. I'd use the early years as an opportunity to be as creative as possible regardless of what you have at hand."

Markus Haase

Carved Wood and Onyx Sculptural Sconces

If faraway planets that gleam in the night sky could be harnessed and brought to earth, they would have a difficult time competing with the beauty of the asymmetrical forms of the carved wood and onyx sculptural sconces that flank the sitting area of the primary bedroom. Made by Markus Haase, who has been represented by Todd Merrill Studio since 2013, they illustrate his remarkable talent and his deep passion for experimentation. Everything that Haase creates is mystical, and these sconces in particular are extraordinary.

With their blades of backlit onyx that are rolled into a wood detail he hand-sculpted, they reflect a gracefulness that reached great heights during the triumphs of Hollywood glamour. We chose them because we had to have statement pieces for the wenge panels that they illuminate because the structural elements are twelve feet tall—anything small would have simply disappeared. The scale of these hold their own brilliantly, as they are five feet tall; and the crisp color of the onyx contrasts with the backdrop to give them a vivid presence on the wall. They read like striking works of art that also happen to be functional objects.

About his inspiration for the luminous fixtures, Haase says, "I am in love with sculpting and they began with the idea of forming different materials from their natural shape into a 'design' that excites my eye. It is something that I feel more than I can tell, and I think it comes across in my work, whether it is furniture or lighting. An important distinction in my discipline is that every piece is unique and hand-built by me in my studio." The evolution of the wood and onyx versions we purchased inspired Haase to combine onyx and bronze in the same profile. "I am one of the only artists I know of today creating one-of-a-kind bespoke lighting in bronze. Rather than using the material I'm casting as a mechanism for producing multiples, each component is first handcarved as a foam model, which I then cast in bronze before setting it with handcarved onyx or alabaster to diffuse the LEDs."

Haase's love affair with unique forms began before he immigrated to New York City from his native Germany, as he had twenty years of experience as a sculptor by then. Though he would have chosen the path of an artist early on, his parents directed him toward a more practical trade education that would provide him with a career as an electrician, a path he followed for nearly eight years. During this apprenticeship, he was working alongside a master stone carver, learning the centuries-old trade as he contributed to historic restorations. This solidified his desire to carve.

"Sculpting was a very natural practice for me, and I was able to take these skills and easily emulate the architectural stone works found on churches and other buildings throughout Europe," he explains. "The detailed elements I replicated from structures that were built centuries ago gave me a strong sense of quality that is close to perfection. This now ingrained excellence is in my process as an artist and designer." When he reached the United States, Haase set up his own studio with clear influences identified.

"My inspiration to create functional art is based on the experience I had when I first saw sculptural furniture and lighting by fellow makers like Michael Coffey and Paul Evans," he explains. "Being an old-school stone sculptor by trade, I wasn't aware of the much bigger spectrum that exists in materials like wood, bronze, stone, glass, or ceramics once you give them purpose. I knew I could sculpt anything I had on my mind, so I started giving 'the form function.'"

This led him to the experimentation from which the design of the penthouse sconces was derived: "They are the result of years I spent reframing my first idea of a sculptural-shaped lamp, which I wanted to make in order to use onyx as a light diffuser because of the unmistakable beauty that is revealed when it is lit. It needed to be elegant, but also simple. So by this distillation of function, I began with two columns of carved and polished onyx, and then found a way

to create a sculpted body of carved wood that would support but also complement them. This form has been one of my most enduring, and many subsequent works pay homage to its simplicity."

Haase has been certain he would be a maker since he can remember: "I always knew that I wanted to work with my hands. For me, there is no better way of connecting one's hands, mind, and soul with a chosen material than by being a sculptor creating functional art." Todd Merrill Studio makes the point that Haase's lighting has no equal in the marketplace today: "He embodies the independent artisan. Each piece bears the distinct mark of the maker's hand. He is not making a piece of furniture that looks like art. He is a sculptor making art that serves functional ends."

Surface magazine said of the installation of Haase's sculptural Stratus chandelier shown during Design Miami/Basel, "Todd Merrill Studio unveils a breathtaking chandelier by the German sculptor, creating a sweeping landscape of radiant sculpted illumination." *Galerie* magazine spotted Haase's Cloud Chandelier No. 1, 2019, during London Design week, calling it "a divine undulating sculpted bronze and onyx chandelier."

His list of exhibitions through Todd Merrill Studio is extensive, the roster striking all the high notes of fairs showing the most avant-garde collectible and limited-edition design, such as Design Miami/, Salon Art & Design, PAD in London and Geneva, FOG Design and Art Fair, Collectible Brussels, and Design Days Dubai. *Incollect*, the online publication by *Antiques & Fine Art Magazine*, celebrates him with this praise: "Combining a mastery of traditional sculpting techniques with a contemporary, material-driven approach to design, Markus Haase creates unique works of art." We couldn't agree more.

Like flowing through a cleft in time, the winged bench opens the imagination to a new world, one that exists deep below the surface of the sea. Its gracefulness contradicts its strength to make it a moody paradox that lives and breathes in its corner of the room. The way the top plane folds beneath the Mobu bench, realized by Sean O'Hara of O'Hara Studio, is a sweeping gesture that pays homage to the graceful creatures whose supple fins move them through oceanic waters.

Sean is a designer and sculptor whose work crosses the boundaries between art and design. He graduated from Rhode Island School of Design (RISD) in 1996; then headed to Vienna, Austria, for his graduate studies. His wife Cynthia, also a graduate of RISD, manages the business and marketing aspects of the remarkable studio. She is also a talented fabricator who loves to experiment with new materials and finishing techniques. We appreciate their drive to create unique pieces and to consistently release new collections.

In fact, it's rare that we don't fall in love with at least one piece in every introduction, and this bench with its continuous mobius strip of handcarved wood is no exception because its natural connections with watery creatures is so poetic. The craftsmanship is exquisite, which makes the organic statement piece a powerful addition to the interiors of the penthouse. We enjoy how the fluid form contrasts with the symmetrical rigid millwork and how the deep tones in the wood draw the eye down to earth from the large wenge structure beside it.

We celebrate the day these two visionaries joined forces, a move that was just as organic as this bench. Cynthia was the catalyst, as Sean had been selling his pieces through other retailers for years. "One day Cynthia came through my studio, observing some wood sculpting I was doing and she really picked up on my concept," he explains. "She said, 'I'd like to market that. Let's build a furniture company,' so from that point on, we began offering the designs to others ourselves." It was the mix of marketing and business training in Cynthia's background intermingled with her art degree

and her involvement in the high-end furnishings industry for more than twenty years that fostered the dynamic potential they have realized.

To say that Sean's work is varied is an understatement. "I feel my work does not neatly fit into a category," he says. "My designs are informed by my sculptural work, and I believe the results are truly unique, setting my work apart from others. It is my belief the materials inform the artisan/designer to guide them toward what they prefer to do, and that this is a critical relationship. You have to get your hands in there in order to hear the materials. To have that conversation with the wood, you have to be willing to sweat through dusty conditions. And most designers are not able to speak on that level with wood, or other materials."

He admits his process is time-consuming: "I spend a good deal of time researching. My form experiments in the workshop translate into designs in an array of materials and a variety of scales—from wooden benches to silver baby rattles and large-scale Corten steel public works to relatively tiny bronze chess sets. I enjoy a wide diversity of projects. I don't think I'd be happy working in a single category, such as specializing in silversmithing, for example. Each project is very different, and each influences the others in ways I could not imagine. This makes for a healthy creative life, as my mind is stretched, and it grows with every request I receive."

About the Mobu, he says, "I discovered a radical way of sculpting wood when I designed my own tool. I'd never seen a piece of furniture built like this, and I needed to design my own tool in order to shape broad planes of rolling wood." He sees the result as a distinctive piece beyond the traditional definition of the word: "The Mobu bench is made from gorgeous wood and the craftsmanship requires a steady hand to sculpt. But, quality from my perspective also means that the piece is completely innovative. When something has never been seen before, that is the highest level of quality in my opinion."

We asked Sean if he had always known he wanted to be a maker and his answer was resolute: "My gift was easily recognizable early in my life. There were many requests when I was young to draw or paint images for others, or to create album covers for bands. I was very fortunate to be supported by my family, and, later in life, by Cynthia and her family. I am very thankful." His gifts came very naturally to him. "This is just the way I am geared," he explains. "I am curious and I am the type to develop form in experimental ways using any material I am able; and each material offers special properties that guide me as they steer me down new exciting paths."

His favorite thing about the unique life he's carved for himself includes the broad range of materials and projects he explores each and every day: "One day to the next, I can shift from sculpting plaster for bronze casting to welding steel. All of the materials and forms influence each other in unexpected ways. Those discoveries are so very satisfying, and they drive my work."

Sean has some clear advice for young artisans who are determined to create their own paths in the world: "Hone your creative process in a manner that ignores categories or current definitions. Those definitions are boundaries that were put in place long ago by those who don't know just how broad a range there is within the creativity spectrum. I think folks are too quick to categorize artists, and we all know that there are many, many shades of gray." As Sean marches into new creative territory, his keen interest in exploring the possibilities for altering the forms in nature will continue: "I pay close attention to how these shapes can visually communicate the unspoken word. I believe that there are undefined universal forms that are able to touch us visually, regardless of culture and background."

Maria Moyer

Porcelain Roses

Whorls of white so perfect they could be the best specimens nature could create, though they are not. These porcelain blossoms sprung from the heart and hands of the talented artist Maria Moyer. They meander along a slice of wall in the primary bedroom suite, pert in the fact that they are not subject to the whims of the seasons. Their fluid rigidity, a contradiction in terms, makes them resolute representations of the fragile petals that rise from the ground on thorny stems.

As you will have read in the presentation of the suite, we found Moyer's artistry when we took the homeowners of the penthouse through BDDW, watching as they studied the floral sculptures and hitting upon the idea that we would purchase them as a gift for these thoughtful clients. Those who have not been introduced to Moyer will be surprised that these delicate creations are some of the smallest and most figurative pieces in her oeuvre, which also includes large-scale ceramic sculpture, painting, and installation.

The roses began as an exercise in material exploration—small, fast, detailed work, between larger, more time-consuming projects. "My work is grounded in nature and science, though the roses are a rare bit of representational work for me," she says. She describes the initial impulse of the exercise as the push to see how thin she could go.

Moyer, who grew up in Los Angeles, spent over a decade living, creating, and exhibiting in New York City. She returned to Los Angeles in 2019 and maintained a bicoastal life until Covid travel obstacles made this impossible. Her studio is in the Frog Town neighborhood (near Silverlake),

but she often works in Malibu where she feels at one with the natural surroundings to which she has been connected since she was a girl.

Her philosophy is remarkably soulful. "I consider my practice an artifact of reverence for the magic and logic of natural systems, including human-sensory perception," she says. "As an artist it's my job to find and execute that which is unique to me and my 'one wild and precious life,' as Mary Oliver expressed so well." She celebrates the history of the discipline that all artists perfect as they work: "I stand on the shoulders of all who came before me and others of my time with whom I am in dialogue." And she is clear about the demands she has on her work: "I try not to let anything out of my studio that doesn't move in the direction of my intention, but I'm not interested in perfection."

We asked her whether she always knew she wanted to be a maker, and her answer is in lock-step with so many of the creatives we are featuring in this book. "I think we all do as children," she explains. "Some of us return to making; some of us never stopped. I've always had some form of creative practice." As to the advice she would have for up-and-coming artists, she says, "Work at it every day; show up even if you only have an hour, and growth and an evolving body of work will happen. Surround yourself with other artists. Read. See!"

The depth of her commitment could serve as a beacon for those yet to be born into a creative existence: "My favorite thing about what I do day-in and day-out is that being an

artist is a practice of freedom. I want to make work that speaks in ways words might not be able to." Though she has a love for and respect of words, she has seen that they don't always hit the emotional or intellectual mark she seeks, which drives her to communicate in a more visual and physical way. The art form she settles on most often is the tactile medium of sculpture. She notes that three-dimensional work and how it affects space hooked her at an early age. "I experiment with painting and photography, but you can't walk around them," she explains. "I don't call myself a ceramist. I love clay and there's an immediacy in clay, but I like working in other materials, too."

Everything for her filters through two seemingly polar opposites that are far from it when considered through a creative lens: with the elemental, it's the "absurd beauty and exquisite weirdness in nature;" with science, it's "ontogeny, phylogeny, and the recapitulation theory"—think of the ebb and flow of a wave juxtaposed against the development of an embryo. There's evolution in both, as there is in her work, which spans aesthetic manifestations and philosophical themes. Proof are the paradoxical profiles of the dainty roses we chose for the penthouse and the large contemporized forms she creates that flow over the imagination in organic abstractions.

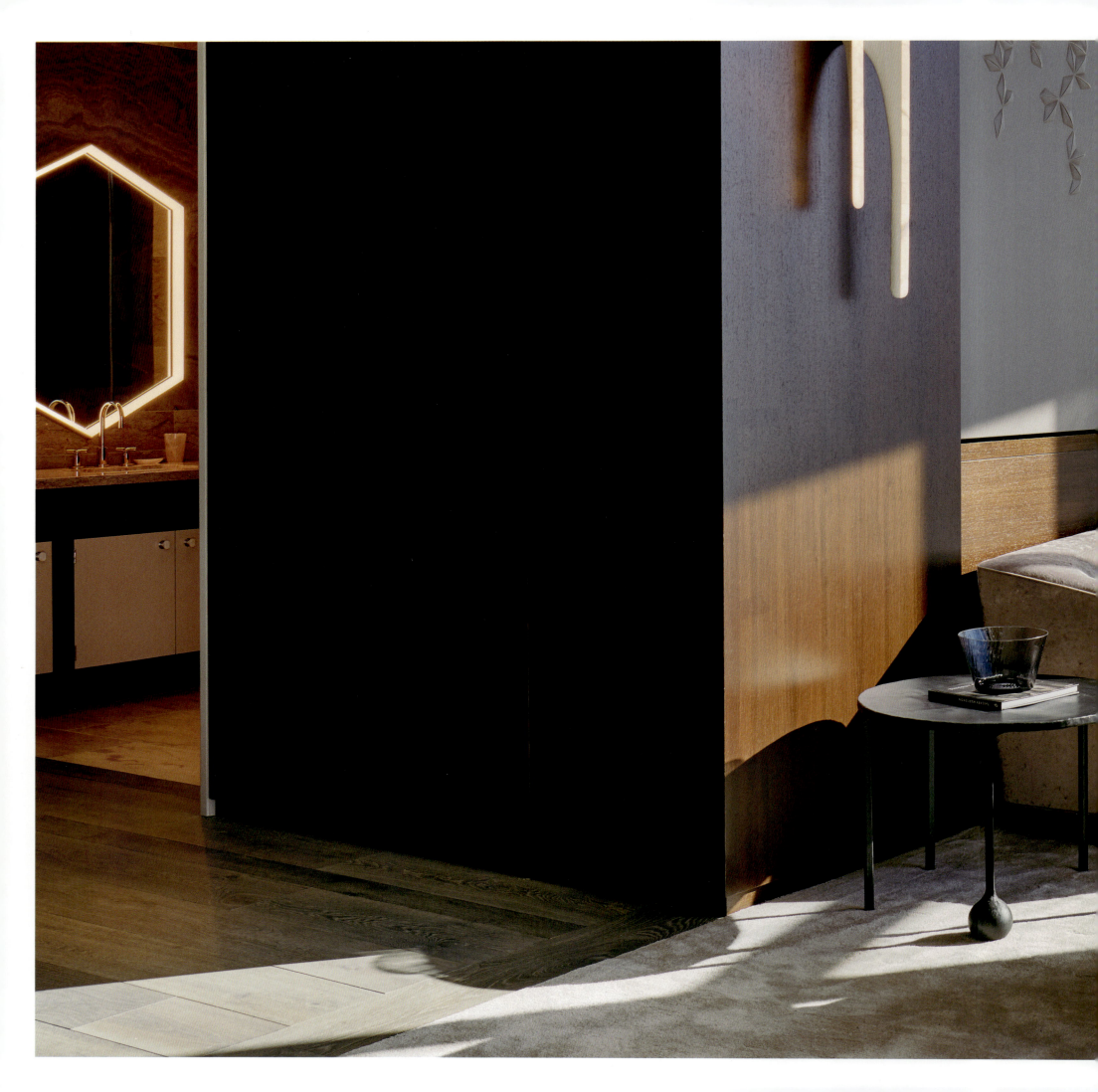

Soft and feminine, her dressing room and bath are celebrations of sophisticated style in pale pinks. With a similar tone and feel as the primary bedroom suite, her dressing room has tailored millwork, hints of floral ornamentation that includes a lush and feminine wallpaper swirling with leaves and a chiaroscuro of colors—from the warmth of wood to pastel finishes and furnishings. Hanging above the Borne Settee that commands the center of the room is a luminous chandelier by Veronese. The Murano glass fixture designed by Piet Hein Eek is in the French company's Past & Future Collection, which has a fascinating story behind it that we share in the full profile of the company in this chapter.

The arrangement of the cabinetry was highly considered because it is the fashion domain of a woman who maintains a boundless social life. Cladding the interiors of the drawers that hold pieces of jewelry is the same marble we chose for the bath, the space an exemplar of mixing stones. Custom hardware by E.R. Butler is also exquisitely feminine—the brooch-like drawer pulls and hammered door knobs could be pieces of jewelry in and of themselves. Hexagonal mirrors repeat in both rooms, luminous when the edges are lit.

The organic patterns on the soft pink panels of onyx in the bathroom, which we sourced from Aria Stone Gallery, create a womb-like atmosphere experienced from the tub. This is one of the spaces in which the stone drove the design and color palette of the room. We hand-selected the slabs in the bathroom like we would pieces of art, and then book-matched them to form the backdrop for her private oasis.

One of the challenges from the start was finding pink marble in a hue that was elegant enough to coexist with the onyx slabs without overwhelming them. Everything we were finding in the United States was this crazy bright pink, so we turned to Italy and found the elegant rose color that reminds us of the spas in the old hotels in Athens that were clad in deep pink stone with spidery veins. The onyx slabs became paintings over the bathtub, in the shower and toilet room, and above the vanity. It was an interesting study in seeing how we could create four different moments from two specimens to compose a serene sense of drama.

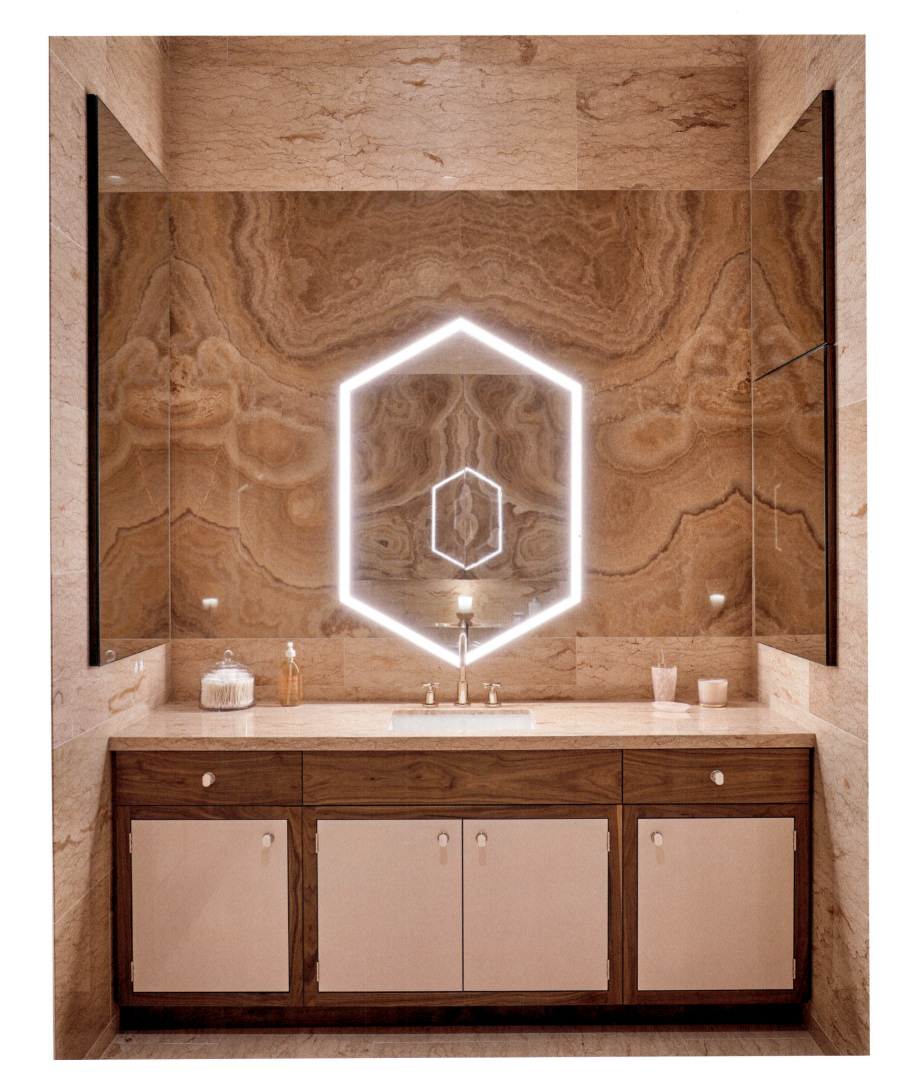

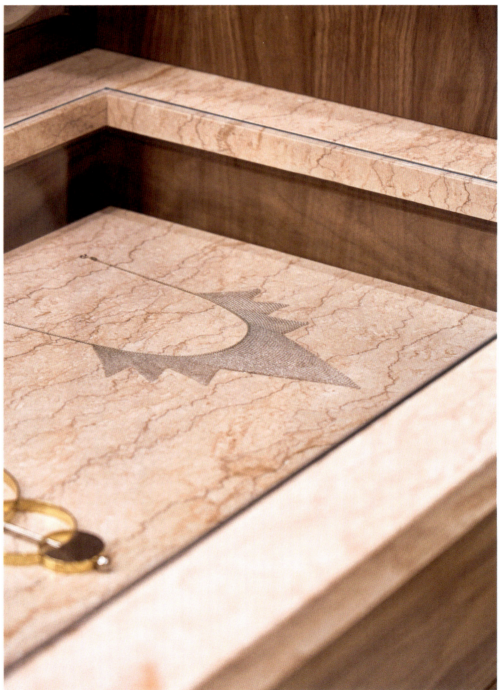

Maison Veronese

Murano Glass Chandelier

It spritzes overhead as it illuminates the dressing space, the sheer whimsy of the scrolls and ornamentations coalescing into a celebration of light. We challenge anyone to be sad while studying its features, the subtle tinges in the glass adding to its fanciful personality. Like a headdress for which a courtier during the ancien régime would have swooned, we knew the femininity of this chandelier from the Veronese Past & Future Collection would be perfect for the wife's dressing room in this residence. Though there are only subtle references to the other pale pink hues in the space, the surroundings draw these out to make this flourish of light a veritable coronation hanging overhead.

There is a fascinating story behind this lighting collection, which is as spirited as this chandelier. Each component in each fixture comprises Murano glass elements from the Veronese archives—pieces that existed because for decades additional shapes were ordered for each fixture produced, which meant there were thousands of pieces that could be repurposed for the new collection. For many years, Ruben Jochimek, the Creative Director of this French design house, wanted to breathe new life into these archived glass elements on the company's shelves because they had been collecting dust since the 1930s. He had long been a fan of the Dutch designer Piet Hein Eek, who is known for creating furniture collections and home accessories from upcycled materials.

When Jochimek approached him and proposed that he create a lighting collection with Veronese's archived glass elements in 2015, Eek loved the idea. They met in Eek's workshop in Eindhoven, the Netherlands; and Jochimek showed the designer, who works with contemporary forms but is a fan of antiques, a small sample of the glass pieces and the collection began to take shape. This is such a special collection because some of the glass elements included in it can no longer be produced as they originally were due to current-day environmental restrictions. This added to the determination Eek and Jochimek felt to find a way to give such elements an opportunity to shine again.

Within no time, Eek devised a Meccano-like cylindrical metal system with circular inserts into which each glass element can be placed freely. The system became the foundation for the collection, which includes various suspensions, table lamps, and candleholders. The metal structure is designed in tiers that can be used to create various lengths, which is one of the most versatile aspects of its function because this creates a wide array of dimensions and arrangements for the varied colors and shapes. There is an endless number of handcrafted Murano glass leaves, flowers, and geometric and abstract shapes from which to draw. This fulfills the Veronese mission that is highly considered when designing collections of lighting and decorative objects: to offer versatile products with untold opportunities for personalization.

We found Maison Veronese through The Future Perfect showroom, which represents the company and carries the Past & Future Collection. The House of Veronese was established in Paris in 1931 with a focus of specializing in timeless Murano glass creations. For nine decades the company has been committed to creating collections that fuse Murano glass craftsmanship and French design sensibilities to create timeless products. Driven by a spirit of discovery and experimentation, the creative forces behind the scenes in the company's atelier today explore innovative ideas and materials that deliver a new perspective of Murano glass to the world.

But the manufacturer is also ever-mindful of being dedicated to its heritage as it produces lighting, mirrors, furniture, vases, and other decorative pieces, many of them highly customized. Its artisans also create new one-of-a-kind pieces for projects. Each design is envisioned and assembled in Paris at the company's atelier using pieces of glasswork produced in Murano, Italy, by master artisans with whom the brand has maintained relationships since 1931.

In 2021, Veronese celebrated its ninety-year anniversary. When the brand was first established, it focused on creating exclusive lighting designs for clients. The company began to introduce its own collections during the early twenty-first century during annual debuts conceived by its in-house design team, some in collaboration with renowned designers. To mark this new period, Veronese introduced products by the renowned French designer André Arbus under a collection bearing his name, the original pieces envisioned by Arbus from the 1930s through the 1950s.

Arbus had been very loyal to Veronese for many years, turning to the company for all of his glass designs, including those for the famed MS *Bretagne* luxury cruise liner, which sailed around the world during the 1960s. The Veronese Concorde wall sconce with gold leaf was designed by Arbus in 1952 for the *Bretagne* and remains a vital part of the iconic collection along with other Arbus designs. The manufacturer still works closely with the Fondation André Arbus to assure that the designer's legacy continues to be honored. Since this collection debuted, several other A-list designers have worked with Veronese to create distinctive new collections.

"Every day at Veronese we work together with our team and collaborators—designers, artisans, architects, and connoisseurs—to bring a new perspective to an old-world craft and to demonstrate its vitality to the world," notes Jochimek. "This is what inspires us. As a family business, we recognize the beauty and significance of heritage, yet we also understand that to preserve both Murano glass and French design know-how, we need to appreciate their essence. It is with that knowledge that we, designers and craftspeople, discover ways to evolve with the times while still remaining true to our past."

As this penthouse came together, we realized that we were drawn to brands with similar philosophies as we scoured the globe for products. We believe the depth that a dedication to quality brings is illustrated in each of the elements we chose to place in our creation of a unified whole, the Veronese chandelier a stellar example. We salute Jochimek and his team for dedicating their efforts to championing a time-honored point of view. "To preserve Murano craftsmanship and remain timeless, we challenge perceptions, ideas, and concepts," Jochimek says. "We cross boundaries, both perceived and geographical, to discover something different and enlightening. When creating, we never allow ourselves to be constrained by anything beyond that which is posed by the laws of nature as they apply to glass and its various forms."

For anyone entering the industry as a young designer or burgeoning executive hoping to create an authentic brand, Jochimek advises, "There is no hierarchy between art and design: they are two separate disciplines that can merge either spontaneously or by intention. When an artisan, craftsperson, or artist chooses to explore the merging of these two worlds, which often happens, it's important that they do not lose sight of the fact that design serves a function whereas art does not. We do not use art, we admire it, discuss it, and even debate about it. Design, on the other hand, exists first and foremost to meet a certain utilitarian purpose, and its beauty serves that objective."

While the creative process is important, he adds, what's even more consequential is character: "I have had the opportunity to work with many designers, artisans, and artists who are at various stages of their careers, and the ones who have stood out were those who understood and appreciated the fact that today there is endless talent within reach and each person is unique. Therefore, to shine they must remain authentic and kind. Success lies more with one's character than with one's artistry."

Primary Bedroom Hallway

Windswept maples yellowed by the advance of fall; paths through forests leading to open fields that beckon; and icy scenes with tree limbs needling skyward. These are the seasons witnessed by Dutch artist Evert Rabbers over a century ago. The old-world sensitivity these darkened palettes bring to the primary bedroom hallway make this a soulful passage. Our aim here was to evoke a very serene morning walk for the husband as he makes his way down the hall to his dressing area to make a cappuccino. There's a coffee bar in his private rooms and a terrace off it where he can sit and enjoy the start to his morning. The windswept settings in the paintings create a nice promenade for him.

We sourced the compositions lining the long walls through John Derian, whom we've known for about twenty years and who we seem to always see when we're combing the Paul Bert section of the Marché aux Puces for finds. Not only do we collect art from the visionary, we also admire the exquisite product line of plates and glassware he has developed. As a collector, he is unusual because he has a knack for finding multiples in so many artists' oeuvres. He had so many paintings by this Dutch artist we were able to sift through them and choose the perfect ones for this space.

For an end-of-the-hallway focal point that perfectly juxtaposes the Dutchman's work, we chose a larger painting by California artist Patrick Dennis. We feel the work of both artists brings a nice cosmopolitan flair to Houston, and the colors in all the paintings complement the handsome wenge paneling. Illuminating the passageway is a Holly Hunt pendant light that effervesces like a lit prism over the long, linear scene.

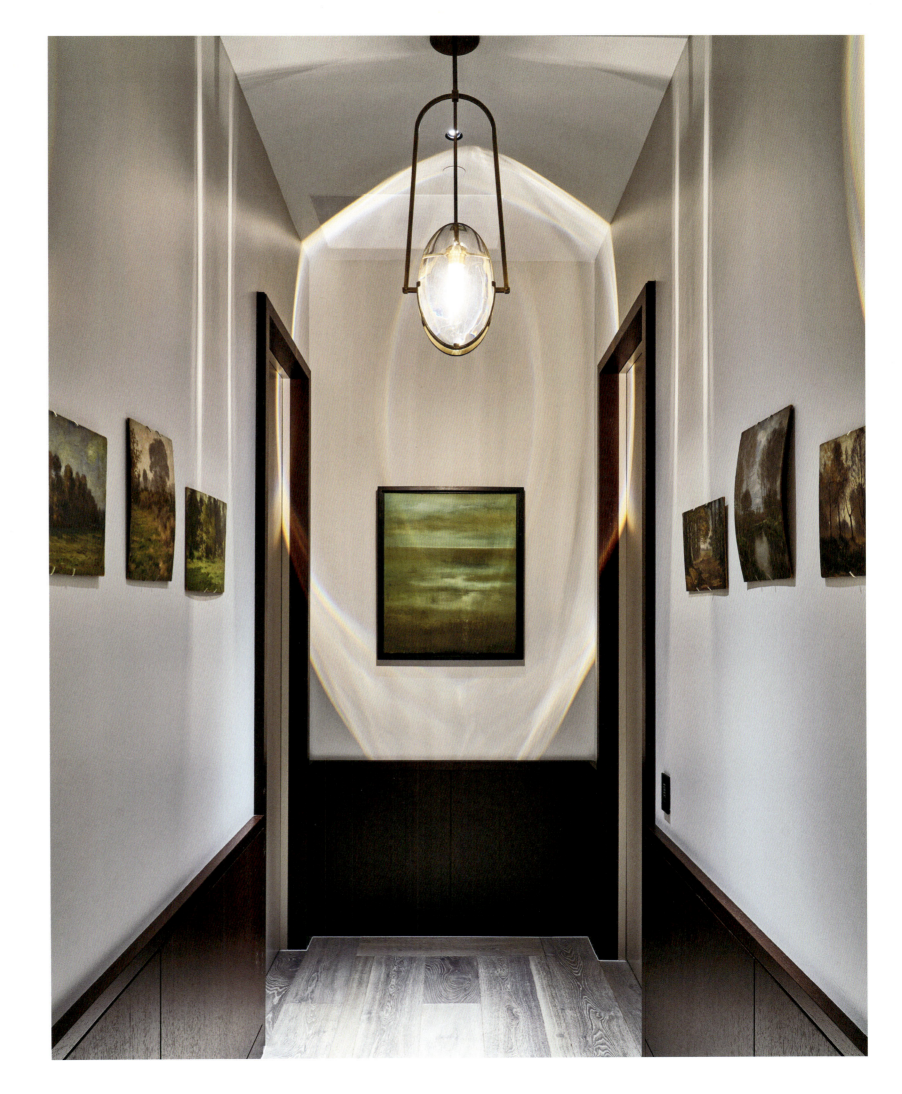

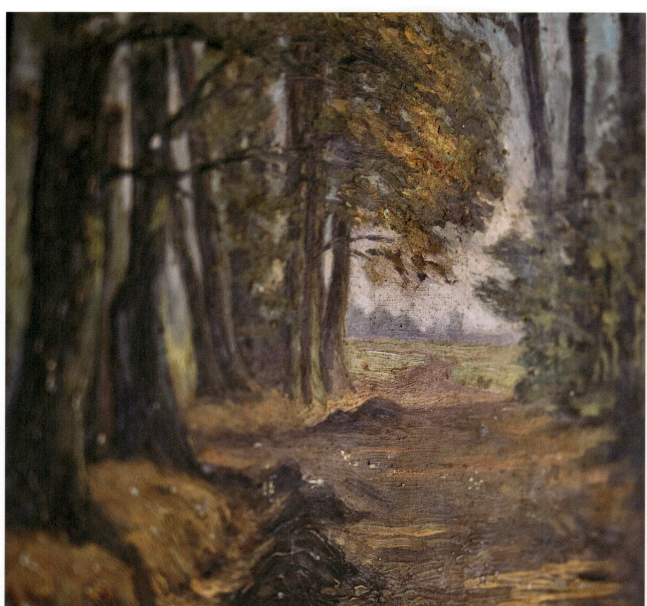

"Why are you putting so much energy into this space and specifying such luxurious materials?" was a question we heard from the workers and subcontractors while we were installing the beautiful millwork in the laundry room created by Gregory Madzio's team at HIICompany Corp. The answer is that moves like these reflect our philosophy that if a homeowner is game, a residence should read "of a piece," regardless how unimportant some builders would consider a room.

The mix of walnut woodgrain and sleek high-gloss lacquered surfaces form a nuanced juxtaposition in the space. Everything is tucked away, even the washer and dryer sit behind cabinetry. The tiles in the room, which has a hint of crinkle to bring it depth, were produced when RW Guild collaborated with Waterworks to design the collection. The countertops are clad in Calacatta Gold marble and we created a framed chalkboard for jotting lists and messages.

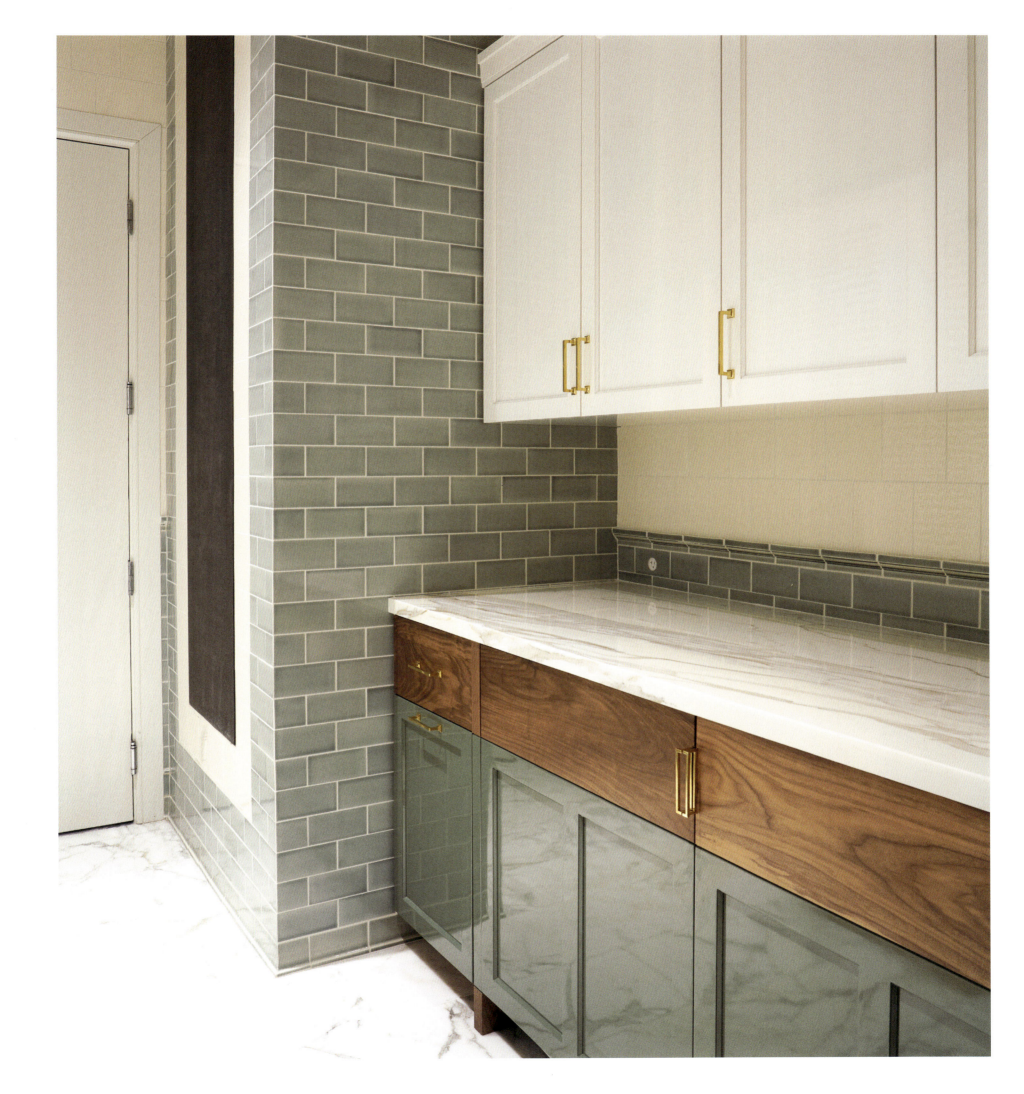

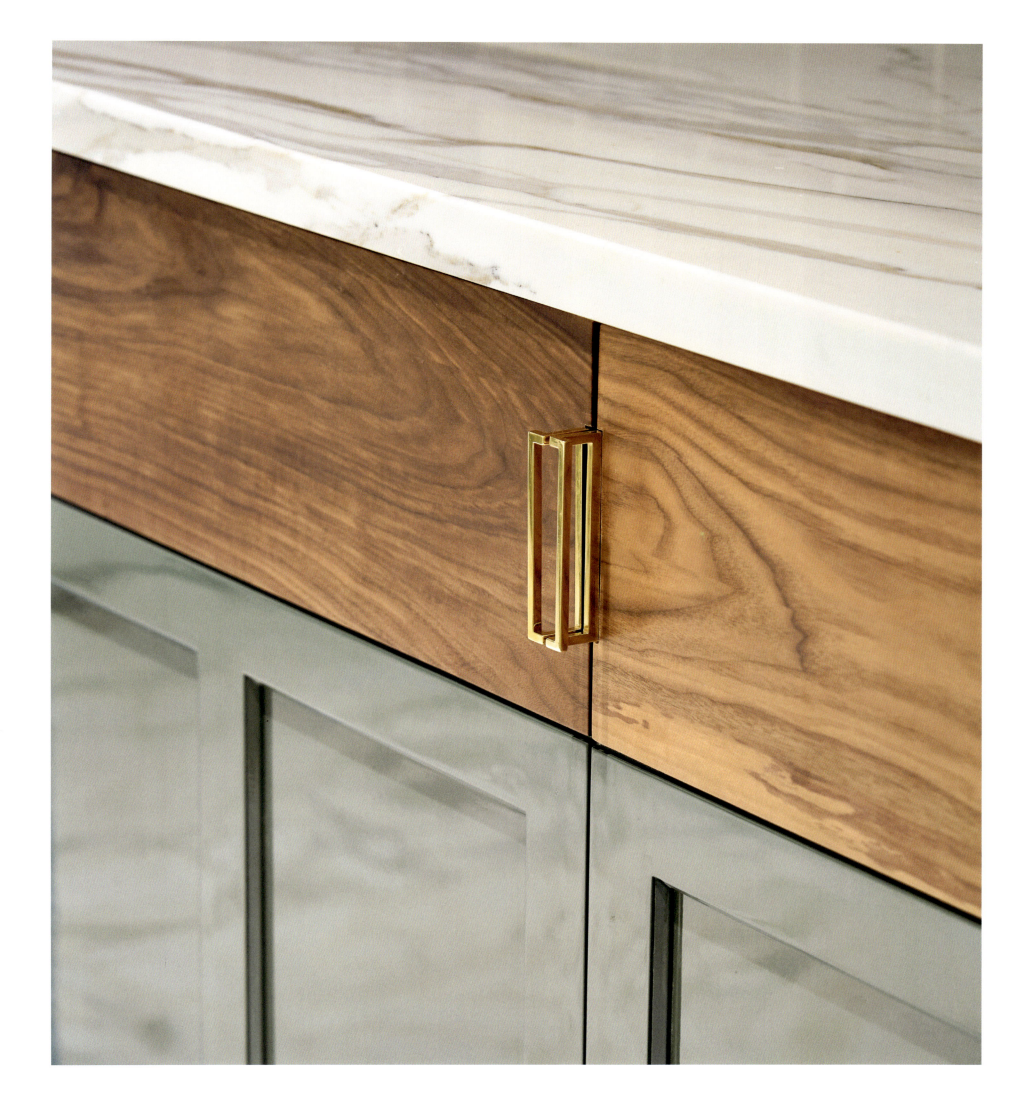

When Zeus asked his daughter Athena to make a wish, the blue-eyed goddess of war requested he make the world see her beauty every day. To achieve this, so the myth goes, he turned the sky blue to match the color of her gaze. The dressing room and bath actualized for the husband in this penthouse would have thrilled the goddess of war! For these private spaces clad in decidedly bold colors of Brazilian marble, we treated the walnut in a gray wash to make the tones more masculine.

In his dressing room, we chose the chandelier and sconces by Gabriel Scott from the Luna Series. We were playful with the glassblown globes that slide along the tubes by mixing the gray and blue ones, though not predictably, on the chandeliers; and juxtaposing blue and gray sconces on each side of the vanity. These fixtures were so perfect for this space, it is as if they were designed specifically for it—we can't imagine any other sconces or chandelier making as strong a statement as they do. The profile of this seriously artisanal brand follows this presentation of the space.

His dressing room has only hints of the Brazilian marble we sourced from Crystal Tile & Marble, Ltd., while the bathroom is drenched in it, the white veining swirling on the walls like cloud drifts on a summer day. By capping the sauna with the stone, we created tonal contrast and provided the homeowner with the illusion he is gazing up at the sky while enjoying the warmth of the steam.

Another playful move we made in the dressing room and bath is choosing hardware by Chris Lehrecke, which we found at E.R. Butler. Each of the drawer pulls varies only slightly in shape and when we began playing around with the placement, they morphed into these wonderful little chess pieces that we chose for his spaces.

They are exquisitely machined and the dark bronze finish resonates so beautifully in the spaces. This is an example of a tack we enjoy taking when creating the ultimate in detailing: choosing hardware that dynamizes doors and drawers. We know that the effort will go unnoticed by some but we also know there are those who will see the subtle detail and say, "Oh, this is slightly different from one drawer to the next!"

Having some fun and being playful in this way reflects the entire theme of the book that is now drawing to a close: it's an essence that includes nuance, notice, and an attention to detail. We know we don't have to be this creative—we could simply have had every piece of hardware be the same, repeating again and again; but in paying homage to the history of our craft of architecture, and interior and product design, we harken back to the days when hardware was handmade, which resulted in each iteration of each design being slightly different. What note would you leave us as we close the last chapter of our exploration of remarkable collaborations with the vast breadth of talent featured here?

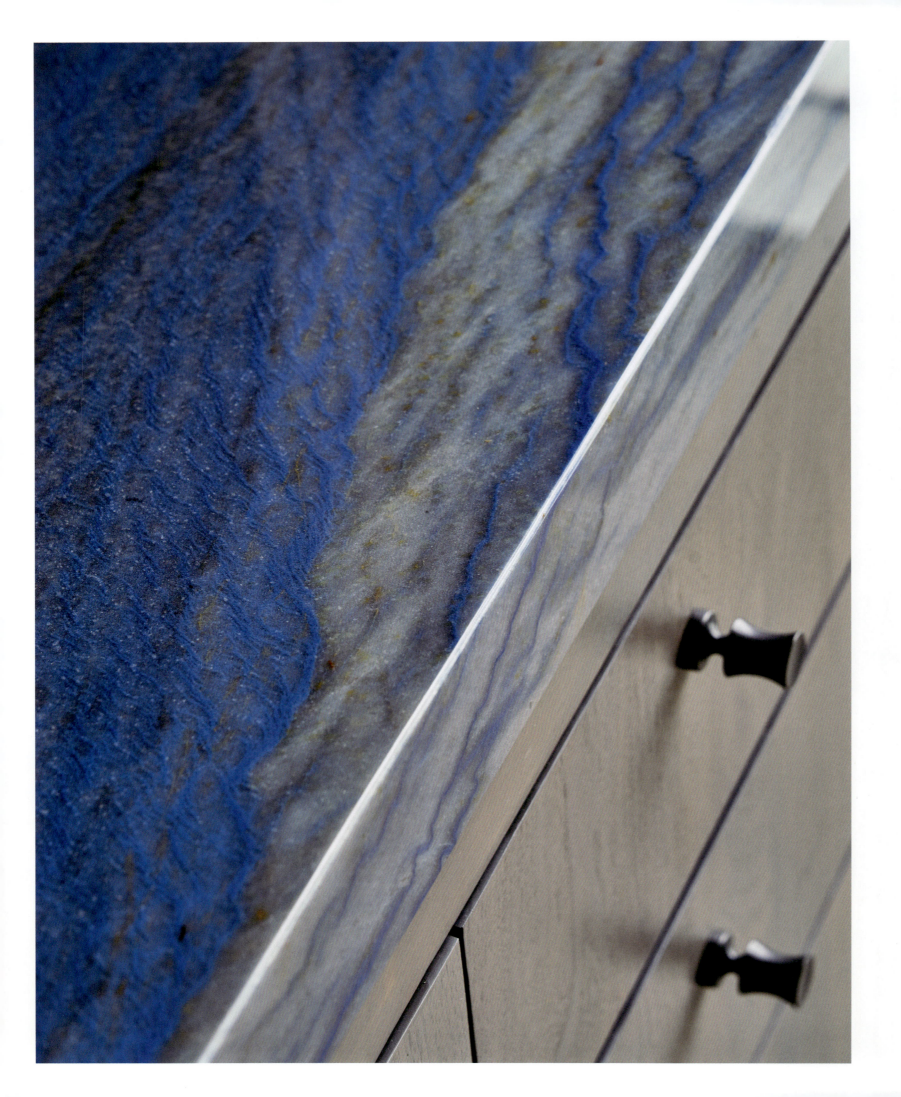

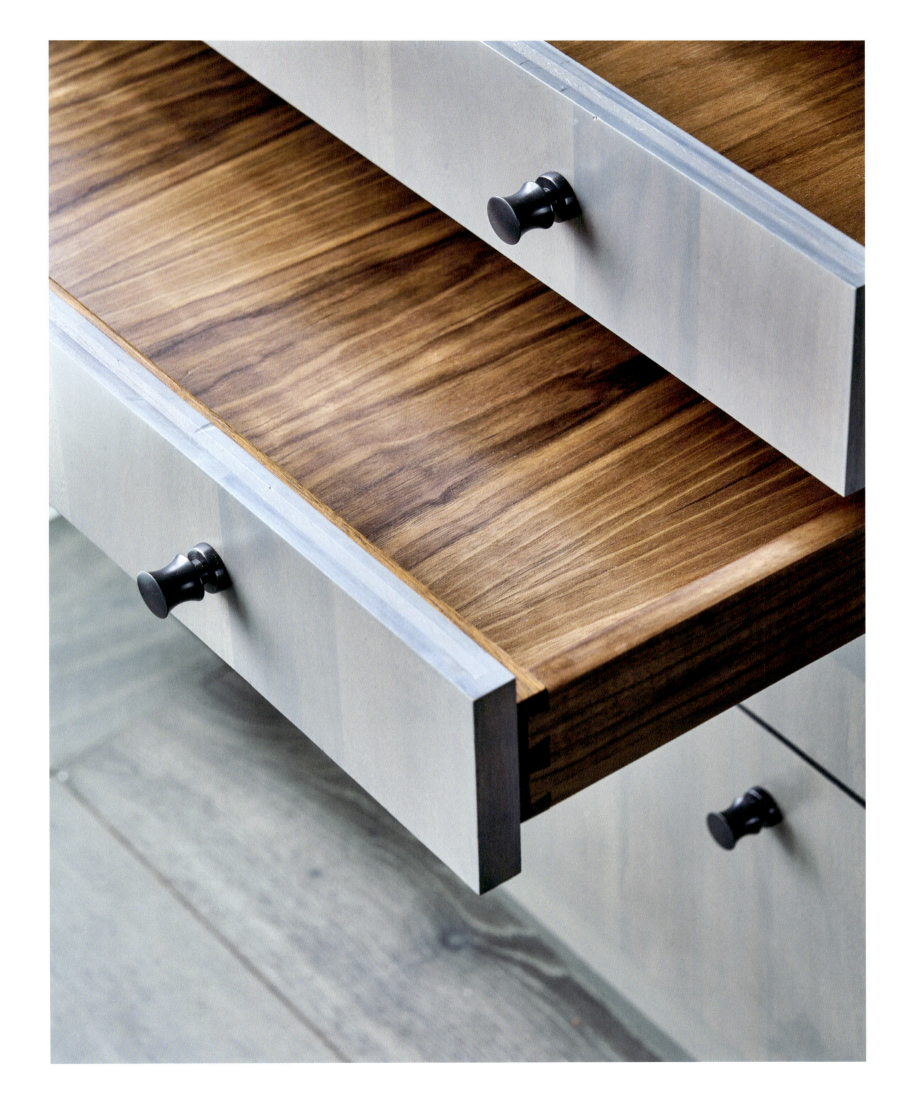

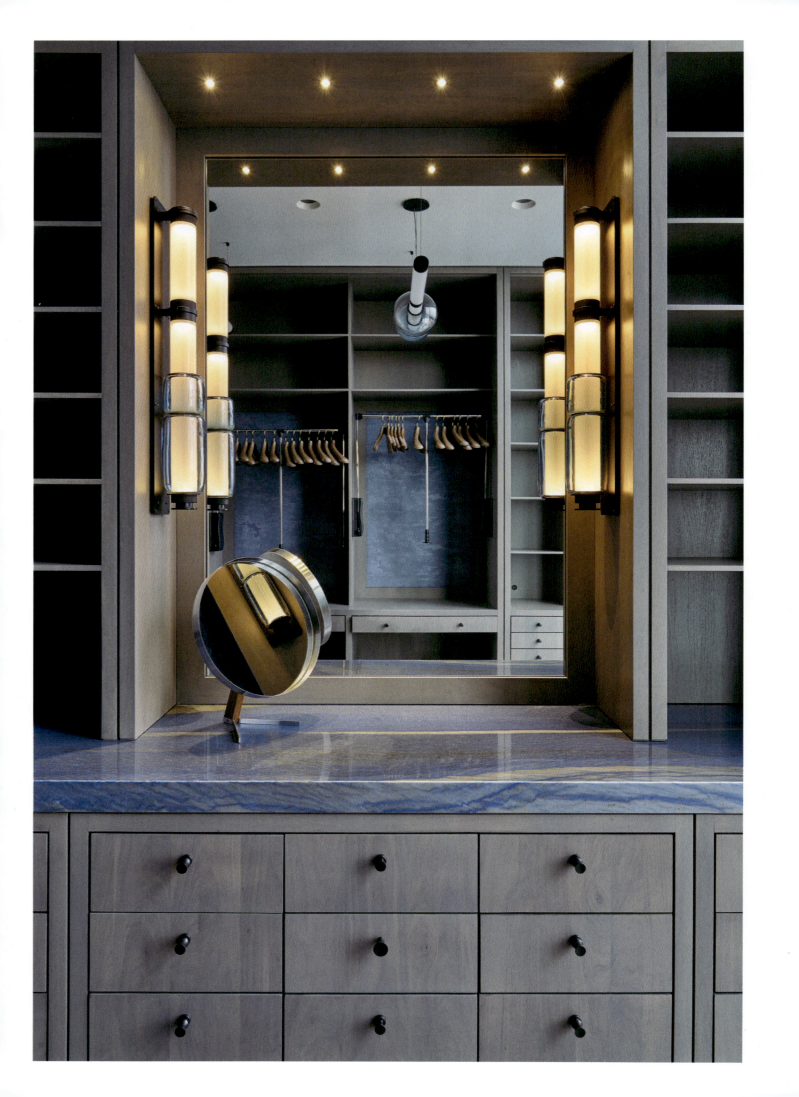

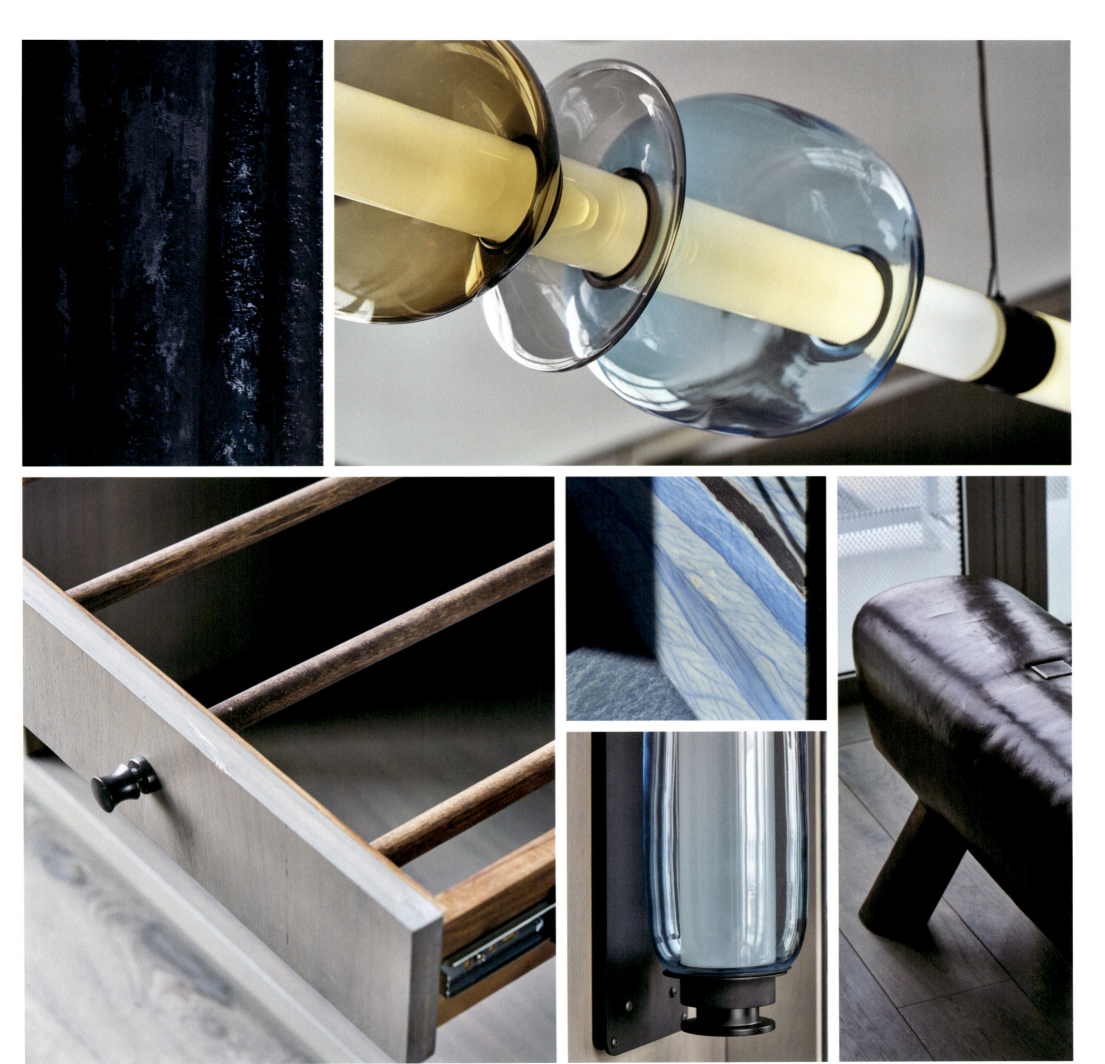

Gabriel Scott

Luna Chandelier and Sconces

Moonglow meets a molten world in the Luna chandelier and sconces we sourced from Gabriel Scott for the husband's dressing room. The pastel glass globes reflect illumination like glowing heavenly bodies in the early morning sky and are testaments to the fact that the phrase "playing with fire" can have a beautiful outcome. It's no surprise that before he turned his attention to lighting, Scott Richler, the founder and creative director of the company, had designed a variety of fashionable products, including jewelry. His concentration was the "nobility of craftsmanship" and exquisite materials.

We asked him what inspired him to found his own brand. "Following my studies in architecture, I spent more than a decade exploring design, and dedicated myself to making in a number of fields ranging from jewelry, fashion, interiors, bespoke furniture, sculpture, and lighting," he says. "Gabriel Scott was a way to blend those experiences. Following a few years designing and building very bespoke furniture pieces and architectural elements, I was looking for a way to create a collection of luxury furnishings that would reach more people the same way my jewelry and fashion had done in years past."

From his design studio and headquarters in Montreal, he began building a business model that has turned the company into a powerhouse in the luxury interiors market. The quality he has achieved is built into Gabriel Scott's design practice, which blends avant-garde and time-honored ideas, and focuses on both storied and innovative methodologies. "Aside from the obvious references to jewelry making found throughout the collection, we also mix materials and techniques in a way as to highlight the heritage of making while at the same time challenging it," Richler says. "For example, the way we approach glassmaking relies on centuries-old techniques but also endeavors to challenge the artisans to express these in new ways."

"The industrial designers and engineers at Gabriel Scott are a tight-knit group," says head designer, Nicolas Pomerleau. "We have a strong team here and everyone's opinion counts,"

he explains. "I'm head of design, but I'm always open to ideas. Custom products and big structures bring us added challenges that we are always eager to tackle—our clients have such high standards that we have become adept at achieving the utmost in refinement for everything we make regardless of scale."

Richler notes that they welcome clients who want to be involved in the creation of their furnishings: "We believe that our clients should be part of the design process because their input results in a feeling of participation in something that was created for them." He adds that this level of collaboration is facilitated by the fact that many of their products utilize forms and a visual language already familiar to their customers. This is why they concentrate on modularity, the principle of repetition, and familiar symbols of ornamentation. "The components that make up a fixture— for example geometric forms that are reminiscent of jewels and details that resemble prongs—have a vocabulary that helps to identify the studio's work, but also sets up a dialogue with the client based on something that already exists in their experience of luxury items."

The Luna series in the penthouse is an example. The globes can be configured in a number of arrangements that make the fixtures extremely versatile. Richler explains that the collection was born of two ideas: "At the studio, we were working on finding a more pleasing solution to linear tube lights while we were also challenging ourselves to develop a fixture inspired by Murano glass beads. After some time, we actually merged these concepts into one when we had the idea of 'threading' the mouth-blown glass beads over the tubes."

Pomerleau remembers when they were fleshing out their concepts for the line of lighting, as it was the first series on which he collaborated when he signed on with the company: "When we worked on Luna, Scott and I printed and cut out colorful shapes that we pinned to a really long wall in the studio. It took us about a year before we were satisfied with the design, a rhythm I'm very familiar with because

the first idea has to process internally to a certain point before it can reach its full potential physically. When you force something, it just doesn't work. We would try small adjustments, then step back and study. It takes a series of these explorations before reaching the point at which the solution becomes clear."

Though Richler points out there is no disputing the beauty of the luminous profiles we chose, he notes that the mechanical attributes are equally stunning: "It's more obvious on inspection that there is a very intentional articulation of details that can only be accomplished with great care and artisanship. Besides the quality of the glassblowing and color rendering, the subtle details in the metal help to define each of the elements with the attention that would otherwise be expected of a jeweler."

This collection also reflects the brand's ability to take one product and manipulate it in untold ways when sizes and configurations grow or shrink. "We are always thinking about how we can adapt so that a product line can grow," Pomerleau explains. "It's fascinating to create designs that have the flexibility to allow us to accomplish that. Also, we see ourselves as a heritage brand so we want to create products that will last more than one lifetime—a modern classic that will be valid far into the future."

It is natural that Richler would amass a team of inventive thinkers like Pomerleau, as he developed a high level of rigor early in his career and infused the company culture with it: "My past consisted of a series of design projects that were all based on one form of artisanship or another. When we used to make handbags in Italy, we enjoyed challenging the best patternmakers in the world as much as they enjoyed the challenges. We continue in that pursuit with our glassblowers, finishers, and builders." What advice does he have for someone hoping to found an artisanal brand? "I would say make things. Don't get stuck in the design. You will learn more by working with real materials than you will ever learn if you don't try."

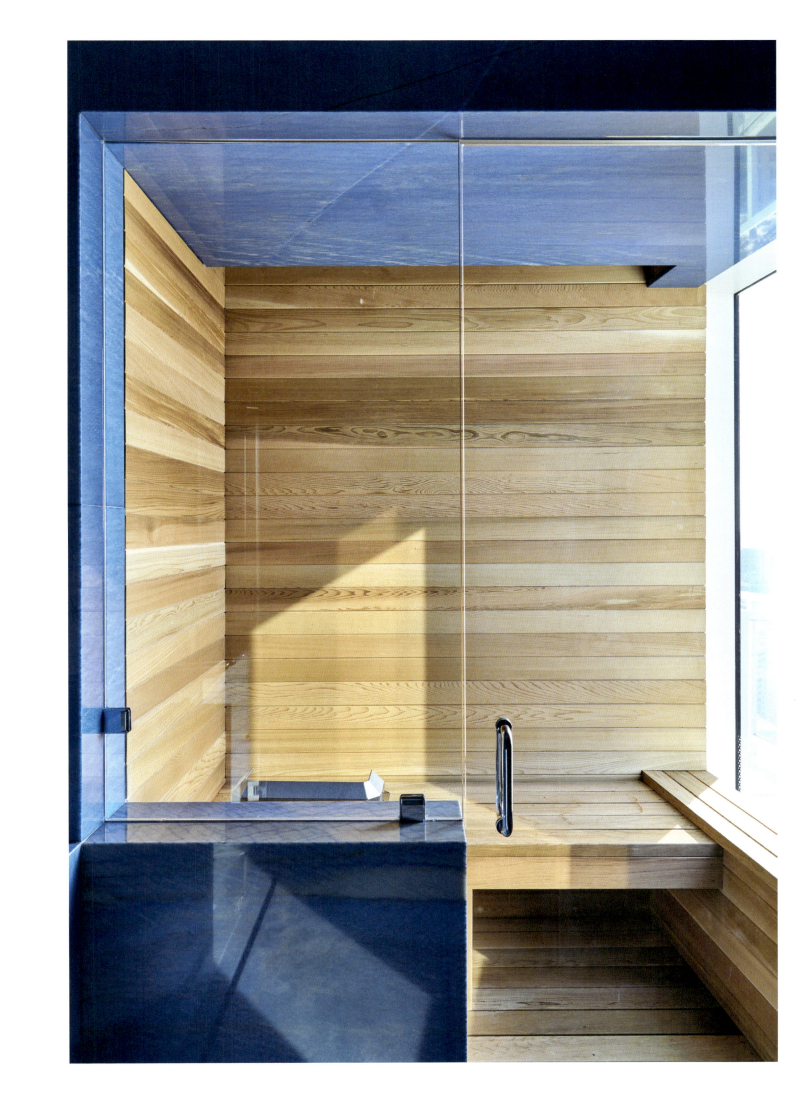

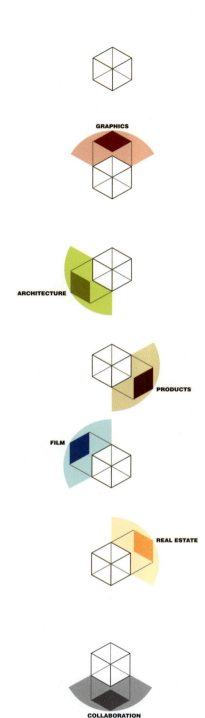

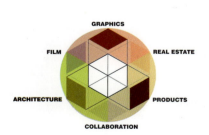

It is our hope that the note you'd be inspired to leave us would be one expressing how it felt as you experienced our passion for relentless experimentation through touring the spaces in the penthouse. We have nurtured this fervor for constructing boundary-pushing, inventive spaces since the beginning. We are proud materialists with a body of work that ranges from the smallest, most meticulously crafted puzzle to a worldwide network of one-of-a-kind luxury commercial spaces. The latter includes hundreds of Christian Louboutin boutiques, each one designed to reflect the cultures surrounding them in locales worldwide.

Also in our portfolio are residential projects like this penthouse, each one exhibiting remarkable nuance. Among the previous residences we've designed is a Da Vinci–style system of elaborate code-breaking games we invented for the children of clients in a New York City apartment, a project that was also illustrated in a book we wrote, designed, and produced, and celebrated by an original score we wrote and produced.

This layered approach illustrates our serious commitment to detail and a rigorously developed sense of play, each of which serves as the foundation for our dedication to thinking outside the box. The reaching past norms began in 2000 when 212box was launched with one of our first explorations, a series of constructs dubbed GlassBoxes installed on the façades of existing structures to illustrate how high the bar could be set when it comes to experimentation. This effort inspired our name. Our perceptiveness was renewed when Eun joined the firm in 2004, and our dedication to investigation has only strengthened since.

Our design ethos is filtered through a holistic approach to problem-solving that operates the same at any scale. We are storytellers with a passion for creating architecture, design, cinematography, and graphics. As we have actualized retail spaces and residential projects around the globe, we have forged relationships with an international network of artists and craftspeople, a number of whom are celebrated here. Our collaborations are extremely important to us, as we could not accomplish what we do alone; and our tireless explorations of materiality require partnerships with highly actualized individuals and manufacturers.

The specificity that emerges as we source and curate elements from these makers or as we design products for them to create is also illustrated here, as this residence is a classic example of one of our strongest attitudes: rather than thinking about any particular style at any point in the process, we allow the style to emerge from the components that are brought together as we create harmonized wholes. A natural outgrowth of this pursuit is that our spaces are timeless and classic; they are neither confined by traditional concepts of beauty nor tethered to a notion of "modern" or "trending."

The fact that we work globally provides us many opportunities to explore cultural craft. As we do, we continue to discover materials that we are eager to interpret in surprising ways. As we have completed built projects throughout North America, Europe, and Asia, we have not only found incredible artistic accomplishments, we have learned that the act of building with people from different parts of the world brings with it a deep dive into understanding the cultures, the places, and other ways of thinking. These immersions have also taught us that the more we share and build together, the more we realize we have in common. The artisans and artisanal brands we chose for the Houston project share the same passion for excellence that drives us as we create and curate. We hope you've enjoyed learning about them and their disciplines that result in such outstanding quality.

CHRISTIAN LOUBOUTIN

CHRISTIAN LOUBOUTIN

Nick Rochowski

Photographer

Capturing the essence of every project we realize is critical to the documentation of our creative journey. This feat is as collaborative as any other aspect of our artistic expression, and we have found a remarkable partner to accomplish this in United Kingdom-based photographer Nick Rochowski, who has recorded the spirit of many of our interiors, including this penthouse. About the shoot during which his unerring eye captured the interiors so alluringly, he says, "I remember going in on the first day and seeing lights." He describes some of the choices he made as he was photographing the penthouse:

"The key starting point for me as an image maker is always the light, whether it's in the studio or in an interior space. Full cascading sunlight is more lurid but I also embrace the subtlety of cloudy weather because it brings with it a mixture of light gradations. With shade, colors read as more natural, objects are not so severely backlit, and the furniture reads differently, particularly when you have such large volumes. To create the filtered light I wanted, I played around with the sheers, opening them and closing them, which I could do because I had multiple days to shoot the residence. With these subtle gestures, different moods are achieved—when the sheers are closed, they filter the light and the spaces become more ethereal. This move is like bouncing light as we often do in studio shoots.

"As I move through the photos of the main living space of the penthouse several years later, they take me from the amazing views to the exquisite layering Eric achieved, which actually transforms the huge volume. I give him a great deal of credit for being able to bring so much warmth to the sizable spaces."

Rochowski was particularly taken by the track of planks embedded in the Foresso floor, and he admired the way the array of objects was integrated to create an intricate shadow play when seen as a whole, the scene particularly effervescent with early sunrise.

"The accessories were like puppets and even the simplest items became sculptures as the light touched them," he explains. "The Curiosity Cabinet was one of the most challenging elements to shoot because when the play of shadow and light reflected on it, it was a real beast to capture!" The curve of the building in the guest and primary bedroom suites was another dilemma: "I have a love for brutalist architecture so I am naturally drawn to a grid structure when I'm shooting. When I noticed how the wall was arcing, I had to adjust the perspective of the shots so the bend wasn't the defining construct of the image."

He credits his ability to create cohesion at this level, in part, to his training in graphic design, which he studied before he gravitated to photography. "I loved working with image and type and I'm always interested in how the visuals will work with text, but taking photos had a bigger draw for me that won out," he says. "Because of that training, I am actually able to crop images as I'm shooting, making notes in my head as I go along as to how certain photos will be edited."

These adjustments come to him soon after he lowers his eye to the viewfinder: "Looking through the lens as I was shooting the dining room, I was particularly interested in documenting the view to downtown because I am always fascinated by how things work on different scales. For this particular project, the residence had quite a prominent position over the cityscape that flowed over the beautiful dining table by Tyler Hays and unfolded beyond the gorgeous pendants. It was like a stage set: the sheers served as a stage curtain and the performance was taking place on the table holding all the sophisticated objects, which became actors in the play."

His aim in bringing this dramatic narrative to life was specific: "I don't like to shoot very wide because I like to capture the sense of how it feels when a person is in a room. Unlike the eye's peripheral vision, a camera flattens things out; if I need to see more, I step back a bit rather than changing to a wide-angle lens." The sumptuousness of his images contained in this book serve as testaments to his ability to provide an experiential perspective—the ability a hallmark in his portfolio.

For anyone who is considering a career in photography, Rochowski advises it's important to continue to grow. "I am always learning, even after doing this for over a decade. Also, being passionate is a necessity because it's so hard in the beginning. All the critical questions are pulling at you: 'Where are clients going to come from? Who is going to take me seriously?' is the refrain. The level of drive I maintained helped me survive the early years." He sees himself as an optimist in the highly competitive field in which he has chosen to create his life's work.

"When I studied photography, one of my professors said at the very beginning of class that 90 percent of us sitting there were not going to make it!" he notes. "When I lecture at universities, I don't say this to the students because there are so many areas within image making that can lead to success. I believe there's room for anyone who has talent and determination." He points out that just a few of these disciplines include editor, art director, creative director, publisher, archivist, retoucher, buyer, producer, and stylist, among others.

"In the beginning, as I was working with an American beauty photographer for a few years, I was pushing to gain access to properties so I could shoot my own portfolio," he says. "I think that's when the passion has to be fully present because initially when you're building your own legacy, you're rarely getting paid correctly, if at all." He also cautions not to be overly focused because burgeoning artists will miss out on the experiences that could inspire them the most: "Keeping your head down as you are working can be isolating because you are daunted by the task, and it's appropriate to be mindful. But allowing people into your process is critical because they can serve as a support network and bring fresh ideas."

He likens a new career to a hilly terrain: "Even if someone has foresight, the road will be up and down because it's difficult to stay with a vision when there are so many uncertainties. It's also easy to be overly rigid in terms of not taking on projects that don't pay as well early on. I've always had a policy of considering the benefit beyond the financial gain, especially with projects that allowed me to stretch. As long as I didn't feel I was being taken advantage of, I always put 100 percent into everything I did."

These moves have certainly paid off for Rochowski, who is now taking on large-scale, prestigious projects like photographing interiors in Buckingham Palace. The award-winning photographer continues to stretch as he works directly with clients and creative agencies across the interior design, luxury, automotive, and architectural industries; and his work has been exhibited in some very prestigious museums and galleries throughout Europe. We're thrilled to be able to showcase this artist's work in this book.

Entries in **bold** *denote images*

Published in Australia in 2023 by
The Images Publishing Group Pty Ltd
ABN 89 059 734 431

Offices
Melbourne
Waterman Business Centre
Suite 64, Level 2 UL40
1341 Dandenong Road,
Chadstone, Victoria 3148
Australia
Tel: +61 3 8564 8122

New York
6 West 18th Street 4B
New York City, NY 10011
United States
Tel: +1 212 645 1111

Shanghai
6F, Building C, 838 Guangji Road
Hongkou District, Shanghai 200434
China
Tel: +86 021 31260822

books@imagespublishing.com
www.imagespublishing.com

The Images Publishing Group Reference Number: 1671

Text © Saxon Henry 2023
Images © 212box and Nick Rochowski 2023, with exception those noted for the following pages:

40–41: © Karen Hsu, Omnivore Inc.; **61:** © Piotr Powietrzynski Photography (top right) | © courtesy HIICompany Corp. (top left); **62:** © courtesy Kyle Bunting (all except top right); **65:** © courtesy Foresso and Eric Clough (top row); **66:** © Elena "Elle" Muliarchyk (top left) | © Troy Mann (middle left, center) | © Eric Clough (top center) | © Lauren Coleman (top right and bottom); **69:** © courtesy Laurence Le Constant; **70:** © courtesy Nathan Allen Glass Studio; **83:** © Boonyakorn Pulsri (top right, middle left and center, bottom center and right | © Visarn Rojsutee (bottom left); **84:** © courtesy BDDW and Tyler Hays; **87:** © courtesy Aria Stone Gallery (top left, bottom) | © Eric Clough (top middle); **93:** © courtesy Cybèle Young; **115:** © Ashley Middleton Photography (top left) | © courtesy Helena Starcevic; **116:** © Ricardo Spizzamiglio; **161:** © Eric Marin et Raphaëlle Carvalho; **162:** © Kate Orne (middle left, bottom right) | © courtesy Christopher Kurtz Studio (top right, middle center, bottom left); **165:** © courtesy RW Guild; **166:** © Brokis Lighting | © Martin Chum (bottom right); **183:** © Jody Kivort (top left, top right, bottom left) | © Eric Clough (top middle, left middle); **201:** © courtesy SHORE; **208:** © courtesy Anasthasia Millot; **229:** © courtesy Area Environments; **230:** © Elodie Dipuis (top left) | © Francis Amiand/La Manufacture Cogolin (top right, far right center) | © House of Tai Ping (top second and third from left, middle left, bottom right); **233:** © courtesy John Hovig; **253:** © Jake Curtis; **254:** © Lars Krüger/LUMIVERE.COM (top left, middle left) | © Studio Been (top center and right, center, bottom center and right); **257:** © Monica Dalmasso (all but top middle) | © courtesy Thierry Martenon (top middle); **258:** © Britney Smith (top left) | © Jenna Bascom (middle left, middle right, bottom left and right) | © courtesy Jake Szymanski (top right) | © Or Harpaz (middle center); **261:** © courtesy Markus Haase; **262:** © courtesy O'Hara Studio; **265:** © Lauren Coleman (middle left) | © Lindsay McAleavy (top left, center, and right; middle right; bottom left, middle, and right); **283:** © courtesy Maison Veronese; **299:** © courtesy Gabriel Scott; **308:** © Jody Kivort (top center and right) | Model: Clelia Montali (bottom left) | © courtesy GARDE (middle right)

A catalogue record for this book is available from the National Library of Australia

Title: Collaborations: A Houston Penthouse // By 212box and Saxon Henry
ISBN: 9781864709513

This title was commissioned in IMAGES' Melbourne office and produced as follows: *Editorial* Georgia (Gina) Tsarouhas, Jeanette Wall *Art direction/production* Nicole Boehringer

Printed on 150gsm Magno Matt paper by Graphius, Belgium

FSC® C014767
MIX
Paper from responsible sources
www.fsc.org

IMAGES has included on its website a page for special notices in relation to this and its other publications. Please visit www.imagespublishing.com